THE COMMUNIST
MANIFESTO

THE COMMUNIST MANIFESTO

Karl Marx and Friedrich Engels

edited and translated by L. M. Findlay

broadview editions

Library and Archives Canada Cataloguing in Publication

Marx, Karl, 1818–1883
      The communist manifesto / Karl Marx and Friedrich Engels ; edited and translated by L.M. Findlay.

Translation of: Manifest der Kommunistischen Partei.
Includes bibliographical references.
ISBN 1-55111-333-3

      1. Communism. I. Engels, Friedrich, 1820–1895. II. Findlay, L. M III. Title.

HX39.5.A224113 2004   335.4'22   C2004-903416-2

Broadview Press Ltd. is an independent, international publishing house, incorporated in 1985. Broadview believes in shared ownership, both with its employees and with the general public; since the year 2000 Broadview shares have traded publicly on the Toronto Venture Exchange under the symbol BDP.

We welcome comments and suggestions regarding any aspect of our publications—please feel free to contact us at the addresses below or at broadview@broadviewpress.com / www.broadviewpress.com

North America
PO Box 1243, Peterborough, Ontario, Canada K9J 7H5
Tel: (705) 743-8990; Fax: (705) 743-8353
email: customerservice@broadviewpress.com
3576 California Road, Orchard Park, NY, USA 14127

UK, Ireland, and continental Europe
NBN Plymbridge
Estover Road
Plymouth PL6 7PY UK
Tel: 44 (0) 1752 202 301
Fax: 44 (0) 1752 202 331
Fax Order Line: 44 (0) 1752 202 333
Customer Service: cservs@nbnplymbridge.com
Orders: orders@nbnplymbridge.com

Australia and New Zealand
UNIREPS, University of New South Wales
Sydney, NSW, 2052
Tel: 61 2 9664 0999; Fax: 61 2 9664 5420
email: info.press@unsw.edu.au

www.broadviewpress.com

This book is printed on 100% post-consumer recycled, ancient forest friendly paper.

Broadview Press Ltd. gratefully acknowledges the financial support of the Government of Canada through the Book Publishing Industry Development Program for our publishing activities.

Series editor: Professor L.W. Conolly
Advisory editor for this volume: Michel W. Pharand

PRINTED IN CANADA

For Norman Feltes (1932–2000)
Teacher, author, activist, comrade, friend

Contents

Acknowledgements

Support for this edition came in several forms and from numerous sources. A grant from the Publications Fund at the University of Saskatchewan enabled me to enlist research and scanning assistance from Tracy Stebner and Siobhan Cox. Another graduate student, Carrie Horachek, helped at an earlier stage. I am grateful also to students in graduate seminars at the University of Toronto and the University of Saskatchewan who worked with me to situate the *Manifesto* within the turbulent currents of the nineteenth century and the dominant political and intellectual tendencies of the twenty-first.

Some of the ideas and analysis presented in the Introduction were first sketched out in a co-presentation with professor Pamela MacCallum to the Victorian Studies Association of Western Canada at the University of Calgary, and at the Marxism 2000 conference at the University of Massachusetts, Amherst. I am grateful to the organizers of both these events and to the audience members who engaged in discussion with me.

My involvement with the *Manifesto* began in meetings of the Young Communist League in Aberdeen, Scotland, in the 1960s, continued in Oxford, and revived once I had found my feet in the Canadian academy. Over the years I have discussed the challenge and relevance of marxian thought with many long suffering or long marching friends and family. The examples of engaged intellectual work set by Norm Feltes of York University and the Ontario Coalition Against Poverty, and by Gary Kelly of the University of Alberta, the guy carrying a copy of Godwin's *Political Justice* into that ever-so-refined Oxford seminar long ago, have inspired me to struggle on through what Norm called "the depth of our ideological winter." Dear friends and colleagues, Sakéj Henderson, Director of the Native Law Centre of Canada, and his partner, Marie Battiste, Director of Indian and Northern Education at the University of Saskatchewan, have taught me much about the presumptions and blind spots in radical European and Canadian thought while helping keep alive the question of the hour in Canada: Why are organized labour and

Indigenous peoples still at loggerheads when they should be uniting against the elites who oppress them both?

My greatest debt is to my partner, Isobel, whose passion for ideas and justice is matched only by the grace and generosity with which she pursues them. Without her counsel and support, not even the flawed and fitful work "I" have so far produced would have seen the light of day.

List of Illustrations

Introduction

The *Communist Manifesto* is one of the most widely read secular texts in any language and it is still eminently readable, and hence usable, today. It continues to provide hope to and for the disadvantaged on the basis of a sociology of the stigma and a political economy of abuse. The stigma in question is poverty and its consequences; and the abuse at issue is the one that keeps elites in power and profits. The 150th anniversary of the *Manifesto*'s publication in 1998 was marked by an extraordinary range of activities across the world. These included discussions first stimulated by the collapse of soviet communism, an event symbolised for many by the removal of the Berlin wall and by the range of liberationist initiatives it nourished or confirmed in nation states within the soviet sphere of influence. There were also exchanges linked to the new millennium (remember Y2K?) and its revolutionary potential, shadowed as it was and is by ultra-capitalist versions of a New World Order in which the "free" market delivers democracy as the ultimate First World commodity to those less "developed" countries willing to endure the tough love purveyed, and structural adjustments demanded, by the World Bank, the World Trade Organization, and the International Monetary Fund (whose website boasts "The World's Largest Online Library"; see also Stiglitz). While millennial fever dissipates, or is transformed into an acute anxiety disorder by the spectres of "terror" and distributive justice, there has been a growing recognition (see, e.g., Amy Chua) that the rigours of economic deregulation demanded of "backward" or "deviant" economies represent in fact an unfair and dangerous double standard: the application of a test which the currently dominant economies themselves never had to meet, namely, the expectation of unrestricted, completely *laissez faire* economic activity.

As well as conferences and colloquia, public celebrations and reviews, and a massively resurgent presence on the internet (more than seventy thousand searchable items for the *Manifesto* alone), there has been extensive coverage of marxist topics in the mainstream media, including Ian Coutts's piece in the Toronto *Globe and Mail* on Saturday July 18, 1998, with its arresting opening line: "Look out—Marx is back." With major international movements currently forming around fair trade, ecology and sustainability, and economic and political justice (see, e.g., Callinicos), interest in the *Manifesto* is probably as high as it has been since the politically turbulent nineteen-sixties. At the same time, the strong impulse to commemorate this particular anniversary in 1998 helped underscore the refusal to abandon the past to Fukuyaman triumphalism and talk of "the end of history" (Niethammer). Not all Americans agreed (or were even consulted) about what a New American Century might be. Meanwhile, not everyone elsewhere identified progress with a world ever more closely resembling the United States in its economic, political, and cultural structures and values.

There are reasons aplenty, therefore, for a revised translation and fresh contextualization of the *Communist Manifesto* which can complicate our sense of options and antecedents by affirming the vitality and pertinence of marxist critique in an age of commodification (Cohen, Tucker, Findlay 2003). Such critique can assist understanding of and encourage participation in intensifying debate about the future of work, about live and dead capital (de Soto), material and immaterial labour (Hardt and Negri); about globalization as aggravated inequality and subversion of national sovereignty, the protean instability and periodic "adjustment" or "correction" of world markets, the fragmentation and dispersal of social and political entities in the name of progress and profitability: in short, the only too predictable global flows of poison and prosperity. Faced with such challenges, concerned citizens of all political stripes, ages, and backgrounds need as much as ever to do their homework, to listen carefully but critically to the voices of the past, and to connect all claims about the post-industrial age to the age of industrialization itself and to the debates it stimulated and was shaped by, most notably those captured in that particular manifesto written by Marx and Engels.

Attentiveness to that past need not be an escape from the present. Indeed, that past is essential to our understanding of where we are and how we are today, what we might become tomorrow, and who that "we" might be. The need for historical knowledge, as a necessary but in itself insufficient condition for individual and collective change, drives much of what follows here in the *Manifesto* and in the editorial materials in which it is nested but to which it cannot and should not be confined. Historical knowledge can of course be disputed by the reader or put to work in ways this editor fervently hoped for or never envisaged. This is all to the good, evincing as it does the productive indeterminacies of education and politics alike, and the profoundly social nature of reflection, exchange, and action. Authors need readers but cannot predict their reactions to what they read; social visionaries need followers but cannot and should not count on their uncritical obedience. A specific and partially recoverable play of dependencies, more or less willingly acknowledged, moderates claims to sovereign subjectivity or statehood at any particular moment in history. Authority has to be earned before it can be justly exercised. And this holds as much for readers as for authors and texts, for intellectual as for moral or political authority. And so read on, but always critically.

The Makers of the Manifesto: The Odd Couple?

The *Manifesto* is the result of a famous and ongoing collaboration by two German men in their late twenties who would become revolutionary icons in their maturity (see Figs. 1 and 2 for the overlay of respectability on this reality). As a summation of several decades of radical thinking by a sizeable number of men (see Appendix L.2–6), and significant numbers of prescient women like Flora Tristan (see Appendix A) and Helen Macfarlane (for a sharp snapshot see Rowbotham), the *Manifesto* might be thought of as an expression of the times that virtually wrote itself. However, that would be to overstate the socially determined nature of this particular text. It was produced in significant measure by general socio-economic structures and the particular pressures of industrial and agricultural crises of the "hungry forties," but it was fully achieved only by dint of individual agency. Indeed, as a distinctive, timely, and unmatchable intervention, the *Manifesto* could have been written only by Marx and Engels. But who were they? And why were they

Fig. 1: Marx in 1880,
International Institute for Social History, Amsterdam

Fig. 2: The Mature Engels,
photo credit David King

charged with the task of producing, in the German language in the first instance, what the work's title-page claimed were the views of the "Communist Party" (see Fig. 11)?

Both authors were born into middle-class families, Marx (1818–83) the eldest son of a lawyer and Engels (1821–95) the eldest son of a textile manufacturer. Both were baptised into the Christian faith, Marx more for the sake of his father's livelihood because his heritage was Jewish and there had been a long tradition of rabbis on both sides of his family. Engels came from a strict and devout Pietistic (i.e., reformed Lutheran) family whose values were shared by many of their immediate neighbours in Barmen (modern Wuppertal). Neither of these young men retained his religious faith long into adulthood, but both continued to recognize the importance of religion to others, including the underclass whose interests they sought to promote. They were equally aware of the prominence of theology in German intellectual life, particularly among many of those whose influence they sought to contest and replace with their own emerging social philosophy and practice. Each had to develop his intellectual independence at first to some degree undercover, Marx pursuing his university studies in the romantic-conservative field of law and then in the significantly depoliticized domain of philosophy, while Engels took advantage of a year's military service in Berlin to defer the demands of commerce while enhancing his capacity for intellectual critique by auditing lectures at the university there. By the time they began collaborating in the early 1840s, however, both men had become much bolder and recognized that they could envisage a more just, post-revolutionary future only by being candid about where they currently stood and persuading others to adopt that stance too. They made their decisive break with Bruno Bauer and the Young (or Left) Hegelians in the jointly authored *The Holy Family; or Critique of Critical Critique* (1845), an experience that was positive enough to fuel their most intensive collaboration up to 1850, including work on *The German Ideology* which, although it remained unpublished until 1932, allowed them not only to elaborate their antipathy to the obscurantist, mystical, and reactionary currents in German intellectual life but also to adumbrate a historical materialist alternative which Engels over-generously ascribed entirely to Marx. After completion of the *Manifesto,* Marx's studies took him in a more solitary and even more rigorous direction into the heart of political economy, while Engels pursued when he could his own interests in military and natural science and in the broader dissemination and defence of marxian thought, while remaining Marx's most trusted confidant and reliable benefactor.

The more intellectually dominant and driven of the two, Marx was a perpetual student, writer, and teacher as well as an incessant (if at times oblique) political activist, while Engels maintained a career in his family business (until 1870) and did his political writing and organization on top of (or sometimes at the expense of) these responsibilities. Engels had the financial means and desire to support Marx in his role as full-time intellectual and devoted family man but, after his retirement from business, and with Marx's health failing, Engels took over effective leadership of the First International (1864–76) for a couple of years. Engels remained unmarried, at least by the bourgeois definition of that institution, but had important, long-term relationships with two working-class sisters, Mary Burns who died in 1863 and Lizzy who succeeded to Mary's uneasy status as Engels' "Mrs." There were elements of male chauvinism as well as political solidarity and mutual education in these relationships, and neither Engels nor Marx (nor many of their political brethren then and since) was free from paternalistic presumptions about women's role in society and as revolutionaries (see Gane). They were rightly contemptuous of bourgeois attempts to link radical politics to sexual promiscuity and moral dissoluteness, and indeed their emphasis on the *scientific* nature of their work was a way of bracketing or avoiding moralistic entanglements and distractions. But sexual mores, like religious belief, were too powerful to ignore completely, and they found themselves, both personally and politically, dealing with such matters more than they wished but not always more than they deserved to! Marx had to deal, for instance, with the consequences of the family housekeeper, Helene Demuth, becoming pregnant while Jenny Marx was visiting relatives in Holland. Bachelor Engels, meanwhile, was often the subject of gossip and scandal on his travels in Europe because of his taste for *grisettes* (see Appendix B).

In early adulthood, the two authors of the *Manifesto* shared similar experiences of disruption, surveillance, and expulsion, before residing more or less permanently in England. Marx chose London where political, financial, and cultural power were concentrated, as well as the growing numbers of radicals exiled from Europe, and where he could use the great research collections of the British Museum (now housed in the new British Library). Engels spent most of his time until 1870 in Manchester, in a major centre of manufacturing and rapid urban growth where his business obligations provided an excellent vantage from which to write his classic study, *The Condition of the Working Class in England* (1845; see Fig. 3 for effects of periodic fluctuations in the cotton trade; for the persistence of child labour in this industry in the United States see the photograph of the "Little Spinner" on the cover of this edition; for Engels' assessment of American labour see Appendix I). *The Condition* was an achievement that, despite being written in German and remaining untranslated into English until 1887, helped Engels gain the trust of British leftists—most prominently Chartists (who were pursuing the six points of a People's Charter through physical and/or moral force) and Owenites (followers of Robert Owen's relatively enlightened views of labour, co-operatives, and social democracy; see Appendix L.6). This work also confirmed Engels' right to be Marx's intellectual partner and collaborator rather than his permanent apprentice.

Several features of this collaboration need to be borne in mind as one reads, and re-reads, the *Manifesto*. First, its authors themselves exemplified the revolutionary potential of the bourgeoisie of which their text makes so much. They had pursued two of the principal middle-class avenues towards respectability and security, commerce and education, and had still become radical critics of bourgeois property relations and the social relations of production that preserved property's sanctity and its owners' sense of virtue. This fact would not be lost on those who knew who they were and something of what they were up to, primarily the tight but fractious circles of European and British radicals. By the time the *Manifesto* and its authorship became widely known, they themselves would have even more impressive credentials, with

Fig. 3: Society of Friends' Soup Kitchen in Manchester:
Preparing the Soup and the Distribution,
Illustrated London News, 22 November 1862

Engels still cutting a revisionary bourgeois figure in the 1860s and Marx retaining his intellectual seriousness and independence despite lacking a "real job" or the considerable private means of many an intellectual "amateur" of the time. Engels could continue to participate in the bourgeois capitalist economy and to critique it. Marx's efforts to provide for his family as well as for the conceptual arsenal of proletarian revolution showed that this new movement could, at least barely, support its own leading thinker, just as the established order could cozen and reward its throng of embedded apologists and ideologues who, as a result of cliques and purges, continued to dominate universities, the public service, the higher journalism, and the mainstream press.

What also needs to be emphasized is that political solidarity could overcome physical, psychological, and social distance (as one can see in the sample letters in Appendices B and F). Still at this time the word "correspondence" (as in the Communist Correspondence Committees established by Marx and Engels from a Brussels base in 1846) remained highly charged because connected to the emergence of liberationist corresponding societies during and after the French Revolution. Written communication expressed the importance of text and literacy to politics, both because power is intimately connected to the production and circulation of information (remember the IMF online library or "embedded" journalism and military videomatics during Operation Iraqi Freedom), and because—censorship, infiltration, and spying notwithstanding—text could and did circulate beyond the knowledge and against the interests of the state and those who dominated its institutions and directed its policies and instruments of intimidation and repression. It was not easy to keep or share a radical faith (see Appendix L.4 and 5), but Marx and Engels kept in constant and productive communication. This was one reason why they were entrusted with the articulation of communist values and a workers' agenda at a moment of immense tension and serious revolutionary promise well summarized by Engels in his posthumously published essay on "The Movements of 1847" (Karl Marx and Friedrich Engels, *Collected Works* 6:520–29; hereafter MECW). This situation would change later in 1848 and in the years thereafter, but in entrusting (at Marx's insistence) the composition of a manifesto to them at this time, some experienced and savvy radicals realized they were placing significant responsibility on these two "scholars" (whose scholarship was both needed and resented; see Appendix B). Here was a major chance to secure change and to establish an international proletarian movement on a more secure intellectual and political foundation. The messengers had to be, as they were, at the height of their powers and unwavering in their commitment. They had to be able to legitimate existing beliefs and class analysis, and somehow go beyond fraternalism in forceful argument, compelling connections, and arresting language.

Both Marx and Engels were experienced and effective political commentators. Each on his own had already produced a body of writing remarkable for its quantity, range, and courage, and they had already shown that they could work effectively together. They would not be worried about originality in a possessive-careerist way, nor about who would get the credit for what on this occasion. They would continue with the productive give-and-take so prominent in their letters to each other as well as in major projects like *The German Ideology*, whose failure to find a publisher did not deter them from further collaboration. And they would work together under the aegis of an anonymity analogous to the transparent anonymity of contributors to major British periodicals like the *Edinburgh* and *Quarterly* reviews. But theirs was not an open secret of authorship tied to personal literary ambition via a blend of particular topics with an unmistakeable prose style like Macaulay's or Carlyle's or Guizot's. It was rather the willing subordination of self to the interests of a collectivist political movement. It was, then, a contribution to a very different disseminative tradition than the one dominating nineteenth-century print culture and increasingly tied to bourgeois forms of property and celebrity (see, e.g., Gross and Bourdieu).

Making the *Manifesto*: Instructions to the Able

But why, more particularly, were Marx and Engels given the task of producing this text, and by whom? The specific commission came from the Communist League in its second Congress, held in London in late November and early December, 1847. This event had come about as a result of intensifying attempts in the 1840s to find the most effective local organizational structures and broader modes of mobilization across regions and national, cultural, and linguistic borders (see Engels' account in Appendix H). They were both experienced in getting the word out in the face of all kinds of harassment, and of setting up new publications in new places when current ones were closed down. They had intimate knowledge of publishers sympathetic to working-class interests in a number of cities across Europe, a knowledge enhanced by Karl Schapper (1812–70), the radical typesetter who took the lead in seeking to merge the League of the Just with the Communist League. They had experience setting up new entities and severing in the process connections that had proved more sentimental than scientific, or otherwise unsatisfactory. They appreciated the need, always, for more than one iron in the fire, for multiple sites of struggle—especially ones that had an elite as well as a popular arm, a place where real thinking could be shared with those whose intellect and commitment were (more or less) up to the challenges of exchange with Marx and Engels, and a more populist site where the objectives were recruitment and mobilization. And this is precisely the case with the Communist League, with its use of the German Workers Educational Association from 1840 onwards as a populist democratic front, while its more hardcore activities evolved through the French secret society tradition as in the (Babeuvist) Society of Equals (see Appendix L.3) nested within the Society of the Pantheon, the (Barbèsian) Society of the Families and (Blanquist) Society of the Seasons, into the German émigré League of the Outlawed and thence (in a reversal of terms) into the League of the Just, whose principals moved to London in 1839 after being expelled from France for participating in the ill fated Blanquist uprising in Paris on May 12.

In the surviving written archive pertinent to the production of the *Manifesto*, one can trace the false starts, or monitor the volatile mix of solidarity and rivalry, the capacities for fracture and self-destruction that are often alleged to be a distinguishing feature of left-wing movements and were certainly in abundant evidence in the 1830s and 40s (but see Appendix I). On the other hand, capital was incurring new dependencies and vulnerabilities as quickly as it was acquiring new sources of profit at home and abroad (see the tensions explored in Appendix L.7) and new sources or degrees of hegemony achieved by such methods as popular visual canonization in the *Illustrated London News* of captains of industry like Isambard Kingdom Brunel (1806–59) and stage-managing of the Great Exhibition of 1851 as the post-Chartist harbinger of prosperity for all in a peaceable kingdom where family values prevail. (See Figs. 4 and 5. Note Brunel's Napoleonic pose and the absence of the human helpers from the garland of notable accomplishments attributed to his "genius." Note also the multi-layered representation of the people by their betters at the Exhibition ceremony, while the only hand raised is the conductor's raised in harmony rather than anger on the balcony behind Queen Victoria and her German-born, science-loving consort, Prince Albert.)

The examples of the American and French revolutions continued to inspire significant portions of the European bourgeoisie to translate their new economic prominence into political clout, and their steady successes fed in turn the aspirations of proletarians and their middle class and aristocratic sympathizers. The new economy required a better educated labour force but could not fully control what that force would do with its expanded literacy and numeracy. Adam Smith had captured this particular dilemma well in *The Wealth of Nations* in 1776 (2.78–8), and later attempts to resolve it by attentive paternalism, sanitized representations of work (as in Fig. 6), limited upward mobility, and gradual political reforms had helped the bourgeoisie to defend its gains while pre-empting proletarian revolution. But fraternal socialism had not done the work of collective justice, and class analysis had to sharpen the sense of solidarity to be achieved and acted on. And so a shift from one slogan to another, from the brotherhood of man to the international proletariat, marks the shift from the League of the Just (and its ten-year attempt to internationalize itself) to the Communist League (and a renewed effort not to sanctify workers as "just" but rather to achieve economic and social justice through their political mobilization). To this end, the

Fig. 4: Isambard Kingdom Brunel,
Illustrated London News, 21 September 1859

Fig. 5: The Royal Opening of the Great Exhibition, London, *Illustrated London News*, 10 March 1851

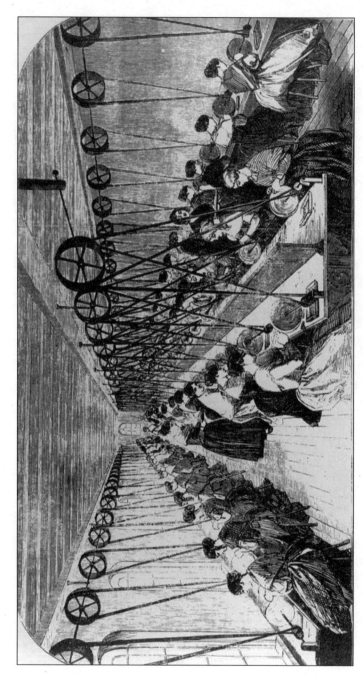

Fig. 6: The Pen-Grinding Room,
Illustrated London News, 22 February 1851

earlier League's leaders, Schapper, Joseph Moll, and Heinrich Bauer, all now based in London, invited Marx and Engels to effect a merger with the Communist League and assist in drafting a program for the new organization.

Engels was a busy participant in the first Congress of the Communist League and had a draft programme (reproduced in Appendix C) and rules approved by the delegates during the final day's business. This draft was then widely circulated in advance of the next Congress. In the meantime, Marx helped effect the break from utopian to scientific socialism and the takeover of the *Deutsche-Brüsselischer-Zeitung* as another organ of the movement with his essay on "The Communism of the *Rheinischer Beobachter*" (see Appendix D). By the end of October, Engels had shown himself once again able to defend the new political line, this time from the counterversion of "true socialism" put forward by Moses Hess at a committee meeting in Paris earlier that month. Consequently, the second iteration of the League's new "Principles [*Grundsätze*] of Communism" (see Appendix F) emerged as the text to be discussed at the upcoming Congress. The scene was thus set for Marx and Engels, together and in person, to underscore the dependency of the Communist League on their theoretical, analytical, and expressive abilities, and for Marx to get League approval to return to Brussels and finish the job with the third iteration of what would now become the *Manifesto* itself.

Making the *Manifesto*: The Politics of Genre

The textual evolution of the *Manifesto* has been effectively discussed by a number of scholars (see, e.g., Andréas, Draper, and Beamish).

Within the broad context of revolutionary literacy one needs to recognize the amplified influence of radical texts achieved through their being read aloud in homes, pubs, and meeting houses where people gathered to share their concerns and knowledge with their less literate intimates, co-workers, and neighbours. The material culture of resistance and dissent included placards, posters, handbills, broadsheets, banners; and also songs of commemoration, critique, and mobilization in the tradition of the *Marseillaise* and anticipating Jim Connell's anthem for the international labour movement composed in 1889, the *Red Flag*: "The banner bright, the symbol plain,/Of human right and human gain." In the tradition of radical literacy, canonical texts—especially the Bible, Shakespeare's plays, Milton's and Bunyan's visions, or in Germany Goethe's *Faust* or the plays of Schiller—were made to yield more or less direct support for particular values and projects (see Rose). Contemporary authors like Percy Shelley, Heinrich Heine, Georg Weerth, and Alphonse de Lamartine (see Appendix L.8) were read in tandem with myriad underclass voices who gave Tom Paine's *Common Sense* fresh inflections and localities in an increasingly inclusive expressive commons, an increasingly aggrieved and outspoken industrial and agrarian muse. In the first half of the nineteenth century labour found its voice(s) as never before (see, e.g., Janowitch, Bowditch, and Ramsland, and Sewell).

When Engels experimented first with the form of a radical catechism (literally a thorough dinning in one's ears, and then associated with concerted oral instruction), he was trying to make a number of forceful points as well as a conciliatory nod in the direction of Schapper's and others' earlier attempt to formulate a "confession of faith" for the League of the Just. Plainly, Engels wished to promote the idea of the secular appropriation of a Christian mode of examining candidates for confirmation. Thus, workers could be tested—in an echo too of the initiation rituals of secret societies—as to their understanding of and commitment to the principles and teachings of communism. Most potential adherents could activate their own memories of religious instruction in a context of its radical redeployment through recurrent performance of a series of questions and answers led by those who knew the text, its inspiration, import, and intended outcomes. Such appropriations drew also on the actual liberatory traditions of some forms of Christianity (like Flora Tristan's, Appendix A) and recent efforts like Wilhelm Weitling's to derive utopian communism from Christ's example in *The Gospel of a Poor Sinner* (1843), as well as on the sad record of complicity between established churches and the politically powerful. The idea of politicizing a religious form appealed enough for instance to Engels' acquaintance and promoter of "true socialism," Moses Hess, that he produced shortly after the *Manifesto* first appeared a *Red Catechism for the German People*. But Hess's effort seems to have had little impact, suggesting that Marx and Engels were correct to move away from rote and confessional forms towards that trusty political genre, the manifesto (see Appendix L for its range of targets and techniques), even though its initial effect was less than they had hoped for.

"Manifesto" literally means a slap or slight blow with the hand, and hence the direct manifestation of opinion or feeling, including reactionary or conciliatory feeling (see Appendix L.1, 7). It therefore connects to the critique of capitalist *manu*facture and the revaluing of the *hands* who worked in the factories now spreading all over Europe from their beginnings in Britain and Belgium. At times of political and social ferment, the manifesto often figures prominently (see Lyons, Cormack, Osborne, Postgate) and it was as popular in the nineteenth century as in the twentieth, figuring "even" in Québec by 1847 in the twenty-six page *Manifeste adressé au peuple du Canada par le Comité Constitutionel de la Réforme et du Progrès* (Appendix L.7). For obvious reasons, much effort has been expended on determining the *originality* of the *Communist Manifesto*. This activity has been predictably partisan, with attempts to stress the work's genius or its embarrassing or culpable indebtedness. But the mystifying and individualising discourse of genius and the sour idiom of the unbelievers are alike invested in the very notions of property and entitlement that Marx and Engels were at such pains to contest. Better to think, then, in terms of critical or strategic contextualism, of the interplay of ethos and idiosyncrasy, memory and inventiveness, in light of the belated but unrivalled success of the work now commonly referred to worldwide as simply "the *Manifesto*." It is very useful to have work like Bert Andréas's on sources, or the detailed comparative scholarship on, for example, Victor-Prosper Considérant's *Manifesto of Peaceful Democracy* (published in French in 1842; see Davidson), and indeed marxist scholarship can hold its head up in any company. But to ascribe too much autonomy to the text or too much directiveness to its immediate historical context, is—like attempting to inflate the claims of Engels or eliminate him altogether from authorship of the *Manifesto*—to miss the point, and also to practice the scholarship of distraction which Marx characterised so bracingly in 1845, in the eleventh and final of his *Theses on Feuerbach*: "The philosophers have only *interpreted* the world in various ways; the point, however, is to *change* it" (MECW 5:8).

In the crucial letter sent to Marx from Engels just before the London Congress began (see Appendix G), the latter describes his most current effort at drafting "Principles"and specifically links the manifesto form to a capacity for historical narrative that catechism lacks. This is a very revealing moment in the evolution of the *Manifesto*. The recognition of the importance of history comes at a time of unprecedented historical activity (see Gooch), including major attempts to reinterpret the profoundly bourgeois French Revolution in a range of progressive and reactionary ways (see Furet). There were also the particular contemporary relations between history and theology to consider. The higher criticism of the Bible had caused as much of a stir among the faithful as Darwinism would later, and Engels was especially attuned to the work of the Young Hegelian David Friedrich Strauss whose use of history in *The Life of Jesus Critically Examined* (1835–36) had for many shifted the ground of scriptural authority from incontrovertible fact to mythopoetic faith. The accommodation of history meant more than ever a move away from the liberal appropriation of formularies of faith to historically informed, secular-scientific methods, language, and genres. Those formularies were designed for the rehearsal of immutable truths and presumed the direction of human history by divine providence. In one of the most brilliantly ironic, intellectually trenchant of all his works, *The Eighteenth Brumaire of Louis Bonaparte* (1852), Marx would soon summarize *homo historicus* in terms even more memorable than those he employed in *The German Ideology* and other works of the 1840s:

> Men make their own history, but they do not make it just as they please; they do not make it under circumstances chosen by themselves, but under circumstances directly encountered, given and transmitted from the past. The tradition of all the dead generations weighs like a nightmare on

the brain of the living. And just when they seem engaged in revolutionising themselves and things, in creating something that has never existed, precisely in such periods of revolutionary crisis they anxiously conjure up the spirits of the past to their service and borrow from their names, battle-cries and costumes in order to present the new scene of world-history in this time-honoured guise and this borrowed language. (MECW 11.1:104)

The constraints and temptations of studying the past inform rather than enfeeble the *Manifesto*. It is not historical narrative that it explicitly disavows, but only "fairy tales" (*Märchen*) alleging the way things "naturally" are or have to be.

Given the traditional brevity of the manifesto form, and the linking of its impact to that brevity, narrative history must needs be abridged, simplified, and buttressed with subheadings and slogans. And this is what happens in the four-part structure employed. As in the case of *The Holy Family*, Marx was only too capable of growing a major text out of a minor provocation, but he had in this case a deadline of which his compatriots in London testily reminded him at the beginning of January 1848, they having already promised in the inaugural number of the *Communist Journal* the previous September that the *Manifesto* would appear in "our next issue" (see Appendix E). That consideration, and Marx's concurrent work on the questions of wages and free trade, made brevity all the more inevitable (as seen particularly in the last section of the *Manifesto*). He also had Engels helping him along, though we have no written record of the final stages of this process. But the job got done and the work appeared virtually simultaneously with the uprising in Paris that helped inaugurate the European "year of revolutions" (see Figs. 7, 8, and 9, the latter two of which record that reaction was still as brutal as ever in 1851; see also Appendix L.8).

With the brevity of the manifesto genre goes a certain directness of style which, at least in the case of Marx and Engels, derives more from a strong sense of audience and political exigency than from any conceptual or expressive crudity. The work is, indeed, a tribute to the productive clarifications of political praxis, of

Fig. 7: Burning the Royal Carriages at the Château d'Eu, *Illustrated London News*, 4 March 1848

Fig. 8: Troops Shooting Insurgents in the Streets of Paris,
Illustrated London News, 3 December 1851

Fig. 9: Troops Shooting the Insurgents in the Streets of Paris, *Illustrated London News*, 13 December 1851

turmoil internal to as well as bearing down from all sides on a particular social movement. Its plot is the history, agency, and socio-political promise of the proletariat, at a time when the relentless invasiveness of the bourgeois mode of production is reducing even children (like the Little Spinner and her many predecessors and successors in the factories and mines of Europe and Empire) to commodities, while communism is being branded a licentious threat to the structures and values of "the" family. The *Manifesto*'s plot conveys the story and certainty of resistance to the lies and contradictions imposed by capital in the "bourgeois epoch." Indeed, its four-part structure serves this end consistently, shifting from the historical development of middle class/labouring class relations in section one to private property rights as the cause of ongoing and intensifying antagonism between capital and wage labour and the main source of stimulus for the proletariat to become more aware, resolute, and internationalist than its underclass predecessors. Section three is a devastating literature review wherein Marx's rigour and irascibility play unsparingly on the reactionary, conservative/bourgeois, and critical-utopian precursors to the movement he is promoting. He constantly shows how moves towards social harmony have been cynical, or sentimental, or sedative, attempting to appeal somehow "beyond" class or to a damagingly vague sense of the exploited masses, or theorizing in advance of the actual social relations of production. His identifying of revolutionary potential and inevitability with the proletariat in the 1840s leads him, finally, to a rapid summary of allegiances and challenges in Germany and other national contexts, with the final exhortation to proletarian unity maintaining the pattern of memorable conclusions to each of the preceding sections of the text. Many readers gain the impression of being drawn into complexity by commitment and reflection. Then they are released, fully awake now, back into political action.

The *Manifesto* refuses the lead of many a pamphlet of the time in seeking community through a form of address too sentimentally in its appeal—as in, e.g., William Benbow's dedication of his pamphlet on behalf of a *Grand National Holiday of the Productive Classes* to "Plundered Fellow-Sufferers!" There are intimate, I/thou residues here; satirical thrusts and stentorian reproofs designed to incense or crush the resistant reader; variations of voice through the evocatively gothic preamble, and then via pedagogical and scientific sobriety to literary sifting and wicked irony, before the final exhortation to an international proletariat in the making—all within the permissive polyglossia (many-voicedness) of historical narrative. The basic notions of displacement and diaspora, the doubling of calculated surplus as uncontrollable excess the pursuit of profit that imperils the profiteer, are multiply intelligible and regularly compelling. Something of the subtlety and power of Marx's writing will be conveyed in detail in the ensuing section on translation. But readers should in general be attentive to the text's enactive syntax, staging disruption or swelling in its own parallel or aggregative structures; and making sequence count as much as substance, so that short or long sentences are not accidentally but strategically so. And the same holds for the dynamic interrelations of literal and figurative language, inventiveness and cliché, old myths of golden apples or of the New Jerusalem feeding into the new myth of bourgeois democracy that consorts with both mechanistic and organic orders of meaning, as in the "wheel of history" and the "putrefaction" of the social body. The violence of the new economy is conveyed by images of "heavy artillery" as well as the wounding powers of hierarchical and exclusionary language, but that violence is also and memorably turned against itself, as the ever industrious bourgeoisie gains ascendancy by digging its own grave (see also Derrida and Sprinker) and preparing the way for the revolutionary proletariat. Marx rings changes on the theme of social control and its limitations, leaving us with an emblem of aristocratic populism as a coat of arms on a bare backside visible to every apparently co-opted commoner; leaving us with productivity's *reductio ad absurdum* in the "crisis" of "overproduction"; and leaving us also with the chilling sobriety of an encounter with the "real conditions of existence," then and now, after the dissolution and dispersal of traditions and illusions designed to legitimate and perpetuate the ruling classes' privileges.

The *Manifesto's* Audiences: Translation as Reception

Translation and interpretation are overlapping but not identical activities. Both are welcomed by authors because they presume the activity of reading. Both are suspected by authors as potentially inaccurate or wrongheaded. Marx, and Engels, and the Communist League wanted to get a particular message out as widely and quickly as possible, and hence the *Manifesto* promises virtually simultaneous translation into "English, French, German, Italian, Flemish and Danish languages." This intention was overtaken by events across Europe but neither completely nor permanently. There was a steady demand among the radical diaspora for the German version, but when the first and second editions of 1848 ran out, a reissue would have to await Sigfrid Meyer's "self-published" version in 1866. Meanwhile, an English translation was completed by Helen Macfarlane for four successive issues of Harney's Chartist weekly, the *Red Republican,* in November 1850, and helped keep alive radical British hopes apparently crushed in 1848. However, the text did not begin to achieve a fully international circulation until the mid 1860s, when the fortunes of political radicalism began to improve once again. As the first volume of Marx's *Capital* also made an impact, the desire to see his already legendary earlier work grew apace. Henceforth, proletarians in Europe, North and South America, and throughout the British Empire produced versions of the *Manifesto* to assist their own thinking and fuel their own political practice (for basic data up to 1959 see Andréas, 374ff). Moreover, as European imperialism extended the domain of understanding of European languages, so colonized peoples sought and found within European languages inspiration for their own resistance movements. During and immediately after the Great War of 1914–18 the *Manifesto* was essential (though not exclusive) reading for radical trade unionists in places like the United States (where the English translation by Helen Macfarlane was reissued in 1871) and Australia (where excerpts of the Engels/Moore translation appeared first in 1893), for political dissidents in Rumania and Croatia, for revolutionaries in Russia and China. The capitalist crisis of the 1930s seemed to validate the *Manifesto*'s major claims, but this was before Stalinism and the enormous resilience and political clout of capitalists created the conditions of resistance to communism (as well as fascism) that gave rise to the Second World War, the Cold War, and the implosion of the Soviet empire. The work has maintained a substantial worldwide readership as a classic of political philosophy and a crucial historical document, while remaining key to many popular struggles for liberation ever since, though often inflected in ways that accommodate local realities (like the presence of José Marti in the Cuban imaginary). This outcome would no doubt have pleased Marx and Engels since they themselves refused to revise and update the *Manifesto*, desiring above all that their work be used rather than fetishized or mummified. *Traditore, traduttore:* to translate is to betray, but not necessarily to betray the values and objectives which the *Manifesto* promotes.

A Note on the Text

The first German edition of the *Manifesto* was (as Kuczynski reaffirms) a 23–page pamphlet in dark green covers typeset from Marx's manuscript which has since disappeared (except for fragments such as the one reproduced in Fig. 10), perhaps in one of the bouts of documentary destruction forced upon revolutionaries by increasingly aggressive police actions in 1848 and the years following. This text appeared at the end of February and was reprinted with fewer typographical errors and better punctuation in a 30-page edition in April–May, while the first edition was still appearing serially in the *Deutsche Londoner Zeitung*. The second edition became the basis of most later German editions, though both editions were alluded to, excerpted, supplemented, paraphrased, pilloried, bowdlerized, and pirated over the course of several decades, as need or opportunity arose and the fact of the work's non-commercial origins and distribution made such open season on it increasingly likely if not apt. The German text used for the translation given here is the 1883 one authorized by the German Social-Democratic Party in exile in Zürich, for which Engels provided his own brief preface (he and Marx had already co-authored seven such prefaces before Marx's death). This edition itself derives from a version of 1873 deriving from the text of the *Manifesto* and read into the court record of a treason trial in Leipzig in that year. One of the defendants, Wilhelm Liebknecht, used the opportunity to elicit a preface from Marx and Engels for this new "edition" and then had to follow through when the authors asked for copies to distribute in England (see Draper 48–52, 62–65; Kuczynski 182ff.).

The 1888 translation of the 1883 German text by Samuel Moore was supervised by Engels who used the occasion to write the longest of his prefaces for the work. Moore came to this task fresh from translating the first volume of *Capital* (where he collaborated with Edward Aveling), and had already proved himself to Engels as intelligent, industrious, and willing to take direction from the principal guardian of Marx's works and reputation. As Hal Draper has argued, it seems likely that Moore did

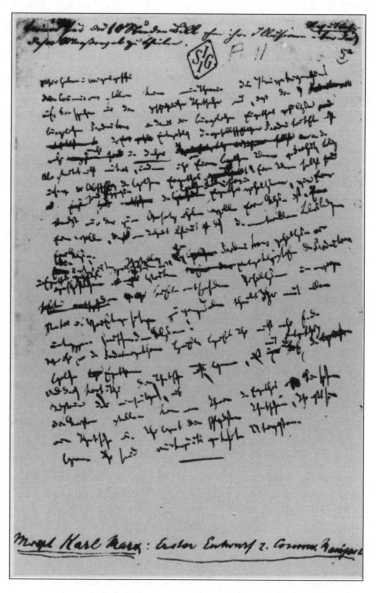

Fig. 10: Fragment of First Manuscript Draft of the *Manifesto*,
International Institute for Social History, Amsterdam

the grunt work while Engels provided both polish and the confidence to depart at times from the literal sense of Marx's German. Engels had published in *The Commonweal* in 1885 an essay on "How Not To Translate Marx" (MECW 21:22–37), which must have given serious pause to anyone thinking to follow H. M. Hyndman's (or his pseudonym John Broadhouse's) lead in taking on Marx without the approval and tutelage of Engels. Moore knew his place, which was not on the title-page of the translation but at the end of Engels' preface, and the two worked effectively together to produce what has deservedly become the standard version of the *Manifesto* in English.

This text is modified here in light of my own and others' interpretations and textual work on the German versions. I am attempting a new rapprochement between resonance and accuracy which I consider true to the attitudes of Marx and Engels towards translations of this text, to their hopes that it would prove prophetic and transformative, and to the growing recognition among scholars that the *Manifesto,* while always attentive to the contemporary currents of European revolution and reaction, is also remarkably prescient about the nature and effects of global capital in the twenty-first century.

The *Manifesto* is, after all, dedicated to countering a myth (of the inevitability and even desirability of uneven development at home and abroad), and to holding national and international elites to account. It urges its own readings of crisis and unity-in-progress as, in fact, the world is "more and more splitting up into two great hostile camps." It is as pertinent as ever today for its refusal to reduce all other forms of freedom to "a single, unconscionable freedom—Free Trade"; for its connection of that "free" market fundamentalism to "everlasting insecurity and mobility" for workers "over the whole surface of the globe"; and for the insight that first-world capital "creates a world after its own image." If new technologies continue to channel benefits disproportionately to the wealthy while increasing workers' "enslavement by the machine," repeating that feminising and infantilizing of labour identified by Marx and Engels as an essential part of the industrial revolution, the *Manifesto* persistently reminds us that education and technologies of communication can be used against those who control access to them. Global capital can be contested in its currently dispersed and rapidly mutating forms almost as readily as in its industrially concentrated forms, and the *Manifesto* continues to inspire and inform the work of resistance.

Above all, I have been guided in my translation by the warning in section three of the *Manifesto* about the complacently eclectic, depoliticizing appropriation [*Aneignung*] of revolutionary ideas via a species of academic translation [*Übersetzung*]. As a transition to the text of the *Manifesto* itself, let me finally give a few examples of the challenges any translator of the *Manifesto* faces, and what I propose by way of a soberly syncretic, historically inflected approach. I have kept the *Manifesto* as editorially uncluttered as possible, but that decision is underwritten by considerations such as the following.

First Translation Sample:

1. a   Ein Gespenst geht um in Europa—das Gespenst des Kommunismus. Alle Mächte des alten Europa haben sich zu einiger heiligen Hetzjagd gegen dies Gespenst verbündet, der Papst und der Czar, Metternich und Guizot, französische Radikale und deutsche Polizisten. (1848)

    b   A frightful hobgoblin stalks throughout Europe. We are haunted by a ghost, the ghost of communism. All the Powers of the Past have joined in a holy crusade to lay this ghost to rest,—the Pope and the Czar, Metternich and Guizot, French Radicals and German police agents. (Helen Macfarlane 1850)

    c   A spectre is stalking [haunting] Europe—the spectre of Communism. All the powers of Old [old] Europe have bound themselves together in [entered into] a crusade [Holy Alliance] against [to exorcise] this spectre; Pope and Czar, Metternich and Guizot, French Radicals and German police spies. (Samuel Moore, with Engels and me, with displaced parts of the 1888 version in square brackets for ease of comparison here.)

Notes to sample:

1. How one renders the opening verb, *umgehen*, is important because it captures boldly the energy and realness of this spectre. The idea of *haunting* pushes unsettlement more in the direction of psychological and moral interiority, whereas Macfarlane's *stalks* retains the necessary energy while humanizing the spectre and preparing for the external evidence of reactionary alliances. *Stalking* has the added advantage of connection to our concerns today with unwanted surveillance and harassment. The open-endedness of *umgehen* has prompted exasperation in some, but the verb's indeterminacy approximates the inclusiveness and inventiveness of revolutonary *mobilité* in general while also suggesting that paranoia increases with power, so that those concerned with homeland or personal security can imagine potential threats anywhere and everywhere and seek without ever achieving what retired US Admiral John Poindexter urged as "total information awareness" in the "War against Terror."

2. *Spectre* should be retained, for its authentic gothic flavour but also for its connections to anxiety and paranoia via the acronyms and code names dear to security agencies fictional and otherwise. However, Macfarlane's *hobgoblin* offers an important reminder that ghosts have specific histories too, and that Shakespeare, Bunyan, Shelley, and folk culture loomed large in the literary sensibility of readers of, and listeners to, *The Red Republican*.

3. Upper case *Old Europe* carries apposite implications of past or quasi-entities like the Holy Roman Empire, Old Corruption, and the *ancien régime,* while its creaky unanimity sits well with the cranky spectrality of Communism. Whether capitalised or not, Old Europe also reminds us of Donald Rumsfeldt's recent distinction between the intransigence of states like Germany and France and the post-soviet states of the "new Europe" who joined the "coalition of the willing" in Operation Iraqi Freedom.

4. As literal a rendering as possible of *verbunden* gestures in passing to the *Bund der Gerechten* (League of the Just) and the general problematic of revolutionary solidarity captured in part by expressions like *Verein* (union), *Gesellschaft* (society) and *das Ensemble des gesellschaftlichen Verhältnisse* (the ensemble of social relations) of which Marx wrote in his *Theses on Feuerbach* and reworked continuously thereafter.

5. *Hetzjagd* is perhaps best rendered here by Macfarlane's *crusade* (without the redundant *holy*). This term conveys the sense of righteous mobilization of specifically Christian forces against an infidel enemy, and gestures back towards old habits and forward to similar attempts at purges during the 1930s, the Cold War, and now the War against Terror. Draper's suggestion of a "witchhunt" has much to recommend it too, while Carver's "in holy alliance for a witchhunt" tries awkwardly and unavailingly to capture every nuance. The holiness of this endeavour is being derided here, as is the likelihood of its proving effective. The Holy Alliance had lasted from 1815 to 1830 and is now beyond resuscitation, despite the fact that the new reactionary configuration includes French Radicals. Compare M and E's first collaborative work published three years earlier, *The Holy Family: A Critique of Critical Criticism*, where holiness is scathingly demystified.

Second Translation Sample:

2 a Alles Ständische und Stehende verdampft, alles heilige wird entweiht, und die Menschen sind endlich gezwungen, ihre Lebensstellung, ihre gegenseitigen Beziehungen mit nüchternen Augen anzusehen. ·

  b Every thing fixed and stable vanishes, everything holy and venerable is desecrated, and men are forced to look at their mutual relations, at the problem of Life, in the soberest, the most matter of fact way. (Macfarlane)

  c All that is set and stolid [solid] turns to vapour [melts into air], all that is holy is profaned, and people are [man is] at last compelled to confront soberly [face with sober sense] their

[real] situation in life, and their interrelatedness to others [his relations with his kind]. (Moore with Engels and me)

Notes to sample:

1. The Moore/Engels translation of this sentence is still a firm part of Marxist discourse and allusion, as in Marshall Berman's sustained meditation on Marxian "melting." Changing it should therefore not be undertaken lightly. The resonance of the phrasing may derive in part from a reworking of Thomas Carlyle's version of Prospero's famous words near the conclusion of Shakespeare's *Tempest* (4.1.148), where the spirit-actors "Are melted into air, into thin air" as part of a larger and more sobering dissolution that will "Leave not a rack behind." (Marx was familiar with Wilhelm Schlegel's translation of this play where the actors "Sind ausgelöst in Luft, in dünne Luft.") Marx may also or alternatively be playing with a passage in his father's favourite, Friedrich Schiller, in the 27th of whose *Letters on the Aesthetic Education of Man* (1795) we find the following claim: "Nothing is more common than to hear from certain petty critics of our age the complaint that all solidity has vanished from the world [*alles Solidität aus der Welt verschwunden sei*] and that being is neglected for appearance." Marx does not opt for mere "solidity" and its passing because such language tends to play down the fact that such change is socially produced and willed (hence "stolid"), a process of mutability both conservative and continuous. Nor does Marx wish to melt bourgeois relations of production into a "timeless" brooding on mortality or a bout of apocalyptic fatalism. The idea of melting into air may not pick up adequately on *verdampfen* as linked perhaps to the defining (and defiling) sign of industrial pollution, which is why Carver smartly favours the notion of going up in smoke rather than melting into air. But this may be straying too far from the literal meaning of turning into vapour, a radical, elementary change of state evocative of the crucible of revolution as well as the furnaces of heavy industry. The *Manifesto* is dealing here not so much with dramatic illusion or environmental critique as with the

self-destabilizing realities of the bourgeois mode of production.

2. I gave some thought here and elsewhere in my translation to gender-sensitive language, because Marx and Engels need to be accountable on an ongoing basis to feminist critique for their androcentric understanding of the worlds of work and politics. I favour the plural "people" to capture the actual inclusiveness of the interrelational challenge posed, while hinting also at historically specific connections between insobriety and working-class women and men alleged by those intoxicated by their own prosperity and respectability.

3. I prefer "existence" to "life" as more suggestive of worldly exigency and privation. As Helen Macfarlane's upper case "Life" indicates, this term can be only too readily generalized, idealized, dehistoricized.

4. My choice of "interrelatedness" is designed to convey the reciprocity denoted by *gegenseitig* and to be faithful to the Marxist stress here and elsewhere on the social relations of production.

Third Translation Sample:

3 a Wir sahen schon oben, dass 'der erste Schritt in der Arbeiter-Revolution die Erhebung des Proletariats zur herrschenden Klasse, die Erkämpfung der Demokratie ist.
   b We have seen that the first step in the proletarian revolution, will be the conquest of Democracy, *the elevation of the Proletariat to the state of the ruling class.* (Macfarlane)
   c We have seen above, that the first step in the revolution by the working class, is to raise the proletariat to the position of the ruling class, to win the battle in [of] democracy. (Moore, Engels, and me)

Notes to sample:

1. Given the importance of the notion of a first step, there have been many attempts to define what is meant by winning what is often rendered as "the battle of democracy." The placing of two statements in apposition to each other suggests their inextricable connection via causality or equivalence. Both are part of a necessary sequence. But the question remains whether democracy is the outcome or destination of proletarian revolution, or rather its interim battleground. Whether, as Hal Draper plausibly suggests, Marx intentionally left ambiguous the meaning of the key phrase, "die Erkämpfung der Demokratie," or whether social and political conditions virtually forbade any clearer and more prescriptive articulation of the place of democratic struggle in the plot of revolution, cannot be fully and finally determined. And even if it were, and it was established that Marx was defining a struggle for a fully proletarian democracy, there is still a case for strategic contextualism trumping authorial intention. The *Manifesto* can be both conciliatory and severe, depending on whether terms like "communism," "revolution," and "democracy" are being understood and applied in a helpful way or appropriated to serve bourgeois interests. Marx's phrasing accommodates the possibility of the Communist League aligning itself with more broadly democratic forces to advance the interests of the proletariat. However, it also discreetly registers reservations about some of the things done in the name of democracy as a bourgeois panacea for the ills of all social classes. It is therefore, as the commodification of democracy in recent years attests (see Findlay 2000), necessary to demystify democracy in the current conjuncture as a seriously imperfect arrangement or aspiration, or as a set of institutions and practice subservient to the transnational, neo-mercantilist interests of major powers. Strategically, now, the *Manifesto* is perhaps most usefully understood as proposing here a battle *within* current democratic structures *for* democracy that will be defined and enjoyed only as the product of proletarian revolution.

Marx and Engels: A Brief Chronology

1818   M born May 5 in Trier

1821   E baptised, January 18, in the Reformed Evangelical faith in nearby Eberfeld

1824   M and his siblings, Sophie, Hermann, Henriette, Louise, Emilie, and Caroline baptised in the Evangelical Church

1829   E enters municipal school in Barmen, remaining there until 1834

1830   M enters Friedrich-Wilhelm-Gymnasium (highschool) in Trier

1835   M graduates from highschool and enrols in Law at Bonn University; continues writing poems; begins corresponding with his father

1836   M transfers to University of Berlin after being disciplined for debts, duelling, and drunkenness; sends his poems to Jenny Westphalen to whom he is secretly engaged

1837   M is already attempting to rethink philosophy, law, history, in part in through an intense engagement with Hegel, in part in the Doctor's club (Young Hegelians), in part in notebooks to which he would continue to confide some of the most important excerpts from his reading throughout his life; writes *Scorpion and Felix* (a "comic novel"), *Oulalam* (a play), *Cleanthes* (a philosophical dialogue), as well as more poetry; his health suffers and he moves outside Berlin on doctor's orders;
E is removed from highschool by his father so he can learn the family business

1838   M's lifelong heart and eye problems begin, and he is certified unfit for a possible year of military service; father dies in May in Trier;
E travels through Netherlands to Britain, likely with his father, to visit the family business (Ermen and

Engels) in Manchester; thereafter begins training as
a commercial clerk in Bremen

1839 M begins work on a doctoral thesis on the
philosophy of Epicurus with the aim of securing a
university position in Bonn;
E continues his training and gets his start as a writer
on socio-political and literary topics for Bremen
newspapers, sometimes using an alias because of
reaction to his liberal views and tastes

1840 M expands the scope of his dissertation while
maintaining contact with Young Hegelians;
E extends his journalistic reputation in more
prominent and influential outlets

1841 M completes his dissertation and receives his Ph.D.
from Jena; the suspension of a mentor, the Young
Hegelian Bruno Bauer, from the faculty at Bonn
makes the rapidly radicalising M realize he has no
future within the conservative and zealously self-
policing German academy;
E returns home from Bremen to Barmen; travels
with his father in Switzerland and Italy before
moving to Berlin for a year's voluntary military
service; attends lectures by Schelling (with whom
he vigorously disagrees in print) and others at
U of Berlin, and attaches himself to a Young
Hegelian group

1842 M writes for and becomes editor in chief of the
Rheinische Zeitung (Rhenisch Times), encountering
and engaging directly with the government
censorship which doomed his university prospects;
he also quarrels with both his employers and the
bombastic leftists seeking to publish in the Times;
his editorial duties entail moving to Cologne where
he begins studying socio-economic matters so that
he can the better rebut all who oppose him;
E completes his military service and goes home
briefly before moving to Manchester where he will
remain for two years, learning the family business

there; en route he stops in Cologne and meets M for the first time; M is wary of E because he thinks him committed to the self-mystifying leftism of the Berlin "Frees"

1843   M resigns as editor of the Times but the Prussian government bans it anyway; June 19 he marries Jenny, refuses a government appointment, and spends next four months in Kreuznach studying the French Revolution with his usual heroic thoroughness; M and Jenny move to Paris where he will join Arnold Ruge in publishing the *Deutsch Französischer Jahrbücher* (Germano-French Annals); completes his essay "On the Jewish Question" while establishing contacts with French leftists and the leaders of secret workers' societies; begins friendship with poet and critic, Heinrich Heine; E begins serious study of British socialism, social conditions in Manchester and the industrial north, and political economy; publishes reports on what he sees in England and makes contact with leaders of the League of the Just, and then with chartist George Julian Harney of *The Northern Star* who reprints his reports on left developments on the continent; writes important essays on Prussia and on political economy as well; becomes friends with the German revolutionary poet, Georg Weerth, another member of the German radical diaspora

1844   M cannot keep the annals going beyond its inaugural double issue because of his ideological split with Ruge, but his contributions to it are enough for the German police to confiscate 800 of the 1,000 copies printed and Prussian government to issue a warrant for his arrest for "high treason and lèse majesté," should he return home; his activities are funded for the first time by German supporters, while his contacts with Russian and French radicals widen; after writing his introduction to Hegel's political theory he embarks

on the *Economic and Philosophical Manuscripts*; the
Silesian Weavers' Revolt of June 4–6 is brutally
repressed but its example will not go away; in
August E joins him in Paris and they collaborate for
the first time, on what will be completed by M as
The Holy Family; M's own family now includes a
daughter, "little Jenny";
E is now a regular contributor to Chartist
publications and a growing authority on both the
Condition of England and European communism

1845 M is expelled from France with other contributors
to *Vorwärts* and settles in Brussels in February;
completes his "Theses on Feuerbach"; M and E
now reading and writing togther, and strengthen
their English and émigré radical ties on visits to
London and Manchester; Jenny gives birth to
another daughter, Laura, future translator of the
Manifesto into French;
E publishes (in German) *The Condition of the
Working Class in England,* a book from which M
will derive much inspiration and guidance; E now
assisting M financially and speaking regularly to
political meetings in Germany as well as England

1846 M and E collaborate on *The German Ideology* for
which no publisher can be found, and establish the
Communist Correspondence Committee to make
Brussels a radical centre to rival London; M's son
Edgar is born;
E strengthens his ties with Harney midst much
turbulence at the top of the Chartist and related
movements; moves to Paris to consolidate ties with
League of the Just

1847 M and E succeed in merging the League of the Just
with their own alliances in a new Communist
League; M publishes his critique of Proudhon, *The
Poverty of Philosophy*; M and E participate (despite
hostility) in the International Congress of Economists
in Brussels in September, after spending two months

together discussing a new communist credo; M and E go to London for the December congress of the CL and are commissioned to write the *Manifesto*; M returns to Brussels to continue this task; E still running foul of the censors for his writings; attends the inaugural congress of the CL in London in June and thereafter begins drafting what will become the *Manifesto*; in Paris begins writing about Chartism for *La Réforme* and is Vice President of the new Democratic Association

1848   *Manifesto* published just after E's expulsion from France and before the February revolution there leading to the abdication of Louis Phillipe and proclamation of a Republic; the *Manifesto* will be serialized between March and July in the German London Times; M expelled from Belgium but welcomed in Paris; the March revolution in Berlin makes Friedrich Wilhelm IV (insincerely) promise a constitution; M and E publish "Demands of the Communist Party in Germany" to be distributed with the *Manifesto*; M and E return to Cologne in April to begin publishing the *New Rhenisch Times* in face of increasing official harassment; June uprising in Paris brutally repressed; M and E prolific in their critique of German reactionaries and in praise of revolutionary developments in Frankfurt, England, Italy, Czechoslovakia, Austria, even after E's enforced move to Switzerland

1849   M expelled from Prussia and then from Paris, residing thereafter in London; E fights for Baden-Palatinate forces before another exile in Switzerland, and then joins M in London

1850–66   These years are marked less by political involvement than by the analysis of what went to wrong in 1848 and how reaction, political economy, and capital can best be combatted (see especially *The Eighteenth Brumaire of Louis Bonaparte* [1852], *Grundrisse* [begun 1857], *Contribution to the Critique of Political Economy*

[1859], and *Theory of Surplus Value* [begun 1862]); M produces a good deal of journalism, including some 8 years of commentary for the *New York Daily Tribune,* and analyses conflicts like the Crimean War, Indian Mutiny, American Civil War, and the Irish Question from an increasingly "marxist" point of view; in preparing for his other most famous work, *Capital,* M reads incessantly in the British Museum and engages with basic concepts of value; E continues in the family business in Manchester while financially supporting M's family, writing regularly on military science and politics; with the founding of the International (Working Men's Association) in London in September 1864, political engagement will intensify once again, and the *Manifesto* will begin its inspirational work in earnest

1867 M publishes first volume of *Capital,* having hand delivered the ms. to Meissner in Amsterdam; the work is largely ignored by the bourgeois German press (though reviewed in four different outlets there by Engels); plans for translation attend the appearance of *Capital* too; M tries to secure English trade-union financial support for striking metal workers in Paris; in Germany M amused but unmoved by persistence of Bismarck's supporters' efforts to buy his formidable talents; M and E intensify their interest in Irish politics

1868 *Capital* I is taken up by workers' publications, including American ones, but not by the mainstream press; M works on *Capital* II midst a recurrent plague of headaches, carbuncles, insomnia, and poverty

1869 M attends the great Hyde Park demonstration of October 24 in defence of the Fenians; he is accompanied, as often on such occasions, by his wife and daughters

1870 Franco-Prussian War is followed by the establishment of the Third Republic in the defeated

France; the Irish Question is seen as key to an English and subsequently global revolution

1871 Paris Commune erupts on March 18, occasioning M's *The Civil War in France*; he intensifies his involvement with the IWMA; the *Manifesto* makes its way officially for the first time into Germany via the published record of the trial of Bebel and Liebknecht for treason in Leipzig; an offprint of this text, with a preface by the authors, is the first one to bear the title, *Das kommunistische Manifest,* a more prudent designation less obviously linked to its banned predecessor; the growth of the IWMA brings with it predictable tensions, squabbles, disciplinary action against Bakunin and others

1872–74 M writing, maintaining an extensive correspondence, keeping the IWMA going, despite chronic health problems

1875 M publishes his *Critique of the Gotha Progam* exposing the concessions made to Lasalleans by the SDSWP when they effected their socialist merger in Gotha

1876 M agrees to write another preface to the *Manifesto*; an updating appendix he still considers premature; M continues to study Russian and American agrarian theories and practices

1881 M's wife Jenny dies in in December

1882 M in Algiers in March-April for health reasons; E first mentions M's famous quip, "What's certain is that I am no Marxist"

1883 M dies March 7; E shelves his own great work (*The Dialectics of Nature*) to become executor, custodian of the legend, expert decoder of M's notoriously illegible handwriting, posthumous benefactor of his friend's memory, surviving works, and family, most notably via seeing two more volumes of *Capital* into print; there is a remarkable multi-lingual funeral for M in Highgate Cemetery but a perfunctory and inaccurate obituary in the *Times* of

London, his long-time home; memorials follow in New York, Paris, Moscow, etc., emphasizing his status as a world figure

1895   E dies August 5 after more than a decade of ceaseless effort on behalf of that revolutionary international proletariat envisioned in the *Manifesto* and now most significantly in evidence in Britain, Russia, France, Germany, and the United States; there is an outpouring of sympathy and solidarity around the world for this remarkable, self-described "second fiddle"; his ashes are spread from a rowboat in the English Channel by Eleanor Marx, her partner Edward Aveling, a comrade from the movement's earliest days, Friedrich Lessner, and an exemplar of "revisionism," Eduard Bernstein, an aptly mixed crew depositing an inert yet immortal cargo in a symbolically apt location.

Fig. 11: Title-Page of the First Edition of the
Manifest der Kommunistischen Partei

A spectre is stalking Europe—the spectre of Communism. All the Powers of Old Europe have bound themselves in a crusade against this spectre: the Pope and the Czar, Metternich and Guizot, French Radicals and German police.[1] Where is the opposition party that has not been denounced as Communistic by its opponents in power? Where the opposition party that has not hurled back the branding reproach of Communism against the more progressive members of the opposition as well as against its reactionary adversaries? Two things stem from this fact:

I. Communism is already acknowledged by all European Powers to be a Power [too].

II. It is high time that the Communists openly set forth before the whole world their perspective, their aims, their tendencies, and meet this fairy tale about the Spectre of Communism with a Manifesto of the Party itself.

To this end, Communists of the most diverse nationalities have assembled in London, and devised the following Manifesto, that is to be published in the English, French, German, Italian, Flemish and Danish languages.

---

[1] Pope Pius IX (1792–1878) was elected in 1846. He maintained the reactionary traditions of the papal office. Czar Nicholas I (1796–1855) had already ruled Russia for more than 20 years. Prince Metternich (1773–1859) masterminded European reactionary measures during and after the Congress of Vienna (1814–15) and via the Holy Alliance, shoring up most particularly what he called the "mouldering edifice" of the Austro-Hungarian Empire. François Guizot (1787–1874), an increasingly conservative historian turned politician, was French Foreign Minister from 1840 to 1848. French Radicals here are not the revolutionary sort but bourgeois moderates, both anti-monarchist and anti-populist, associated with *Le national*. Police powers, not only in Germany, continued to be exercised in the interest of elites.

I

BOURGEOIS AND PROLETARIANS

The history of all society hitherto is the history of class struggles.[1]

Freeman and slave, patrician and plebeian, lord and serf, guild-master and journeyman, in short, oppressor and oppressed, situated in constant opposition to one another, carried on an uninterrupted, now hidden, now open conflict, a fight that each time ended in a revolutionary transformation of the entire society or in the common ruin of the contending classes.

In the earlier epochs of history, we find almost everywhere a comprehensive articulation of society into various orders, a manifold gradation of social ranks. In ancient Rome we have patricians, knights, plebeians, slaves; in the Middle Ages, feudal lords, vassals, guild-masters, journey-men, apprentices, serfs; and in almost all of these classes further specific gradations.

The modern bourgeois society that has sprouted from the ruins of feudal society has not done away with class antagonisms. It has but established new classes, new conditions of oppression, new forms of struggle in place of the old ones.

However, our epoch, the epoch of the bourgeoisie distinguishes itself by the fact it has simplified the class antagonisms. Society as a whole is more and more splitting up into two great hostile camps, into two great classes directly confronting each other: Bourgeoisie and Proletariat.

From the serfs of the Middle Ages sprang the chartered

---

[1] That is, all *written* history. In 1847, the pre-history of society, the social organization existing previous to recorded history, was all but unknown. Since then Haxthausen discovered common ownership of land in Russia, Maurer proved it to be the social foundation from which all Teutonic races started in history, and by and by village communities were found to be, or to have been the primitive form of society everywhere from India to Ireland. The inner organization of this primitive Communistic society was laid bare, in its typical form, by Morgan's crowning discovery of the true nature of the *gens* and its relation to the *tribe*. With the dissolution of these primaeval communities society begins to be differentiated into separate and finally antagonistic classes. I have attempted to retrace this process of dissolution in: "Der Ursprung der Familie des Privateigenthums und des Staats," 2nd edit, Stuttgart, 1886. [Engels' note to 1888 translation]

burghers of the earliest towns. From this bourgeoisification the first elements of the bourgeoisie were developed.

The discovery of America, the rounding of the Cape, opened up a new terrain for the rising bourgeoisie. The East-Indian and Chinese markets, the colonisation of America, trade with the colonies, the increase in the means of exchange and in commodities generally, gave to commerce, to navigation, to industry, an impulse never before known, and thereby, to the revolutionary element in the tottering feudal society, a rapid development.

The hitherto existing feudal or guild system of industry could no longer cope with the growing needs of the new markets. The manufacturing system took its place. The guild-masters were pushed to one side by the manufacturing middle class; the division of labour between the different corporate guilds vanished before the division of labour within the selfsame workshop.

But the markets kept constantly growing, the demand constantly rising. Even manufacture no longer coped. Thereupon, steam and machinery revolutionised industrial production. The place of manufacture was taken by modern big industry, the place of the industrial middle class by industrial millionaires, the leaders of whole industrial armies, the modern bourgeois.

Big industry has established the world market, for which the discovery [sic] of America prepared the way. This market has given an inestimable development to commerce, to navigation, to communication by land. This development has, in its turn, reacted on the extension of industry; and in proportion as industry, commerce, navigation, railways extended, in the same proportion the bourgeoisie extended, increased its capital, and pushed into the background all of the classes handed down from the Middle Ages.

We see, therefore, how the modern bourgeoisie is itself the product of a long course of development, of a series of revolutions in the modes of production and of exchange.

Each of these steps in the development of the bourgeoisie was accompanied by a corresponding political advance of that class. An oppressed cohort under the sway of the feudal nobility, armed and self-governing associations in the commune; here independent urban republic, there taxable third estate of the monarchy, afterwards, in the period of manufacture proper, serving either the semi-feudal or the absolute monarchy as a counterpoise against the nobility, and as cornerstone of the great monarchies in general. The bourgeoisie has at last, since the establishment of big industry and of the world market, acquired for itself, in the modern representative State, exclusive political sway. The executive of the modern State is but a committee for managing the common affairs of the whole bourgeoisie.

The bourgeoisie has played an intensely revolutionary part in history.

The bourgeoisie, wherever it has got the upper hand, has put an end to all feudal, patriarchal, idyllic relations. It has remorselessly torn asunder the motley feudal ties that bound people to their natural superiors, and has left remaining no other nexus between two people than naked self-interest, than callous "cash payment." It has drowned the heavenly ecstasies of religious fervour, of chivalrous enthusiasm, of philistine sentimentalism, in the ice-cold water of egotistical calculation. It has dispersed personal worth into exchange value, and in place of the numberless chartered, fully earned freedoms has set up a single, unconscionable freedom—Free Trade. In a word, in place of exploitation, veiled by religious and political illusions, it has substituted public, shameless, direct, blatant exploitation.

The bourgeoisie has stripped of its halo every occupation hitherto honoured and looked up to with reverent awe. It has converted the physician, the lawyer, the priest, the poet, the researcher, into its paid wage-labourers.

The bourgeoisie has torn away from the connectedness of the family its consoling veil, and has reduced it to a merely monetary relation.

The bourgeoisie has disclosed how the brutal display of vigour in the Middle Ages, which reactionaries so much admire, found its fitting complement in the most slothful indolence. It has been the first to show what human effort can achieve. It has worked wonders of a different order than Egyptian pyramids, Roman aqueducts, and Gothic cathedrals; it has conducted expeditions of a different order than all diasporas of peoples and crusades.

The bourgeoisie cannot exist without constantly revolutionising the instruments of production, thereby the relations of production, and hence social relations in their entirety. Retaining the old mode of production in unaltered form, was, by contrast, the first condition of existence for all earlier industrial classes. Constant, radical transformation of production, uninterrupted disturbance of all social conditions, everlasting insecurity and mobility distinguish the bourgeois epoch from all earlier ones. All relations fixed, corroded fast, with their retinue of ancient and venerable thinking and opinion, are dispersed, all new-formed ones become antiquated before they can ossify. Everything set and stolid turns to vapour, all that is holy is profaned, and people are at last compelled to confront soberly their situation in life, their relations to others.

The need for a constantly expanding market for its products chases the bourgeoisie over the whole surface of the globe. It must nestle everywhere, settle everywhere, establish connexions everywhere.

The bourgeoisie has through its exploitation of the world market given a cosmopolitan character to production and consumption of all countries. To the great chagrin of reactionaries, it has removed from under the feet of industry the national ground. All venerable national industries have been destroyed or are daily being destroyed. They are dislodged by new industries, whose introduction becomes a life-and-death question for all civilised nations, by industries that no longer work up native raw material, but raw material drawn from the remotest zones; industries whose products are consumed not only at home but in every part of the world. In place of the old wants, satisfied by the productions of the country, emerge new wants requiring for their satisfaction the products of the most remote lands and climes. In place of the old local and national seclusion and self-sufficiency, there emerges multifaceted intercourse, a comprehensive interdependence of nations. And as in material, so also in intellectual production the intellectual products of individual nations become common property. National one-sidedness and narrow-mindedness become more and more impossible, and from the numerous national and local literatures a world literature forms itself.

The bourgeoisie, by the rapid improvement of all instruments of production, by the immensely facilitated means of communication, draws all nations, even the most barbarian, into civilisation.

The cheap prices of its commodities are the heavy artillery with which it batters down all Chinese walls, with which it forces the barbarians' most entrenched hatred of foreigners to capitulate. It compels all nations, if they are not to be overwhelmed, to adopt the bourgeois mode of production; it compels them to introduce what it calls civilisation into their midst, i.e., to become bourgeois themselves. In a word, it creates a world after its own image.

The bourgeoisie has subjected the country to the rule of the towns. It has created enormous cities, has greatly increased the urban population as compared with the rural, and has thus rescued a considerable part of the population from the idiotism of rural life. Just as it has made the country dependent on the town, so it has made barbarian and semi-barbarian countries dependent on the civilised ones, nations of peasants on nations of bourgeois, the East on the West.

The bourgeoisie keeps more and more doing away with the scattered state of the population, of the means of production, and of property. It has agglomerated the population, centralised means of production, and concentrated property in a few hands. The necessary consequence of this was political centralisation. Independent or but loosely connected provinces with separate interests, laws, governments and systems of taxation, were pressed together into one nation, one government, one code of laws, one national class-interest, one tariff-zone.

The bourgeoisie, during its rule of scarce one hundred years, has created more massive and more colossal productive forces than have all preceding generations together. Subjection of Nature's forces to man, machinery, application of chemistry to industry and agriculture, steam-navigation, railways, electric telegraphs, clearing of whole continents for cultivation, making river-traffic possible, whole populations conjured out of the ground—what earlier century had even a presentiment that such productive forces slumbered in the lap of social labour?

We have seen then, that the means of production and of exchange, on whose foundation the bourgeoisie built itself up, were generated in feudal society. At a certain stage in the development of these means of production and of exchange, the conditions under which feudal society produced and exchanged, the feudal organisation of agriculture and manufacturing industry, in a word, the feudal relations of property became no longer compatible with the already developed productive forces; they transformed themselves into so many fetters. They had to be burst asunder; they were burst asunder.

Into their place stepped free competition, accompanied by the social and political constitution adapted to it, and by the economical and political sway of the bourgeois class.

A similar movement is going on before our very eyes. Modern bourgeois society with its relations of production, of exchange and of property, a society that has conjured up such gigantic means of production and of exchange, is like the sorcerer who is no longer able to control the powers of the nether world whom he has summoned by his spells. For many a decade past the history of industry and commerce is but the history of the revolt of modern productive forces against the modern conditions of production, against the property relations that are the conditions of existence of the bourgeoisie and of its rule. It is enough to mention the commercial crises that by their political return put on trial, ever more threateningly, the existence of the entire bourgeois society. In these commercial crises a great part not only of the products produced but also of the previously created productive forces, are regularly destroyed. In these crises there breaks out a social epidemic that in all earlier epochs would have seemed an absurdity—the epidemic of over-production. Society suddenly finds itself returned to a state of passing barbarism; it appears as if a famine, a universal war of devastation had cut off the supply of every means of subsistence; industry and commerce seem to be destroyed. And why? Because there is too much civilisation, too much means of subsistence, too much industry, too much commerce. The productive forces at our disposal no longer tend to further the development of the relations of bourgeois civilisation; on the contrary, they have become too powerful for these relations by which they are encumbered, and so soon as they overcome these encumbrances, they bring into disorder the whole of bourgeois society, then endanger the existence of bourgeois property. The relations of bourgeois society have become too narrow to comprise the wealth created by them. And how does the bourgeoisie get over these crises? On the one hand by the enforced destruction of a mass of productive forces; on the other by the conquest of new markets, and by the more thorough exploitation of the old ones. And by what means? By preparing the way for more general and more destructive crises, and by diminishing the means whereby crises are prevented.

The weapons with which the bourgeoisie felled feudalism to the ground are now turned against the bourgeoisie itself.

But not only has the bourgeoisie forged the weapons that bring death to itself; it has also called into existence the people who are to wield those weapons—the modern workers, the proletarians.

To the same degree as the bourgeoisie, i.e., capital, is developed, so is the proletariat, the modern working class, developed—a class of labourers, who live only so long as they find work, and who find work only so long as their labour increases capital. These workers who must sell themselves piecemeal are a commodity, like every other article of commerce, and are consequently exposed equally to all the vicissitudes of competition, all the fluctuations of the market.

Owing to the expanded use of machinery and to division of labour, the work of the proletarians has lost all individual character, and, consequently, all charm for the worker. He [or she] becomes a mere appendage of the machine, and it is only the most simple, most monotonous, and most easily acquired dexterity that is required of them. The cost of production of workers is restricted, almost entirely, to the means of subsistence that they require to maintain themselves and reproduce their stock [Race]. But the price of a commodity, and therefore also of labour, is equal to its cost of production. In proportion, therefore, as the repulsiveness of the work increases, the wage decreases. Nay more, in proportion as the use of machinery and division of labour increases, in the same proportion the burden of toil also increases, whether by extension of the working hours, by increase of the work exacted in a given time, by increased speed of the machinery, etc.

Modern industry has converted the little workshop of the patriarchal master into the great factory of the industrial capitalist. Masses of workers, pressed together in the factory, are organised like soldiers. As ordinary soldiers in the industrial army they are placed under the command of a comprehensive hierarchy of sub-officers and officers. Not only are they slaves of the bourgeois class, and of the bourgeois state; they are daily and hourly enslaved by the machine, by the overseer, and, above all, by the individual bourgeois manufacturer himself. The more openly this despotism proclaims gain to be its ultimate goal, the more petty, hateful and the more embittering it is.

The less the skill and exertion of strength implied in manual labour, in other words, the more modern industry becomes developed, the more is the labour of men superseded by that of women. Differences of age and sex have no longer any social validity for the working class. They are only instruments of labour, more or less costly to use, according to their age and sex.

No sooner is the exploitation of the labourer by the manufacturer, so far, at an end, and he receives his wages in cash, than he is set upon by the other portions of the bourgeoisie, the landlord, the shopkeeper, the pawnbroker, etc.

The lower strata of the middle class—the small tradespeople, shopkeepers, and retired tradesmen, the handicraftsmen and peasants—all these cohorts sink into the proletariat, partly because their meagre capital does not suffice for the scale on which big industry is carried on, and is swamped in the competition with the bigger capitalists, partly because their skill is rendered worthless by new methods of production. Thus the proletariat is recruited from all classes of the population.

The proletariat goes through various stages of development. With its birth begins its struggle with the bourgeoisie.

At first the contest is carried on by individual labourers, then by the workpeople of a factory, then by the operatives of one trade, in one locality, against the individual bourgeois who directly exploits them. They direct their attacks not only against the bourgeois conditions of production, but they direct them against the instruments of production themselves; they destroy imported wares that compete with their labour, they smash machinery, they set factories ablaze, they seek to restore by force the vanished status of the worker in the Middle Ages.

At this stage the workers form a mass scattered over the whole country and fragmented by competition. Uniting to form more compact bodies is not yet the consequence of their own active union, but the uniting of the bourgeoisie, which, in order to attain its own political ends, is compelled to set the whole proletariat in motion, and is yet for a time able to do so. At this stage, then, the proletarians do not fight their enemies, but the enemies of their enemies, the remnants of absolute monarchy, the landowners, the non-industrial bourgeois, the petty bourgeoisie. In this fashion, the whole historical movement is concentrated in the hands of the bourgeoisie; every victory so obtained is a victory for the bourgeoisie.

But with the development of industry the proletariat not only increases in number; it becomes concentrated into greater masses, its strength grows, and it feels its strength more. The interests and conditions of life within the ranks of the proletariat are more and more alike, in proportion as machinery obliterates distinctions of labour, and nearly everywhere reduces wages to the same low level. The growing competition among the bourgeois, and the resulting commercial crises, make the wages of the workers ever more fluctuating. The unceasing improvement of machinery, ever more rapidly developing, makes their situation in life more and more precarious; the collisions between individual workers and individual bourgeois take more and more the character of collisions between two classes. Thereupon the workers begin to form combinations against the bourgeois; they club together in order to keep up wages. They enter into long-term associations in order to make provision beforehand for these occasional revolts. Here and there the struggle breaks out into riots.

From time to time the workers are victorious, but only for a time. The real fruit of their struggles lies, not in the immediate result, but in the ever more inclusive union of the workers. It is assisted by the enhanced means of communication that are created by big industry and that place the workers of different localities in contact with one another. It was just this contact that was needed to centralise the numerous local struggles, all of the same character, into one national struggle between classes. But every class struggle is a political struggle. And that union, to attain which the burghers of the Middle Ages with their miserable highways required centuries, the modern proletarians by means of railways achieve in a few years.

This organisation of the proletarians into a class, and consequently into a political party, is at every instant unsettled again by the competition between the workers themselves. But it always rises up again, stronger, firmer, mightier. It compels legislative recognition of particular interests of the workers by making use of the divisions within the bourgeoisie itself. And so the Ten Hours Bill in England.[1]

Overall, collisions within the old society further, in many ways, the course of development of the proletariat. The bourgeoisie is embroiled in an ongoing struggle: at first with the aristocracy; later on with those portions of the bourgeoisie itself whose interests have been set at odds with the progress of industry; at all times, with the bourgeoisie of all foreign countries. In all these struggles it sees itself required to appeal to the proletariat, to ask for its help, and thus to propel it into the political arena. The bourgeoisie itself, therefore, supplies the proletariat with its own elements of education, that is to say, with weapons usable against itself.

Moreover, as we saw, entire sections of the ruling classes are by the advance of industry precipitated into the proletariat or are at least threatened in their conditions of existence. These also supply the proletariat with a significant amount of educational elements.

Finally, in times when the class struggle nears decision, the process of dissolution inside the ruling class, within the whole of old society, assumes such a violent, glaring character, that a small section of the ruling class cuts itself adrift to join the revolutionary class, the class that holds the future in its hands. Just as, therefore, at an earlier period, a section of the nobility went over to the bourgeoisie, so now a portion of the bourgeoisie goes over to the proletariat, and in particular a portion of the bourgeois

---

[1] In 1847 an Act was passed limiting the work of women and children to 10 hours per day and 58 hours per week. When first proposed, this legislation produced a major split between aristocratic populists and the industrial bourgeoisie. The complex and shifting economic and political allegiances that made the Bill's passage possible, and its enforceability questionable, are well analysed by E in two articles in 1850 (MECW 10:288–300 and 271–76). For M's manuscript draft of this passage, see Fig. 10.

ideologists, who have raised themselves to a theoretical understanding of the historical in its entirety.

Of all the classes that stand face to face with the bourgeoisie today, the proletariat alone is a really revolutionary class. The other classes decay and go under in the presence of big industry; the proletariat is its very own product.

The middling levels—the small manufacturer, the small trader, the artisan, the peasant—all these fight against the bourgeoisie to save from extinction their existence as fractions of the middle class. They are therefore not revolutionary, but conservative. Nay more, they are reactionary, for they try to roll back the wheel of history. Should they be revolutionary, they are so in view of their impending transfer into the proletariat; they thus defend not their present but their future interests, they abandon their own standpoint in order to set themselves on proletarian ground.

The lumpenproletariat, that passive putrifying of the lowest layers of old society, may here and there be swept into the movement by a proletarian revolution; its lot in life, however, disposes it more readily to be bought for the cause of reactionary intrigue.

The conditions of existence of old society are already nullified in the conditions of existence of the proletariat. The proletarian is without property; his relation to wife and children has nothing else in common with bourgeois family relations; modern industrial labour, modern subjection to capital, the same in England as in France, in America as in Germany, has stripped him of every trace of national character. Law, morality, religion, are to him so many bourgeois prejudices, behind which lurk many bourgeois interests.

All the preceding classes that got the upper hand, ought to secure their already acquired status by subjecting society at large to their conditions of appropriation. The proletarians cannot take command of the productive forces of society, except by abolishing their own previous mode of appropriation, and thereby also every other previous mode of appropriation. The proletarians have nothing of their own to protect; their mission is to destroy all hitherto existing protection and insurance for private holdings.

All previous historical movements were movements of minorities, or in the interest of minorities. The proletarian movement is the independent movement of the immense majority in the interest of the immense majority. The proletariat, the lowest stratum of our present society, cannot raise itself up, cannot stand up straight, without exploding the whole stratified superstructure of official society.

Though not in substance, yet in form, the struggle of the proletariat with the bourgeoisie is at first a national one. The proletariat of each country must naturally first of all settle matters with its own bourgeoisie.

In depicting the most general phases of the development of the proletariat, we traced the more or less concealed civil war within existing society, up to the point where that war breaks out into open revolution, and where the forceful overthrow of the bourgeoisie lays the foundation for the sway of the proletariat.

Hitherto, every form of society has been based, as we have already seen, on the antagonism of oppressing and oppressed classes. But in order to oppress a class, certain conditions must be assured to it under which it can, at least, continue its slavish existence. The serf, in the period of serfdom, raised himself to membership in the commune, just as the petty bourgeois, under the yoke of feudal absolutism, managed to develop into a bourgeois. The modern worker, on the contrary, instead of rising with the progress of industry, sinks deeper and deeper below the conditions of existence of his own class. He becomes a pauper, and pauperism develops more rapidly than population and wealth. And here it becomes evident that the bourgeoisie is unfit any longer to be the ruling class in society, and to impose its conditions of existence upon society as directive law. It is unfit to rule because it is incompetent to assure an existence to its slave within his [or her] slavery, because it cannot help letting them sink into such a state that it has to feed him instead of being fed by him. Society can no longer live under it; i.e., its existence is no longer compatible with society.

The most essential condition for the existence and for the sway of the bourgeois class is the accumulation of riches in private hands, the formation and augmentation of capital. The condition for capital is wage-labour. Wage-labour rests exclusively on competition between the labourers. The advance of industry, whose unwilling and unstoppable instrument is the bourgeoisie, replaces the isolation of the workers due to competition by their revolutionary combination due to association. The development of big industry, therefore, cuts from under its feet the very foundation on which the bourgeoisie produces and appropriates products. It produces, above all, its own grave-diggers. Its fall and the victory of the proletariat are alike inevitable.

II
PROLETARIANS AND COMMUNISTS

In what relation do the Communists stand to the proletarians in general?

The Communists do not constitute a party distinct from other workers parties.

They have no interests separate from those of the proletariat as a whole.

They do not lay out any principles peculiar to themselves, through which they wish to mould the proletarian movement.

The Communists are distinguished from the other working-class parties by this only, that, in the various national struggles common to the proletarians, they point out and bring to prominence the shared interests of the entire proletariat, independent of nationality; and that, on the other hand, in the various stages of development which the struggle of the working class against the bourgeoisie passes through, they always represent the interests of the movement as a whole.

The Communists, therefore, are in effect, the most resolute section of the workers parties of every country, always pressing further; on the other hand, they have over the great mass of the proletariat the theorising edge in understanding the conditions, heading, and the general results of the proletarian movement.

The immediate aim of the Communists is the same as that of all the other proletarian parties: formation of the proletariat into a class, overthrow of the bourgeois rule, conquest of political power by the proletariat.

The theoretical conclusions of the Communists are in no way based on ideas or principles that have been invented, discovered by this or that global improver.

They are simply general versions of actual relations in an existing class struggle, in a historical movement going on before our eyes. The abolition of existing property relations is not an indicator exclusive to Communism.

All property relations have been subject to continual historical change, a persistent historical alteration.

The French Revolution, for example, abolished feudal property in favour of bourgeois property.[1]

What distinguishes Communism is not the abolition of property generally, but the abolition of bourgeois property.

But modern bourgeois private property is the final and most complete expression of the production and appropriation of products based on class antagonisms, on the exploitation of some by others.

In this sense, the Communists can sum up their theory in this one motto: abolition of private property.

We Communists have been reproached for wishing to abolish the right to acquire personal property by working for it oneself, which property is alleged to be the foundation of all personal freedom, activity and independence.

Hard-won, self-acquired, self-earned property! Do you mean the property of the petty bourgeois and the small peasant, a form of property that preceded bourgeois property? We have no need to abolish it; the development of industry has abolished it and abolishes it every day.

Or do you speak of modern bourgeois private property?

But does wage-labour, the work of the proletarian, produce any property for him [or her]? Not a bit. It produces capital, i.e., the property which exploits wage-labour, which cannot increase except when it begets fresh wage-labour. Property, in its current form, derives from the antagonism of capital and wage-labour. Let us examine both sides of this antagonism.

To be a capitalist is to have not only a purely personal, but a

---

[1] Compare Appendix L.3.

social status in production. Capital is a collective product, and only by the united action of many members, nay, in the last resort, only by the united action of all members of society, can it be set in motion.

Therefore, capital is not a personal but a social power.

When, therefore, capital is converted into common property, into the property of all members of society, personal property is not transformed into social property. Only the social character of the property is changed. It loses its class character.

We come now to wage-labour.

The average price of wage-labour is the minimum wage, i.e., the amount of the means of subsistence necessary to keep the worker functioning as a worker. What, therefore, the wage-labourer appropriates by means of his labour, suffices merely to prolong and reproduce his [or her] bare existence. We are by no means inclined to abolish this personal appropriation of the products of labour for the reproduction of human life, an appropriation that leaves no surplus wherewith to command the labour of others. We want to do away only with the miserable character of this appropriation, through which the labourer lives merely to increase capital and lives only in so far as the interest of the ruling class requires it.

In bourgeois society, living labour is simply a means to increase accumulated labour. In communist society, accumulated labour is simply a means to expand, to enrich, to promote the workers' way of life.

In bourgeois society, therefore, the past dominates the present; in communist society, the present dominates the past. In bourgeois society capital is independent and individualized, while the living individual is dependent and depersonalized.

And the elimination of these conditions is called by the bourgeois the death of individuality and freedom! And rightly so. It is undoubtedly a matter of making bourgeois individuality, independence, and freedom disappear.

By freedom, under the present bourgeois conditions of production, is understood free trade, free buying and selling.

But if dealing disappears, the free dealing disappears as well. The talk about free dealing, like the rest of our bourgeoisie's bold hyping of freedom, is generally meaningful only in contrast with restricted dealing, with the fettered traders of the Middle Ages, but not when opposed to the communistic elimination of dealing, of the bourgeois conditions of production, and of the bourgeoisie itself.

You are horrified by our intending to do away with private property. But in your existing society, private property is no longer an option for nine-tenths of the population; it exists precisely because for nine-tenths it does not exist. You charge us, therefore, with intending to do away with a form of property whose necessary precondition is that the immense majority of society should have no property at all.

In a word, you charge us with intending to put an end to your property. Precisely so; that is just what we intend.

From the moment when labour can no longer be converted into capital, money, or ground rent, in short into a social power that may be monopolised, i.e., from the moment when individual property can no longer be transformed into bourgeois property, into capital, from that moment, you claim, individuality is suspended.

You therefore confess that by the individual you mean none other than the bourgeois, the bourgeois owner of property. And this person must certainly be eliminated.

Communism deprives no one of the power to appropriate the products of society; it deprives one only of the power to subjugate others' labour by means of such appropriation.

It has been objected that with the abolition of private property all effort will cease and universal laziness take over.

According to this, bourgeois society ought long ago to have succumbed to idleness; for those of its number who work in it acquire nothing, and those who do not make acquisitions. This objection expresses in sum the tautology that there can no longer be any wage-labour when there is no longer any capital.

All objections urged against the communistic mode of producing and appropriating material products, have similarly been urged against the communistic modes of producing and appropriating intellectual products. Just as for the bourgeois the disappearance of class property is the disappearance of production itself, so the disappearance of class culture is to him [and her] identical with the disappearance of culture more generally.

The culture whose loss he laments, is, for the enormous majority, training to be machines.

But don't wrangle with us by judging our intended abolition of bourgeois property against your bourgeois notions of freedom, culture, law, &c. Your very ideas are born of the conditions of bourgeois production and property, just as your law is but the will of your class made into regulation for all, a will, whose content is determined by the material conditions of existence of your class.

The selfish notion you use to transform into eternal laws of nature and of reason the social forms springing from your current relations of production and property—historical relations that come and go in the course of production—this misconception you share with every ruling class that has preceded you. What you understand about ancient property, what you understand about feudal property, you are yet unwilling to grasp about bourgeois.

Abolition of the family! Even the most radical flare up at this infamous proposal of the Communists.

On what foundation is today's family, the bourgeois family, based? On capital, on private gain. Fully developed, it exists only among the bourgeoisie; but it finds its complement in the lack of family imposed on proletarians and in public prostitution.

The bourgeois family will vanish as a matter of course when this its complement vanishes, and both will vanish with the vanishing of capital.

Do you charge us with wanting to stop the exploitation of children by their parents? To this crime we plead guilty.

But, you say, we destroy the most revered relations when we replace home education by social.

And is not your education also social—determined by the social conditions under which you educate, by the intervention, direct or indirect, of society, by means of schools, &c? The Communists have not invented the intervention of society in education; they do but alter its character, seizing education from the influence of a ruling class.

The bourgeois discourse of the family and education, about the revered bond between parent and child, becomes all the more disgusting, the more, by the action of big industry, all family ties among the proletarians are torn asunder and the children transformed into simple articles of commerce and instruments of labour.

But you Communists would introduce community of women, screams the whole bourgeoisie at us in chorus. The bourgeois sees in his wife a mere instrument of production. He hears that the instruments of production are to be exploited in common, and, naturally, can come to no other conclusion than that the lot of being common to all will likewise fall to women.

He has not a clue that it is exactly a matter of erasing the status of women as mere instruments of production.

At any rate, nothing is more ridiculous than the ultra-righteous indignation shown by our bourgeois at the alleged community of women ratified by the Communists. The Communists have no need to introduce community of women; it has existed almost always.

Our bourgeois, not content with having the wives and daughters of their proletarians at their disposal, not to mention official prostitution, take considerable pleasure in seducing each others' wives.

Bourgeois marriage is in reality a communality system of wives. At most, the Communists can be reproached with desiring to replace a hypocritically concealed community of women with an openly approved one. Besides, it is self-evident that the abolition of the present relations of production must entail the passing of the community of women deriving from them, i.e., of official and unofficial prostitution.

The Communists are further reproached with desiring to abolish countries and nationality.

The workers have no fatherland. One cannot take from them what they have not got. In that the proletariat must first acquire political supremacy, must elevate itself to be the national class, must constitute itself the nation, it is itself yet national, though by no means in the bourgeois sense.

National differences and antagonisms between peoples are daily vanishing more and more with the development of the bourgeoisie, with freedom of trade, the world market, uniformity in industrial production and in the corresponding conditions of existence.

The supremacy of the proletariat will cause them to vanish still more. United action of the leading civilised countries at least, is one of the first conditions for the emancipation of the proletariat.

In proportion as the exploitation of one individual by another is prohibited, the exploitation of one nation by another will also cease.

Along with the antagonism between classes within the nation, the hostility of nations towards each other also ceases.

The charges against communism made from a religious, philosophical, and generally ideological standpoints do not deserve a detailed response.

Does it require deep insight to comprehend that people's ideas, views and conceptions—in a word, their consciousness—changes with their conditions of existence, their social relations and their life in society?

What does the history of ideas indicate other than that intellectual production changes along with material production? The ruling ideas of any age are always the ideas of the ruling class.

People speak of ideas that revolutionise an entire society; in this they do but express the fact that within the old society the elements of a new one have been developed, that the dissolution of the old ideas proceeds at the same pace as the dissolution of the old conditions of existence.

When the ancient world was in its last throes, the ancient religions were overcome by Christianity. When Christian ideas succumbed in the 18th century to Enlightenment ideas, feudal society engaged in its mortal struggle with the then revolutionary bourgeoisie. The ideas of freedom of conscience and religion conveyed merely the domination by free competition of the realm of conscience.

"But," it will be said, "religious, moral, philosophical, juridical ideas, etc. have indeed been modified in the course of historical development. Religion, morality, philosophy, politics, law, constantly survived this exchange."

"There are, besides, eternal truths, such as Freedom, Justice, etc., that are common to all states of society. Communism, however, abolishes eternal truths; it abolishes all religion and all morality instead of remodelling them afresh; it therefore contradicts all historical experience hitherto."

What does this accusation reduce itself to? The history of all society to date has taken the path of class antagonisms, antagonisms that assumed different forms in different epochs.

But whatever form they may have taken, the exploitation of one part of society by the other is a fact common to all preceding centuries. No wonder, then, that the social consciousness of all centuries, notwithstanding all the multiplicity and variety it displays, moves in certain common forms, forms of consciousness, which cannot completely vanish except with the total disappearance of class antagonisms.

The Communist revolution is the most radical rupture with traditional property relations; no wonder that in the course of its development there occurs the most radical rupture with traditional ideas.

But let us have done with the bourgeoisie's objections to communism.

We have already seen above that the first step in the worker-revolution is the raising of the proletariat to the ruling class, prevailing in democracy.

The proletariat will use its political supremacy to wrest all capital gradually from the bourgeoisie, to centralise all instruments of production in the hands of the State, i.e., of the proletariat organised as the ruling class, and to increase the body of productive forces as rapidly as possible.

Of course, in the beginning this cannot be achieved except by means of despotic inroads on the right of property, and on the relations of bourgeois production; by means of measures, therefore, which appear economically insufficient and untenable, but which, in the course of implementation outstrip themselves and are unavoidable as a means of transforming the whole mode of production.

These measures will of course be different in different countries.

Nevertheless, in the most advanced countries the following will be pretty generally applicable.

1. Expropriation of landed property and application of ground rent of land to state expenditures.
2. A heavy progressive tax.
3. Abolition of right of inheritance.
4. Confiscation of the Property of all emigrants and rebels.
5. Centralisation of credit in the hands of the state through a national bank with state capital and an exclusive monopoly.
6. Centralisation of all modes of transportation in the hands of the state.
7. Expansion of national factories and instruments of production owned by the state; reclamation and improvement of estates according to a common plan.
8. Equal liability of all to labour. Establishment of industrial armies, especially for agriculture.
9. Combination of agriculture and industry, to effect the gradual undoing of the opposition between town and country.
10. Free public education for all children. Doing away with children's factory labour in its present form. Combination of education with material production, etc., etc.

When, in the course of development, class distinctions have disappeared, and all production is concentrated in the hands of associated individuals, public power loses its political character. Political power in the proper sense is the organised power of one class for the subjugation of another. When the proletariat during its struggle with the bourgeoisie is compelled to organise itself as a class, by means of a revolution makes itself the ruling class, and as the ruling class forcibly removes the old conditions of production, then, along with these conditions, it eradicates the conditions for the existence of class conflict and of classes generally, and thereby its own supremacy as a class.

In place of the old bourgeois society, with its classes and class antagonisms, there emerges an association, in which the free development of each is the condition for the free development of all.

III
SOCIALIST AND COMMUNIST
LITERATURE

1. Reactionary Socialism

a. *Feudal Socialism.* Owing to their historical position, the aristocracies of France and England were called upon to write pamphlets against modern bourgeois society. In the July revolution of 1830 in France, and in the English reform movement, they once again succumbed to the hateful upstart. Thenceforth, a serious political contest was out of the question. A literary battle alone remained possible. But even in the realm of literature the old discourse of the restoration period had become impossible. In order to arouse sympathy, the aristocracy were obliged to lose sight apparently of their own interests, and to formulate their list of grievances against the bourgeoisie in the interest of the exploited working class alone. Thus they prepared for restitution by singing lampoons about their new master, and permitting themselves to whisper in his ear more or less ominous prophecies.

In this way arose feudal Socialism: half lamentation, half squib; half echo of the past, half menace of the future; at times, by its bitter, witty and incisive criticism striking the bourgeoisie to the heart; always comic in effect through total inability to grasp the operation of modern history.

They brandished the proletarian alms-bag like a banner, in order to rally the people behind them. But every popular following saw on their hindquarters the old feudal coats of arms and broke ranks midst loud and irreverent laughter.[1]

A section of the French Legitimists and Young England exhibited this spectacle best.[2]

---

[1] M borrows this image from Heinrich Heine's satirical poem, *A Winter's Tale* (1844), a work he had been instrumental in publishing in *Vorwärts.*

[2] Draper points out that the image of heraldic hindquarters comes from Heine's satirical poem of 1844, *Germany, a Winter's Tale,* which pokes fun at the neo-mediaeval spiked helmets of the Prussian cavalry. Marx sees analogous tendencies among the Bourbonists who resented the Orleanist reign of Louis Philippe from 1830 to 1848, but would have replaced him with more of the same under another name. And the

In pointing out that their mode of exploitation was cast otherwise than that of the bourgeoisie, the feudalists simply forgot that they exploited under circumstances and conditions wholly different and now outmoded. In demonstrating that under their rule the modem proletariat never existed, they simply forget that the modern bourgeoisie was the necessary offspring of their social structure.

At any rate, they conceal the reactionary character of their criticism so little that their chief grievance against the bourgeoisie amounts to this, that under their regime a class is emerging which will explode the whole of the old social order.

What they reproach the bourgeoisie more for is producing not so much a proletariat as a revolutionary one.

In political practice, therefore, they join in all coercive measures against the working class; and in ordinary life, despite their inflated rhetoric, they stoop to pick up the golden apples and to barter truth, love, and honour for traffic in wool, sugar beets, and schnapps.

As the parson has ever gone hand in hand with the feudalist, so has clerical socialism with feudal socialism.

Nothing is easier than to give Christian asceticism a socialist coating. Has not Christianity come out strongly against private property, against marriage, against the State? Has it not preached in the place of these, charity and mendicancy, celibacy and mortification of the flesh, monastic life and the Church? Religious socialism is but the holy water with which the priest consecrates the aristocrat's ire.

b. *Petty-Bourgeois Socialism.* The feudal aristocracy was not the only class brought down by the bourgeoisie, or whose conditions of existence wasted away and perished in modern bourgeois society. The medieval burgesses and small peasantry were the precursors of the modern bourgeoisie. In countries which are little developed, industrially and commercially, these classes still vegetate beside the rising bourgeoisie.

In countries where modern civilisation has developed, a new

---

same holds for the aristocratic nostalgia and selective philanthropy and reform, including the Ten Hours Act (1847), of a Tory faction in England commonly associated with Benjamin Disraeli and Lord Shaftesbury.

petty bourgeoisie has been formed which floats between proletariat and bourgeoisie while renewing itself constantly as a supplementary part of bourgeois society. The individual members of this class, however, are constantly hurled down into the proletariat by the action of competition; assuredly as modern industry develops, they even see the moment approaching when they completely disappear as an independent section of modern society, to be replaced in commerce, manufacturing, and agriculture by overseers and shopmen.

In countries like France, where the peasant class constitutes far more than half of the population, it was natural that writers who sided with the proletariat against the bourgeoisie should use, in their criticism of the bourgeois regime, the standard of the small peasant and petty bourgeois, and took up the cause of the working class from the standpoint of the petty bourgeoisie. Thus arose petty-bourgeois socialism. Sismondi is the chief among its authors, in France as well as England.[1]

This school of Socialism dissected with great acuteness the contradictions in modern relations of production. It laid bare the hypocritical alibis of economists. It proved, incontrovertibly, the disastrous effects of machinery and division of labour; the concentration of capital and landed property; overproduction, crises, the unavoidable ruination of the petty bourgeois and peasants, the misery of the proletariat, anarchy in production, the crying inequalities in the distribution of wealth, the industrial war of extermination between nations, the dissolution of old moral bonds, of old family connections, of old nationalities.

In its positive import, however, this socialism aspires either to restoring the old means of production and of exchange, and with them the old property relations, and the old society, or to forcibly reconfining modern means of production and of exchange within the framework of the old property relations which they exploded, had to explode. In either case, it is at the same time reactionary and utopian.

---

[1] Slightly overstated. But Léonard Simonde de Sismondi (1773–1842), Swiss-born and prolific writer on historical and economic topics, was frequently praised by Marx for his critique of capitalism's crises and contradictions, but as often chided for false reasoning and unnecessary political moderation.

Its last words are: corporate guilds for manufacture; patriarchal relations in agriculture.

In its fuller expression, this commitment ended with a hangover for the uncourageous.

c. *German or True Socialism.* The Socialist and Communist literature of France, which originated under the pressure of a bourgeoisie in power, and that was the expression of the struggle against this power, was introduced into Germany at a time when the bourgeoisie had just begun its struggle against feudal absolutism.

German philosophers, semi-philosophers, and *beaux esprits* seized eagerly on this literature, only forgetting that when these writings emigrated from France French social conditions did not emigrate along with them. In the German context, this French literature lost all immediate practical significance and assumed a purely literary aspect. It was sure to look like idle speculation about the True Society, about the realization of Human Nature. Thus, for the German philosophers of the eighteenth century, the demands of the first French Revolution were nothing more than the demands of Practical Reason[1] in general, the disclosure of the will of the revolutionary French bourgeoisie representing in their eyes the laws of pure Will, of Will as it was bound to be, of true human Will.

The work of the German *literati* consisted solely in bringing the new French ideas into harmony with their ancient philosophical conscience, or rather, in annexing the French ideas from their own philosophic point of view.

This annexation took place in the same way in which a foreign language is appropriated, in and as translation.

We are familiar with how the monks wrote silly lives of Catholic saints over the manuscripts on which the classical works of ancient heathendom had been transcribed. The German littérateurs reversed this process with the profane French literature. They wrote their philosophical nonsense underneath the French original. For instance, underneath the French criticism of money relations they wrote "Alienation of Humanity," and

---

[1] See Immanuel Kant's *Critique of Practical Reason* (1788).

underneath the French criticism of the bourgeois State they wrote "Abolition of the Category of the General," and so forth.[1] This insertion of their philosophical language underneath the French contributions they dubbed "Philosophy of Action," "True Socialism," "German Science of Socialism," "Philosophical Foundation of Socialism," and so on.

The French-socialist, communist literature was thus in effect emasculated. And since it ceased in German hands to express the struggle of one class against the other, the German felt conscious of overcoming French one-sidedness,[2] of representing not true needs but the needs of Truth; not the interests of the proletariat but the interests of Human Nature, of Humanity in general who belong to no class in the real world but only in the misty firmament of philosophical fantasy.

This German Socialism, which took its awkward school work so seriously and solemnly, and pitched its value like a coster-monger, meanwhile gradually lost its pedantic innocence.

The struggle of the German, and especially the Prussian bourgeoisie against the feudalists and absolute monarchy—in sum, the liberal movement—became more earnest.

True Socialism was thus offered the longed-for opportunity to confront the political movement with the Socialist demands: the traditional anathemas against liberalism, against representative government, bourgeois competition, bourgeois freedom of the press, bourgeois legislation, bourgeois liberty and equality, and of preaching to the masses that they had nothing to gain and everything to lose from this bourgeois movement.[3] German Socialism conveniently forgot that the French criticism, whose silly echo it was, presupposed the existence of modern bourgeois society with its corresponding material conditions of existence

---

[1] This paragraph, and the next two, play with the notion of the palimpsest, or that which can be reclaimed as a textual surface and written over more than once, in a way both more playful and more politically purposeful than can be claimed by many deconstructionists in our own time.

[2] German claims to "many-sidedness" are strongly associated with Wilhelm von Humboldt (1767–1835), the first Prussian Minister of Education and founder of the University of Berlin.

[3] See also Appendix D.

and political constitution adapted thereto, the very goals in dispute for the first time within the German struggle.

To the German absolute governments, with their claque of priests, teachers, cabbage-boors and bureaucrats, it served as a welcome scarecrow against the increasingly threatening bourgeoisie.

It represented a sweet completion after the bitter floggings and shootings to which these same governments treated German working-class uprisings.

While this True Socialism thus served the governments as a weapon for fighting the German bourgeoisie, it also represented directly a reactionary interest, the interest of middle-class German Philistines. In Germany the petty-bourgeois class, a relic of the sixteenth century, and since then constantly cropping up here again under various forms, is the real social basis of the existing state of things.

Its preservation is the preservation of the German status quo. From the industrial and political supremacy of the bourgeoisie it anticipates certain destruction: on the one hand, in the wake of capital concentration; on the other, from the rise of a revolutionary proletariat. True Socialism appeared to kill two birds with one stone. It spread like an epidemic.

The robe of speculative cobwebs, embroidered with the rhetorical flowers of *beaux esprits*, drenched with the dew of erotic sentiment—this overwrought robe in which the German socialists wrapped some of their emaciated eternal truths, merely increased the sale of their wares to this public.

For its part, German socialism recognised more and more its vocation as the stilted stand-in for this middle-class Philistine.

It proclaimed the German nation to be the typical nation, and the German petty Philistine to be the typical man. To each of his deficiencies it gave a hidden, higher, socialistic spin so as to signify its opposite. It extracted the extreme conclusion from directly countering the brutally destructive tendency of communism while proclaiming its own ability to rise impartially above all class struggles. With very few exceptions, all the so-called socialist and communist publications that now circulate in Germany belong to the domain of this foul, enervating literature.

2. Conservative, or Bourgeois, Socialism

A part of the bourgeoisie wishes to redress social grievances in order to secure the continued existence of bourgeois society. To this cohort belong economists, philanthropists, humanitarians, improvers of the condition of the working class, organisers of charity, preventers of cruelty to animals, temperance societies, hole-and-corner reformers of every imaginable kind.

This form of Socialism has, moreover, been worked out into complete systems. We cite Proudhon's *Philosophie de la Misère* as an example.[1]

The socialistic bourgeois want the conditions of existence without the struggles and dangers necessarily resulting therefrom. They want the existing state of society minus its revolutionizing and disintegrating elements. They want the bourgeoisie without the proletariat. Bourgeois socialism conceives the world of its ascendancy to be naturally the best world; and bourgeois Socialism contrives from this consoling conception a semi- or complete system. When it calls on the proletariat to implement such a system in order to enter the New Jerusalem, it is basically asking only that the proletariat remain within existing society while rejecting its odious ideas about it.

A second, less systematic and more practical form of socialism sought to make the working class recoil from every revolutionary movement by showing that neither this nor that political change but only a change in the material conditions of existence, in economical relations, could be of advantage to them. By change in the material conditions of existence, however, this socialism by no means understands the eradication of the bourgeois relations of production, which is achievable only by way of revolution, but rather administrative improvements that advance on the basis of these relations of production, that therefore change not at all the relation between capital and wage-labour, but in the best case for the bourgeoisie lessen the cost of its rule and simplify the ways in which it is administered.

---

[1] Pierre Joseph Proudhon (1809–65) published in 1846 *Système des Contradictions Economiques ou Philosophie de la Misère*. M replied in 1847 with *Misère de la Philosophie* whose tone is echoed here.

Bourgeois socialism finds fit expression only when it becomes a mere figure of speech.

Free trade!—in the interests of the working class. Protective duties!—in the interests of the working class. Prison cells now!—in the interests of the working class. This is the last, the only earnestly intended word of bourgeois Socialism.

Its socialism resides precisely in the proposition that the bourgeois are bourgeois—in the interests of the working class.

3. Critical-Utopian Socialism and Communism

We do not here refer to that literature which, in every great modern revolution, has always given voice to the demands of the proletariat (writings of Babeuf and others).[1]

The first direct attempts of the proletariat, in a time of general excitement, when feudal society was being overthrown, necessarily foundered because of the undeveloped state of the proletariat itself, as well as the absence of the material conditions for its emancipation, conditions unproducible in advance of the bourgeois era. The revolutionary literature that accompanied these first movements of the proletariat is unavoidably reactionary in content. It teaches a general asceticism and rude levelling.

The Socialist and Communist systems proper, the systems of Saint-Simon, Fourier, Owen and others, emerge in the early undeveloped period of the struggle between proletariat and bourgeoisie we described above.[2]

The creators of these systems admittedly see the class antagonisms, as well as the action of the fragmenting elements in the

---

[1] François Noël ["Gracchus"] Baboeuf (1760–97) exemplifies for Marx intellectual interventionism at its best, both for his attempt to keep the French Revolution on track (which he paid for with his life), and for the inspiration he provided posthumously via the promotion of his work on equality by his disciple Buonarotti and by the Chartist, Bronterre O'Brien. Draper points out astutely that Marx refuses to name living "others" for fear of putting them in danger from the authorities. See also Appendix L.3.

[2] Count Claude Saint-Simon (1760–1825) exerted great influence on 19th-century socialism through his extensive writings on systematic social planning. Charles Fourier (1772–1837) was another prolific writer in French on social reform, socialist association, and model communities (phalansteries). Robert Owen (1771–1858) was a leading British advocate and organizer of co-operatives and model industrial villages.

dominant society itself. But they witness no historical self-determination on the part of the proletariat, no political movement particular to it.

Since the development of class antagonism proceeds in step with the development of industry, they do not as yet encounter the material conditions for the emancipation of the proletariat, and therefore seek after a social science, after new social laws, in order to bring about these conditions.

Social action has to yield to their personal inventive action; historical conditions of emancipation to those born of phantasy; and the gradual class-formation of the proletariat to a privately contrived shaping of society. Future world-history resolves itself for them into propaganda for, and practical implementation of, their social plans.

In their planning they are conscious of capturing mainly the interests of the working class as the class that suffers most. Only from this perpective of being the most suffering class does the proletariat exist for them.

The undeveloped state of the class struggle, as well as their own situation in life, brings them to believe themselves far superior to the class antagonism referred to above. They want to improve the life situation of every member of society, even those best off. Hence, they habitually appeal to the whole of society without distinction; nay, preferably to the ruling class. Assuredly, to see their system is to understand it as the best possible plan of the best possible society.

They consequently reject all political, and especially all revolutionary, action; they wish to attain their objective by peaceful means, and endeavour, by minor experiments that fail as a matter of course, by the force of example to clear the path for the new social gospel.

Such phantasizing about the society of the future, at a time when the proletariat is still in a very undeveloped state and can but fancifully conceive of its own position, corresponds to its earliest, fully prescient impulses towards a general reconstruction of society.

But these socialist and communist publications contain critical elements too. They attack all the foundations of existing society. Hence they have furnished most valuable materials for the enlightenment of the workers. Their positive proposals for the society of the future—for example, the abolition of the distinction between town and country, of the family, of private accumulation, of wage labour, the proclamation of social harmony, the conversion of the state into a mere superintendence of production—all these proposals of theirs signify solely the disappearance of class antagonism which is only just forming and which they register only in its earliest, inchoate forms. These proposals, therefore, retain a purely utopian significance.

The meaning of critical utopian socialism and communism bears an inverse relation to historical development. In proportion as the class struggle unfolds and takes definite shape, this imaginary elevation above it, these phantastic attacks upon it, lose all practical value, all theoretical justification. Therefore, although the originators of these systems were in many respects revolutionary, their disciples form reactionary sects all the time. They hold fast to the old views of their masters as opposed to the further historical development of the proletariat. They therefore endeavour consistently to deaden the class struggle and to resolve conflicts. They still dream of experimental realisation of their social utopias, of founding separate phalansteries, of establishing home colonies, of setting up a little Icaria—duodecimo editions of the New Jerusalem;[1] and to construct all these castles in the air, they are compelled to appeal to the hearts and money-bags of the bourgeois. By degrees they sink into the category of the aforementioned reactionary or conservative socialists, differing from them only by more systematic pedantry, by fanatical superstitious belief in the miraculous effects of their social science.

They therefore violently oppose all political action on the part of the workers, such action as could result only from blind unbelief in the new Gospel.

The Owenites in England and the Fourierists in France opposed the Chartists and the *Réformistes* repectively.

---

[1] As in the *Communist Journal* (Appendix E), the utopian (Icarian) immigration schemes of Étienne Cabet (1788–1856) are tied to the larger difficulties shared by Fourier's phalansteries and Owen's home colonies. Note the witty particularity of Marx's "duodecimo" reference, implying an easily portable and concealable copy of a social gospel.

POSITION OF THE COMMUNISTS IN RELATION TO THE VARIOUS EXISTING OPPOSITION PARTIES

From Section II the relation of the Communists to the already constituted workers parties is plain, and accordingly their relation to the Chartists in England and the agrarian reformers in North America.[1]

They battle for the attainment of the immediate aims and interests of the working class; but in the current movement they at the same time represent the future of the movement. In France the Communists ally themselves with the Social-Democrats, against the conservative and radical bourgeoisie, without relinquishing the right to critique the phrases and illusions born of the revolutionary tradition.

In Switzerland they support the Radicals, without losing sight of the fact that this party consists of antagonistic elements, partly of democratic socialists in the French sense, partly of radical bourgeois.

Among Poles the Communists support the party that insists on an agrarian revolution as essential to national emancipation, the same party that brought about the Cracow insurrection in 1846.

In Germany, as soon as the bourgeoisie acts in a revolutionary fashion the Communist party battles along with them against the absolute monarchy, feudal land tenure, and the petty bourgeoisie.

But they do not for an instant cease to nourish among the workers the clearest possible awareness of the hostile antagonism of bourgeoisie and proletariat, so that the German workers can instantly appropriate and adapt the social and political features which the bourgeoisie must introduce along with its dominance as so many weapons against the bourgeoisie, so that after the overthrow of the reactionary classes in Germany the struggle against the bourgeoisie itself can at once commence.

It is to Germany that the Communists are most attentive because Germany stands on the eve of a bourgeois revolution,

---

[1] The National Reform Association was founded in the United States in 1845 by George Henry Evans but included many radical German immigrants. It aimed at the nationalizing and equitable redistribution of land, the abolition of slavery and wage slavery, among other things, and, despite its utopianism, represented a growing working-class consciousness of the implications of capitalist development.

and, because it is undertaking this radical change amid the more advanced conditions of European civilization generally and with a much more developed proletariat than England's in the seventeenth and France's in the eighteenth century, Germany's bourgeois revolution will thus be only the immediate forerunner of a proletarian revolution.

In a word, the Communists everywhere support every revolutionary movement against the existing social and political order of things.

In all these movements they foreground the property question as the fundamental question for the movement, no matter its degree of development.

Finally, the communists labour everywhere for the solidarity and agreement of the democratic parties of all countries.

The Communists disdain to conceal their views and aims. They openly declare that their objectives can be attained only by the forcible overthrow of all existing social orders. Let the ruling classes tremble at a communist revolution. In it proletarians have nothing to lose but their chains.

Proletarians of all lands unite!

Appendix A: From Flora Tristan's Tour de France, *September 1844*

[Flora Tristan (1803–44) was a multi-talented writer, feminist, and international socialist activist whose life and works attest both to the ubiquity of sexism across the nineteenth-century political spectrum, and to the multiple sources of radical thought and agency in the 1840s. She died before the great year of revolution, but was instantly recognized as a martyr to the causes of freedom and justice. Workers raised a monument to her memory in 1848 and her contribution to the advancement of working people was praised in the works of others, including Marx. In recent decades her reputation has been effectively revived and revised by feminist scholars, and many of her works translated into English, but her accomplishments deserve to be better known, not only as anticipating the *Manifesto's* call for proletarian unity in her *Worker's Union* (1843) or for rivalling Engel's talent for social observation, but also for the subtlety of her accommodation of religious and political thought and her strategic use of personal charisma to mobilize and guide working-class opinion. In the following excerpt, part of a posthumously published record of a tour of France in which she functioned as a "travelling book-seller" as well as socialist networker and orator, she displays her acerbic attentiveness to consistency in politics, and her attribution of chameleon behaviour to its sources in poverty and desperation. She places herself firmly within the French revolutionary tradition before offering a theory of popular politicization and aligning herself with the notion of political catechism with which Marx and Engels experimented before deciding on the manifesto form as most appropriate for their purposes in 1847. Note the enforced curtailment of her writing under the pressure of events, epitomising the predicament of radical writers in general, and of the women among their number in particular.]

Lafitte at Toulouse. He said it himself.—In Carcassone Lafitte is a proletarian democrat, a revolutionary—because he is assured of dinner at his mother's, but in Toulouse Lafitte is a bourgeois Fourierist—wearing yellow gloves because he has to find three francs every day so he can eat.—Thus one encounters the same necessity for every individual: to eat. Give every man and woman the right to work (the possibility of food), the right to be educated (the possibility for a reflective life), the right to bread (the possibility of living completely independently) and humanity which is currently so vile, so repulsive, so hypocritically vicious, will transform itself accordingly and will become noble, proud, independent, free! and attractive! and happy!

These three rights plainly correspond to the three words uttered in order to achieve the revolution of 1789: 1—equality—first the right to work, 2—liberty—second the right to bread—3—fraternity—third the right to education.—Because in order to achieve equality everyone has to work—in order to achieve liberty everyone has to be able to live—in order to live in brotherhood everyone has to have an education so that they can sympathise with each other.

Our fathers marched in the name of these three vague words to whose meaning they had no access.—in this fashion ideas are produced first on the instinctive level—then on the sentimental level—then on the level of understanding—today people feel a need of rights—but only a very few understand what this means.—For that to happen will take another decade—although my Tour of France will be a *catechism* which will facilitate the diffusion of ideas.

I am in the middle of writing and I have to stop.

—What a supplication!

(*Le Tour de France: État actuel de la classe ouvrière sous l'aspect moral, intellectuel et matériel.* E. Jules-L. Puech with Michel Collinet and Stephane Michaud. 2 vols. Paris: François Maspero, 1980. II.192. Emphasis added; my translation. For more on Tristan see, e.g., Susan Grogan, *Flora Tristan: Life Stories.* London: Routledge, 1998.)

Appendix B: Letter from Engels to Marx, November–December 1846

[This long letter is a typical mix of the high-brow and the low-brow. Engels' German is peppered with French, Dutch, Danish, Swedish, in a display of wry cosmopolitanism and Germanophilia. By turns rake and radical, he is as unguarded with Marx as he is wary of the generic "Straubingers" or naïve artisans clinging to the guild and craft illusions which will be treated so severely in the *Manifesto*, or of the police spies that hound him constantly. Engels shows how thoroughly immersed he and Marx are in the worlds of resistance and surveillance, and the international distribution of their allies and adversaries. We register the importance of Paris as a revolutionary site and fleshpot, the benefits and drawbacks of any form of political "party," and the ongoing struggle to get the fruits of collaboration published. The uneven politicization of European countries, combined with the uneven mental capacities of Marx and Engels' current allies, leaves the latter in no doubt about the magnitude of the struggle ahead, and the need to make pragmatic compromises while strategically flourishing, moderating, or concealing the nature and tendencies of their own scholarship. Engels gives Marx the benefit of his own observation and analysis, while being completely at ease with the likelihood that his friend has already acted on his own. There is clearly a strong friendship underlying their voluminous correspondence, as well as a steely political resolve.]

ENGELS TO MARX
IN BRUSSELS
[Paris, middle of November–December 1846]

Dear Marx

The reasons for the brief letter I recently sent [Philippe] Gigot[1] are the following. During the investigation into the disturbances [bread riots] in the Faubourg St. Antoine in October, a multitude of Germans were arrested and questioned, the whole of the second

---

[1] Philippe Gigot (1819–60), member of the Communist League while working (until purged in 1848) in the Belgian Ministry of the Interior in Brussels.

batch consisting of Straubingers. Some of these numbskulls, who have now been sent across the border, must have talked a great deal of nonsense about [Hermann] Ewerbeck[1] and myself; in fact, in view of their paltriness, nothing else could have been expected of the Straubingers than that they should have been scared to death and have given away all that they knew and more. On top of that, such Straubingers as I was acquainted with, secretive though they were concerning their own miserable affairs, shamefully sounded the alarm about my meetings with them. That's how these lads are.

At the Barrière, as I have already written and told you, the noble Eisermann delivered himself of a further, detailed *avis aux mouchards* [warning to informers] in which he attacked me. [Adolph] Junge[2] was also guilty of some gross indiscretions; the fellow is a trifle swollen-headed, he wishes to be sent to Calais and London at the expense of the French government. In short, M. Delessert set one spy after another at the heels of myself and Ewerbeck, who has long been under suspicion and has an expulsion order hanging over his head. These spies succeeded in following us to the *marchand de vins* [wine shop], where we sometimes foregathered with the Faubourg stalwarts. This was proof enough that we were the leaders of a dangerous clique, and not long afterwards I learned that M. Delessert had requested M. Tanneguy Duchâtel to issue an expulsion order against me and Ewerbeck, and that there was a splendid pile of documents relating to the case in the Prefecture, almost next door to the place where the whores are medically examined. Needless to say, I had no desire to let myself be banished on the Straubingers' account. I had already anticipated something of the kind when I noticed the nonchalance with which the Straubingers were holding forth for all to hear and arguing all over the place about who was right, [Karl] Grün[3] or I. I was sick and tired of the whole business, there was no putting the lads to rights; even in discussion they wouldn't speak their minds frankly just like the people in London, and I had achieved my main object, the triumph over Grün. It was an excellent opportunity of honourably ridding myself of the Straubingers, vexing as the whole affair was in other

---

1   Hermann Ewerbeck (1816–60), German physician, journalist, and member of the CL.
2   Member of the CL, artisan who emigrated to the US in 1848.
3   Karl Grün (1817–77) was a leading advocate of the True Socialism mocked in the *Manifesto*.

respects. I therefore let it be known to them that I could no longer remain their tutor and that, furthermore, they should watch their step. Ewerbeck at once decided to go on a journey and appears, indeed, to have departed forthwith—at any rate, I haven't seen him since. Where he has gone, I do not know. The police had also been looking for the little man [Karl] (Bernays)[1] who, however, had withdrawn to his old place [Sarcelles] because of a variety of escapades (it's remarkable what mad scrapes he gets into as soon as he sets foot in the civilised world). When he will return to Paris, I don't know, but in no circumstances will he move into lodgings where he had intended to, hence *the address that was given you is useless*. He has safely received his manuscript [article on crimes and criminal law]. Meanwhile I can thank the noble police for having reft me from the arms of the Straubingers and reminded me of the pleasures life has to offer. If the suspicious individuals who have been following me for the past fortnight are really informers, as I am convinced some of them are, the Prefecture must of late have given out a great many entrance tickets to the *bals* Montesquieu, Valentino, Prado, etc., etc. I am indebted to Mr Delessert for some delicious encounters with *grisettes* and for a great deal of pleasure, *car j'ai voulu profiter des journées et de nuits qui pouvaient être mes dernières à Paris. Enfin* [since I wanted to take advantage of the days and nights which might well be my last in Paris. Anyway] since in other respects I've been left in peace up till now, everything would appear to have quietened down. But in future address all letters to Monsieur A. F. Körner, artiste-peintre, 29, rue neuve Bréda, Paris, with an envelope inside bearing my initials, taking care that nothing shows through.

You will understand that, in the circumstances, I have had to leave W. Weitling[2] entirely to his own devices. Having seen none of our people, I have no idea whether he has been or still is here. Nor does it matter. I don't know the Weitlingians at all and, he'd get a fine welcome amongst those I know; because of their eternal clashes with his tailor friends, they feel the most frightful animosity towards him.

The affair with the London people [in the League of the Just] is annoying precisely because of Harney[3] and because they, of all the

---

[1] Karl Bernays (1815–79), lawyer and radical journalist, was another who settled in the US.

[2] Wilhelm Weitling (1808–71), much traveled exile, utopian communist, and briefly a rival theorist to M and E.

[3] George Julian Harney (1819–97), leading radical Chartist and publisher.

Straubingers, were the only ones with whom one could attempt to make contact frankly and without arrière-pensée [mental reservation]. But if the fellows are unwilling, *eh bien* [well then], let them go. In any case one can never know if they won't produce another address as miserable as the one to Mr [Johann] Ronge or to the Schleswig-Holsteiners. On top of that, there's their perpetual envy of us as 'scholars'. By the way, we have two methods by which we can rid ourselves of them should they rebel: either make a clean break with them, or simply allow the correspondence to lapse. I would be for the latter, if their last letter admits of an answer which, without giving undue offence, is lukewarm enough to rob them of any desire to reply quickly. Then another long delay before answering—and two or three letters will be enough to consign this drowsy correspondence to its last sleep. For how and why should we ridicule these fellows? We have no press organ and even if we had one, they are no writers but confine themselves to an occasional proclamation which no one ever sees, still less cares about. If we are to ridicule the Straubingers *at all,* we can always avail ourselves of their fine documents; if the correspondence finally does lapse, well and good; the rupture will be gradual and attract no great attention. In the meantime we shall quietly make the necessary arrangements with Harney, taking care that *they* owe us the final letter (which they will in fact do, once they have been made to wait the 6–10 weeks for an answer), and then leave them to clamour. An immediate rupture with the fellows would bring us neither gain nor *gloire* [glory]. *Theoretical* disagreements are hardly possible with the fellows since they have no theory and, *sauf* [save] for their possible unspoken misgivings, so that all discussion with them is impossible except, perhaps, face to face. In the case of an open rupture they would bring up against us all that generalised communist thirst-for-learning stuff: we'd have been glad to learn from the learned gentlemen, if they'd have something decent, etc. *Practical* party differences would—since there are only a few of them on the committee and a few of us too—soon degenerate into mere personalities and ill-natured exchanges, at least on the face of it. As a party we can enter the lists against literary men, but not against Straubingers. They are, after all, a couple of 100 strong, vouched for among the English by Harney, proclaimed in Germany by the *Rheinischer Beobachter*, etc., etc., [see Appendix D] a rabid and by no means impotent communist society; they are, furthermore, the most tolerable of the

Straubingers, and can certainly not be bettered so long as there is no change in Germany. We have learnt from this business that, in the absence of a proper movement in Germany, nothing can be done with the Straubingers, even the best of them. It is better after all to let them quietly go their own way, attacking them as a whole, *en bloc*, than to provoke a dispute which might only serve to sully our reputations.Vis-à-vis ourselves, these lads declare themselves to be 'the people,' 'the proletarians,' and we can only appeal to a communist proletariat which has yet to take shape in Germany. In addition, the Prussian Constitution is in the offing, and we might then be able to make use of the fellows' signatures, etc., etc.— Anyways, my words of wisdom will doubtless arrive too late and you will already have passed and acted on a resolution in this matter. I would, by the way, have written earlier, but I was waiting to see what turn the affair with the police would take.

I have just received a reply from the Swiss publisher [Johann Michael Schläpfer]. The letter, enclosed herewith, only confirms my belief that the fellow's a scoundrel. No ordinary publisher would accept so amiably after keeping one waiting x weeks. Now we shall have to see what the Bremen man [Kuhtmann] says, and then we can always do as we think fit. Then again there's the fellow [Johann Marmor or August Schmid] at Belle-Vue near Constance; perhaps something might be arranged with him; I could try him again if the Bremen man's not agreeable. Meanwhile I make some more enquiries in Herisau—if only we had a decent fellow in Switzerland to whom one could send the manuscript [of *The German Ideology*] with instructions to hand it over only against payment in cash [Dutch *baar Geld*]. But the only one there is that thirsty paterfamilias Püttmann!

During the recent bad spell, one of my innocent, incidental pastimes, besides girls, has been to concern myself to some extent with Denmark and the other northern countries. What an abomination! Rather the smallest German than the biggest Dane! Nowhere else is the *misère* of morality, guilds and estates still carried to such a pitch. The Dane regards Germany as a country which one visits in order to "keep mistresses and squander one's fortune on them" *(imedens at han reiste i Tydskland, havde han en Maitresse, som fortärede ham den bedste del af hans Midler,* we read in a Danish school book). He calls the German a *tydsk* windbag, and regards himself as the true representative of the Teutonic soul—the Swede in turn despises the Dane as "Germanised" and degenerate, garrulous and effete—the Norwegian looks down on the Gallicised Swede and his aristocracy and rejoices in the fact that at home in *Norge* [Norway] exactly the same stupid, peasant economy is dominant as at the time of the noble Canute, and he, for his part, is treated *en canaille* [disdainfully] by the Icelander, who still continues to speak exactly the same language as the unwashed Vikings of anno 900, swills whale oil, lives in a mud hut and goes to pieces in any atmosphere that does not reek of rotten fish. I have several times felt tempted to be proud of the fact that I am at least no Dane nor yet an Icelander, but merely a German. The editor of the most advanced Swedish newspaper, the *Aftonbladet*, has twice been here in Paris to seek enlightenment on the organisation of labour, has for years taken the *Bon Sens* and the *Démocratie pacifique*: he solemnly conferred with Louis Blanc and Considérant,[1] but found himself out of his depth, and returned home none the wiser. Now as before he loudly advocates free competition or, as the Swedes have it, freedom of *nourishment* or else *själfförsörjningsfrihet*, freedom of self-supply (which sounds even better than freedom to pursue a *trade*). Of course, they're still up to their necks in the guild nonsense and, in the parliaments, it's precisely the bourgeois who are the most rabid conservatives. Throughout the whole country there are only two proper towns, à 80,000 and 40,000 inhabitants respectively, the third, Norrköpping, having only 12,000 and all the rest perhaps 1,000, 2,000, 3,000. At every post station there's one inhabitant. In Denmark things are scarcely better, since they have only one solitary city there, in which the guilds indulge in the most ludicrous proceedings, madder even than in Basle or Bremen, and where you aren't allowed on the promenade without an entrance ticket. The only thing these countries are good for is to show what the Germans would do if they had freedom of the press, viz., what the Danes have actually done, immediately found a "society for the proper use of the free press," and print almanacs full of Christian good intentions. The Swedish *Aftonbladet* is as tame as the *Kölner Zeitung*, but considers itself "democratic in the true sense of the word." On the other hand the Swedes have the novels of Fröken [Miss] Bremer and the Danes of Councillor of State (Eta traad)

---

[1]   Louis Blanc (1811–82), prolific French journalist, historian, and democratic socialist. Victor Considérant (1808–93), leading French Fourierist and editor of the *Démocratie pacifique* mentioned here.

Oehlenschläger, Commander of the Order of the Dannebrog [Society of Knights founded 1671]. There's also a terrific number of Hegelians there and the language, every third word of which is filched from the German, is admirably suited to speculation. A report was begun long ago and will follow within the next few days [but has not survived]. Write and tell me if you have Proudhon's book [*Système des contradictions économiques, ou Philosophie de la misère*].[1]

If you wish to make use of Proudhon's book, which is bad, for your own book, I will send you the very extensive excerpts I have made. It's not worth the 15 francs it costs.

(MECW: 38.89-94)

---

[1] Pierre Joseph Proudhon (1809-65), whose muddle-headed "philosophy" of libertarianism elicited a devastating response from M in *The Poverty of Philosophy* (1847).

Appendix C: Engels, Draft of a Communist Confession of Faith, 9 June 1847

[Discovered in its fullest form, and in Engels' hand, only in 1968 by Bert Andréas, this document records what was being debated at the first Congress of the Communist League in London, June 2-9, 1847. Engels shows his political acumen as well as his secretarial and compositional abilities in having completed this draft by the final day of the Congress, and thus claiming a crucial role for himself and the absent Marx in producing what later became the *Manifesto*. The draft made major concessions to the confessional and catechetical traditions with which the League of the Just were familiar, while leaving himself and Marx with a source to cannibalize and sharpen—to their own liking and in light of the reactions from the broader potential membership of the new League to whom the document was circulated along with draft Rules. The Confession is multiply abolitionist, and attentive to the varieties of historical and contemporary forms of exploitation in rural and urban settings. It is uncompromising too in its linking of property, class, and competition, its insistence on the newness of the proletariat as social formation, and the inevitable, self-destructive dependency of the bourgeoisie on proletarian labour.]

DRAFT OF A COMMUNIST CONFESSION OF FAITH

Question 1: *Are you a Communist?*
Answer: Yes.

Question 2: *What is the aim of the Communists?*
Answer: To organize society in such a way that every member of it can develop and use all his capabilities and powers in complete freedom and without thereby infringing the basic conditions of this society.

Question 3: *How do you wish to achieve this aim?*
Answer: By the elimination of private property and its replacement by community of property.

Question 4: *On what do you base your community of property?*

Answer: Firstly, on the mass of productive forces and means of subsistence resulting from the development of industry, agriculture, trade and colonisation, and on the possibility inherent in machinery, chemical and other resources of their infinite extension. Secondly, on the fact that in the consciousness or feeling of every individual there exists certain irrefutable basic principles which, being the result of the whole of historical development, require no proof.

Question 5: *What are such principles?*

Answer: For example, every individual strives to be happy. The happiness of the individual is inseparable from the happiness of all, etc.

Question 6: *How do you wish to prepare the way for your community of property?*

Answer: By enlightening and uniting the proletariat.

Question 7: *What is the proletariat?*

Answer: The proletariat is that class of society which lives exclusively by its labour and not on the profit from any kind of capital; that class whose weal and woe, whose life and death, therefore, depend on the alternation of times of good and bad business; in a word, on the fluctuation of competition.

Question 8: *Then there have not always been proletarians?*

Answer: No. There have always been *poor* and *working classes*; and those who have worked were almost always the poor. But there have not always been proletarians, just as competition has not always been free.

Question 9: *How did the proletariat arise?*

Answer: The proletariat came into being as a result of the introduction of the machines which have been invented since the middle of the last century and the most important of which are: the steam-engine, the spinning machine and the power loom. These machines, which were very expensive and could therefore only be purchased by rich people, supplanted the workers of the time, because by the use of machinery it was possible to produce commodities more quickly and cheaply than could the workers with their imperfect spinning wheels and hand-looms. The machines thus delivered industry entirely into the hands of the big capitalists and rendered the workers' scanty property which consisted mainly of their tools, looms, etc., quite worthless, so that the capitalist was left with everything, the worker with nothing. In this way the factory system was introduced. Once the capitalists saw how advantageous this was for them, they sought to extend it to more and more branches of labour. They divided work more and more between the workers so that workers who had formerly made a whole article now produced only a part of it. Labour simplified in this way produced goods more quickly and therefore more cheaply and only now was it found in almost every branch of labour that here also machines could be used. As soon as any branch of labour went over to factory production it ended up, just as in the case of spinning and weaving, in the hands of the big capitalists, and the workers were deprived of the last remnants of their independence. We have gradually arrived at the position where almost *all* branches of labour are run on a factory basis. This has increasingly brought about the ruin of the previously existing middle class, especially of the small master craftsmen, completely transformed the previous position of the workers, and two new classes which are gradually swallowing up all other classes have come into being, namely:

I.   The class of the big capitalists, who in all advanced countries are in almost exclusive possession of the means of subsistence and those means (machines, factories, workshops, etc.) by which these means of subsistence are produced. This is the *bourgeois* class, or the *bourgeoisie*.

II. The class of the completely propertyless, who are compelled to sell their labours to the first class, the bourgeois, simply to obtain from them in return their means of subsistence. Since the parties to this trading in labour are not *equal*, but the bourgeois have the advantage, the propertyless must submit to the bad conditions laid down by the bourgeois. This class, dependent on the bourgeois, is called the class of the *proletarians* or the *proletariat*.

Question 10: *In what way does the proletariat differ from the slave?*

Answer: The slave is sold once and for all, the proletarian has to sell himself by the day and by the hour. The slave is the property of one master and for that very reason has a guaranteed subsistence, however wretched it may be. The proletarian is, so to speak, the slave of the entire bourgeois *class*, not of one master, and therefore has no guaranteed subsistence, since nobody buys his labour if he does not need it. The slave is accounted a *thing* and not a member of civil society. The proletarian is recognised as a *person*, as a member of civil society. The slave *may*, therefore, have a better subsistence than the proletarian but the latter stands at a higher stage of development. The slave frees himself by *becoming a proletarian*, abolishing from the totality of property relationships only the relationship of *slavery*. The proletarian can free himself only by abolishing *property in general*.

Question 11: *In what way does the proletarian differ from the serf?*

Answer: The serf has the use of a piece of land, that is, of an instrument of production, in return for the handing over a greater or lesser portion of the yield. The proletarian works with instruments of production which belong to someone else who, in return for his labour, hands over to him a portion, determined by competition, of the products. In the case of the serf, the share of the labourer is determined by his own labour, that is, by himself. In the case of the proletarian it is determined by competition, therefore in the first place by the bourgeois. The serf has guaranteed subsistence, the proletarian has not. The serf frees himself by driving out his feudal lord and becoming a property owner himself, thus entering in to competition and joining for the time being the possessing class, the privileged class. The proletarian frees himself by doing away with property, competition, and all class differences.

Question 12: *In what way does the proletarian differ from the handi-craftsman?*

Answer: As opposed to the proletarian, the so-called handi-craftsman, who still existed nearly everywhere during the last century and still exists here and there, is at most a *temporary* proletarian. His aim is to acquire capital himself and so to exploit other workers. He can often achieve this aim where the craft guilds still exist or where freedom to follow a trade has not yet led to the organisation of handwork on a factory basis and to intense competition. But as soon as the factory system is introduced into handwork and competition is in full swing, this prospect is eliminated and the handicraftsman becomes more and more a proletarian. The handicraftsman therefore frees himself *either* by becoming a bourgeois or in general passing over into the middle class, or, by becoming a proletarian as a result of competition (as now happens in most cases) and joining the movement of the proletariat—i.e., the more or less conscious communist movement.

Question 13: *Then you do not believe that community of property has been possible at any time?*

Answer: No. Communism has only arisen since machinery and other inventions made it possible to hold out the prospect of an all-sided development, a happy existence, for all members of society. Communism is the theory of a liberation which was not possible for the slaves, the serfs, or the handicraftsmen, but only for the proletarians and hence it belongs of necessity to the 19th century and was not possible in any earlier period.

Question 14: *Let us go back to the sixth question. As you wish to prepare for community of property by the enlightening and uniting of the proletariat, then you reject revolution?*

Answer: We are convinced not only of the uselessness but even of the harmfulness of all conspiracies. We are also aware that revolutions are not made deliberately and arbitrarily but that everywhere and at all times they are the necessary consequence of circumstances which are not in any way whatever dependent either on the will or on the leadership of individual parties or of whole classes. But we also see that the development of the proletariat in almost all countries of the world is forcibly repressed by the possessing classes and that thus a revolution is being forcibly worked for by the opponents of communism. If, in the end, the oppressed proletariat is thus driven into a revolution, then we will defend the cause of the proletariat just as well by our deeds as now by our words.

Question 15: *Do you intend to replace the existing social order by community of property at one stroke?*

Answer: We have no such intention. The development of the masses cannot be ordered by decree. It is determined by the development of the conditions in which these masses live, and therefore proceeds gradually.

Question 16: *How do you think the transition from the present situation to the community of property is to be effected?*

Answer: The first, fundamental condition for the introduction of community of property is the political liberation of the proletariat through a democratic constitution.

Question 17: *What will be your first measure once you have established democracy?*

Answer: Guaranteeing the subsistence of the proletariat.

Question 18: *How will you do that?*

Answer: I. By limiting private property in such a way that it gradually prepares the way for transformation into social property, e.g., by progressive taxation, limitation of the right of inheritance in favour of the state, etc., etc.

II. By employing workers in national workshops and factories and on national estates.

III. By educating all children at the expense of the state.

Question 19: *How will you arrange this kind of education during the period of transition?*

Answer: All children will be educated in state establishments from the time when they can do without the first maternal care.

Question 20: *Will not the introduction of community property be accompanied by the proclamation of the community of women?*

Answer: By no means. We will only interfere in the personal relationship between men and women or with the family in general to the extent that the maintenance of the existing institution would disturb the new social order. Besides, we are well aware that the family relationship has been modified in the course of history by the property relationships and by periods of development, and that consequently the ending of private property will also have a most important influence on it.

Question 21: *Will nationalities continue to exist under communism?*

Answer: The nationalities of the people who join together according to the principle of community will be just as much compelled by this union to merge with one another and thereby supersede themselves as the various differences between estates and classes disappear through the superseding of their basis—private property.

Question 22: *Do communists reject the existing religions?*

Answer: All religions which have existed hitherto were expressions of historical stages of development of individual peoples or groups of peoples. But communism is that stage of historical development which makes all existing religions superfluous and supersedes them.

In the name and on the mandate of the Congress.

Secretary: President:

Heide   *Karl Schill*
[alias of Wilhelm Wolff][1]   [alias of Karl Schapper][2]

London, June 9, 1847

(MECW 6: 96–103)

---

[1] Wilhelm Wolff (1809–64), nicknamed Lupus, a seasoned radical and collaborator of
     M and E who settled in London after having to leave Silesia when the weavers' rising
     there was put down in 1844.
[2] Karl Schapper (1812–70), German émigré and key figure in the merging of radical
     entities and agendas in the CL.

Appendix D: Marx, "The Communism of the Rheinischer Beobachter," September 1847

[In this essay Marx shows he is at least as zealous as Engels in defending communism against bourgeois co-option. He does so by a devastating process of citation and analysis, by ironic empathising with the difficulties of a writer much his inferior, and by the unmasking of connections between reactionary government and a compliant press, apparently progressive taxes and the reintroduction of economic injustice. Like Engels, he uses the category of the proletariat (rather than the vague and treacherously populist "people"), and his knowledge of greater press freedoms in England and France, to underscore the mendacity of "Prussian liberalism." No wonder those forces tried (unsuccessfully) to recruit Marx as an apologist for their policies! In claiming that the bourgeoisie creates for the proletariat the "status of a recognized party," Marx anticipates the title-page of the *Manifesto* and that strategically premature designation, "Communist Party." His growing command of economic issues wrests the concept of value from the hands of government bureaucrats and bourgeois politicians alike and returns it to the realm of social relations. He concludes in a way that prepares for the opening of the *Manifesto* where absolutists and reactionaries are listed and ridiculed.]

Karl Marx
THE COMMUNISM
OF THE *RHEINISCHER BEOBACHTER*

Brussels, September 5,—In issue No. 70 of this newspaper an article from the *Rh[einischer] Beobachter* is introduced with the words:

"In issue No. 206 the Rh[einischer] B[eobachter] preaches communism as follows."

Whether or not this comment is intended ironically, Communists must protest against the idea that the *Rheinischer Beobachter* could preach "communism," and especially against the idea that the article communicated in issue No. 70 of the D[eutsche]-B[russler]-Z[eitung] is communist.

If a certain section of German socialists has continually blustered against the liberal bourgeoisie, and has done so, in a manner which has benefited nobody but the German governments, and if at present government newspapers like the *Rh[einischer] Beobachter*, basing themselves on the empty phrases of these people, claim that it is not liberal bourgeoisie but the government which represents the interests of the proletariat, then the Communists have nothing in common with either the former or the latter.

Certain people have admittedly wished to lay the responsibility for this on the German Communists, they have accused them of being in alliance with the government, for the simple reason that all of the revolutionary parties in Germany the Communists are by far the most revolutionary, and that the government knows this better than anyone else.

Can Communists unite with a government which has pronounced them guilty of high treason and treats them as such?

Can the government propagate in its press principles, which, in France, are considered to be anarchistic, incendiary and destructive of all social relations, and to which this same government continually ascribes the very same characteristics?

It is inconceivable. Let us examine the so-called communism of the Rheinischer Beobachter, and we shall find it is very innocent.

The article begins:

"If we examine our (!) social condition, then the greatest distress and the most pressing want reveal themselves everywhere (!), and we have to admit that much has been neglected. This is, indeed, a fact, and the only (!) question which arises, is what causes it. We are convinced that our constitution does not bear the responsibility for this, for (!) as far as social conditions are concerned matters are (!) still worse in France and England. Nevertheless (!) liberalism seeks the remedy in representation alone; if the people were represented, it would help itself. This is quite illusory to be sure, but nonetheless (!) extremely (!!) plausible."

In this paragraph we see the Beobachter [observer] before us, in the flesh—the way he chews his pen, at a loss for an introduction, speculates, writes, crosses out, writes again, and then finally, after some considerable time, produces the above magnificent passage. In order to arrive at liberalism, his own inherited hobby-horse, he begins with "our social condition," that is, strictly speaking, the social condition of the Beobachter, which may very well have its unpleasantness. By means of the extremely trivial observation that our social condition is miserable and that much has been neglected, he arrives, by way of some very thorny sentences, at a point where the only question which arises for him, is what causes it. This question arises for him, however, only to disappear again at once. The Beobachter does not, in fact, tell us what causes it, neither does he tell us what does not cause it, and that is, of course, the Prussian constitution. From the Prussian constitution, by means of a bold "for," he arrives at France and England, and from here to Prussian liberalism is for him of course only a trifling leap, which, supported by the least motivated "nevertheless" conceivable, he accomplishes with ease. And thus at least, he has reached his favourite terrain, where he can exclaim, "This is quite illusory to be sure, but nonetheless extremely plausible." But nonetheless extremely!!!

Besides the "Old General," Arnold Ruge,[1] there are only a few men in Germany who can write in this way, and these few are all Consistorial Counsellors in Herr Eichhorn's ministry.

We cannot be required to go into the contents of this introductory passage. It has no content other than the awkwardness of its form, it is merely the portal through which we step into the hall where our observing Consistorial Counsellor[2] is preaching a crusade against liberalism.

Let us listen:

> "Liberalism has above all the advantage that its approach to the people takes easier and more pleasant forms than does that of the bureaucracy." (Indeed, not even Herr Dahlman or Gervinus writes such clumsy and angular prose.) "It speaks of the welfare and the rights of the people. In reality, however, it only pushes the people forward in order thereby to intimidate the government; it considers the people only as cannon fodder in the great onslaught against the power of the government. To seize the power of the state — this is the true tendency to liberalism, the welfare of the people is only of secondary importance to it."

Does the Herr Consistorial Counsellor believe he has told the people anything new with this? The people, and in particular the communist section of the people, knows very well that the liberal bourgeoisie is only pursuing its own interests and that little reliance should be placed on its sympathy for the people. If, however, the

---

[1] Arnold Ruge (1802–80), activist, writer, and academic who collaborated with M on the *Deutsch-Französiche Jahrbücher* before their final falling out in 1844.

[2] Probably Councillor Wagener.

Consistorial Counsellor concludes from this that the liberal bour-geoisie exploits the people for its own ends in so far as the people participates in the political movement, then we must answer him: "That is quite plausible for a Consistorial Counsellor, to be sure, but nonetheless extremely illusory."

The people, or, to replace this broad and vague expression by a definite one, the proletariat, has quite another way of reasoning than the gentlemen of the ecclesiastical ministry permit themselves to imagine. The proletariat does not ask whether the welfare of the people is a matter of secondary or primary importance to the bour-geoisie, or whether the bourgeoisie *wishes* to use proletarians as the common fodder or not. The proletariat does not ask what the bour-geoisie merely *wishes* to do, but what it *must* do. It asks whether the present political system, the rule of the bureaucracy, or the liberals are striving for, the rule of the bourgeoisie, will offer it the means to achieve its own purposes. To this end it only has to compare the political position of the proletariat in England, France and America with that in Germany to see that the rule of the bourgeoisie does not only place quite new weapons in the hands of the proletariat for the struggle *against* the bourgeoisie, but that it also secures for it a quite different status, the status of a recognised party.

Does the Herr Consistorial Counsellor then believe that the proletariat, which is more and more adhering to the Communist Party, that the proletariat will be incapable of utilizing the freedom of the press and the freedom of association? Let him just read the English and French working men's newspapers, let him just attend some time in a single Chartist meeting!

But in the ecclesiastical ministry, where the *Rh[einischer] Beobachter* is edited, they have queer ideas about the proletariat. They think they are dealing with Pomeranian peasants or with the Berlin loafers. They think they have reached the greatest depths of profundity when they promise the people no longer *panem et circenses* [bread and circuses],[1] but *panem et religionem* [bread and religion] instead. They delude themselves that the proletariat wishes to be helped, they do not conceive that it expects help from nobody but itself. They do not suspect that the proletariat sees through all these empty consistorial phrases about the "welfare of the people" and bad social conditions just as well as through the similar phrases of the liberal bourgeoisie.

---

[1] Juvenal, *Satires* x.80.

And why is the welfare of the people only of secondary importance to the bourgeoisie? The *R[heinischer] Beobachter* replies:

"The United Diet[1] has proved it, the perfidy of liberalism is exposed. The Income Tax was the acid test of liberalism, and it failed the test."

These well-meaning Consistorial Counsellors, imagining in their economic innocence that they can use the Income Tax to throw dust in the eyes of the proletariat!

The Slaughter and Milling Tax directly affects wages, the Income Tax affects the profit of capital. Extremely plausible, Herr Consistorial Counsellor, isn't it? But the capitalists will not and cannot allow their profits to be taxed with impunity. This follows from competition itself. So within a few months after the introduction of the Income Tax, wages will therefore have been reduced to precisely the extent by which they were actually raised by the abolition of the Slaughter and Milling Tax and by the reduced food prices resulting from this.

The level of wages expressed, not in terms of money, but in terms of the means of subsistence necessary to the working man, that is the level of *real*, not of *nominal* wages, depends on the relationship between demand and supply. An alteration in the mode of taxation may cause a momentary disturbance, but will not change anything in the long run.

The only economic advantage of the Income Tax is that it is cheaper to levy, and this the Consistorial Counsellor does not mention. Incidentally the proletariat gains nothing from this circumstance either.

What, then, does all this talk about the Income Tax amount to?

In the first place, the proletariat is not at all, or only momentarily, interested in the whole matter.

In the second place, the government, which in levying the Slaughter and Milling Tax comes daily into contact with the proletariat and confronts it in a hateful fashion, the government remains in the background where the Income Tax is concerned, and forces the bourgeoisie to assume in full the odious business of pressing down wages.

---

[1]   Convening by Frederick William IV of the 8 provincial diets of Prussia. This unity disintegrated after two months.

The Income Tax would thus be of benefit to the government alone, hence the anger of the Consistorial Counsellors at its rejection.

But let us concede even for a moment that the proletariat has an interest in the matter; should this Diet have granted it?

By no means. It ought not to have granted moneys at all, it should have left the financial system exactly as it was so long as the government had not fulfilled all of its demands. The refusal of moneys is, in all parliamentary assemblies, the means by which the government is forced to yield to the majority. This consistent refusal of moneys was the only thing in which the Diet behaved energetically, and that is why the disappointed Consistorial Counsellors have to try and render it suspicious in the eyes of the people.

"And yet," the *Rh[einischer] Beob[achter]* continues, "the organs of the liberal press quite appropriately raised the matter of the Income Tax."

Quite correct, and it is indeed a purely bourgeois measure. For this very reason, though, the bourgeoisie is able to reject it when it is proposed to it at the wrong time by ministers whom it cannot trust an inch.

We shall, incidentally, add this confession concerning the paternity of the Income Tax to the record; we shall find it useful later on.

After some exceptionally vacuous and confused twaddle the Consistorial Counsellor suddenly stumbles over the proletariat in the following manner:

"What is the proletariat?" (This is yet another of those questions which arise *only* to remain unanswered.) "It is no exaggeration when we" (that is, the Consistorial Counsellors of the *Rh[einischer] B[eobachter]*, not, however, the other profane newspapers) "state that one-third of the people has no basis for its existence, and another third is on the decline. The problem of the proletariat is the problem of the great majority of people, it is the cardinal question."

"Thrice happy people," continues the Consistorial Counsellor, "you have at least won the question of principle! And if you do not understand what this is, then let your representatives explain it to you; perhaps you will forget your hunger in the course of their lengthy speeches!"

Who still dares to claim that the German press is not free? The *Rh[einischer] Beob[achter]* employs here with complete impunity a turn of phrase which many a French provincial jury would without more ado declare to be an incitement of the various classes of society against one another and cause to be punished.

The Consistorial Counsellor behaves, incidentally, in a terribly awkward manner. He wishes to flatter the people, and does not even credit it with knowing what a question of principle might be. Because he has to feign sympathy for the people's *hunger*, he takes his revenge by declaring it to be stupid and politically incompetent. The proletariat knows so well what the question of principle is that it does not reproach the Diet for having won it, but for *not* having won it. The proletariat reproaches the Diet for having stayed on the defensive, for not having attacked, for not having gone ten times further. It reproaches it with not having behaved decisively enough to make possible the participation of the proletariat in the movement. The proletariat was certainly incapable of showing any interest in the *Privileges of the Estates*. But a Diet demanding trial by jury, equality before the law, the abolition of the corvée [forced labour] system, freedom of the press, freedom of association and true representation, a Diet having once and for all broken with the past and formulating its demands according to the needs of the present instead of according to the old laws — such a Diet could count on the strongest support from the proletariat.

The *Beobachter* continues:

"And may God grant that this Diet should not absorb the power of the government, otherwise an insuperable brake will be put upon all social improvements."

The Herr Consistorial Counsellor may calm himself. A Diet that could not even get the better of the Prussian government will be given short shrift by the proletariat when the need arises.

"It has been said," the Consistorial Counsellor observes further, "that the Income Tax leads to revolution, to communism. To revolution, to be sure, that is to say, to a transformation of social relations, to the removal of limitless poverty."

Either the Consistorial Counsellor wishes to mock his readers and merely say that the Income Tax removes *limitless* poverty in order to replace it with limited poverty, and more of a similar kind of bad Berlin jokes—or he is the greatest and most shameless ignoramus in Economic matters alive. He does not know that in England the Income Tax has been in existence for seven years and has not transformed a single social relation, has not removed the least hair's breadth of limitless poverty. He does not know that it is precisely where the *most limitless* poverty exists in Prussia, in the weaving villages of Silesia and Ravensberg, among the small peasants of Silesia, Posen, the Mosel and the Vistula, that the Class Tax, that is, the Income Tax, is in force.

But who can reply seriously to such absurdities? It is further stated:

> "Also to *communism*, as it happens to be understood.... Where all relations have been so intertwined with one another and brought into flux by trade and industry that the individual loses his footing in the currents of competition, by the nature of the circumstances he is *thrown upon the mercy* of society which *must* compensate in respect of the *particular* for the consequences of the *general* fluctuations. Hence society has a *duty of solidarity* in respect of the existence of its members."

And there we are supposed to have the communism of the *Rh[einischer] Beobachter!* Thus—in a society such as ours, where nobody is secure in his existence, in his position in life, society is duty bound to *secure* everybody's existence. First the Consistorial Counsellor admits that the existing society *cannot* do this, and then he demands of it that it should nevertheless perform this impossible feat.

But it should compensate in respect of the particular for that for which it can show no consideration in its general fluctuations, this is what the Consistorial Counsellor means.

"One-third of the people has no basis for its existence, and another third is on the decline."

Ten million individuals, therefore, are to be individually *compensated for.* Does the Consistorial Counsellor believe in all seriousness that the *pauvre* [poor] Prussian government will be able to achieve this?

To be sure, and what is more by means of the Income Tax, which leads to communism, as it *happens to be understood* by the *Rh[einischer] Beobachter.*

Magnificent. After bemusing us with confused balderdash about alleged communism, after declaring that society has a duty of solidarity in respect of the existence of its members, that it *has to* care for them, although it cannot do so, after all these aberrations, contradictions and impossible demands, we are urged to accept the Income Tax as the measure which will resolve all contradictions, make all the impossibilities possible and restore the solidarity of all members of society.

We refer to Herr von Duesberg's memorandum on the Income Tax, which was presented to the Diet. In this memorandum employment had already been found for the last penny of the revenue from the Income Tax. The hard-pressed government had not a farthing to spare for the compensation in respect of the particular for general fluctuations, for the fulfillment of society's duties of solidarity. And if, instead of ten million, only ten individuals had been through the nature of circumstances thrown upon Herr von Duesberg's mercy, Herr von Duesberg would have rejected all ten of them.

But no, we are mistaken; besides the Income Tax the Herr Consistorial Counsellor has yet another means for introducing communism, as he happens to understand it:

> "What is the Alpha and Omega of the Christian faith? The dogma of original sin and redemption. And therein lies the association in solidarity of humanity in its highest potential: One for all and all for one."

Thrice happy people! The *cardinal question* is solved for all eternity! Under the double wings of the Prussian eagle and the Holy Ghost, the proletariat will find two inexhaustible springs of life: first, the surplus from the Income Tax above the ordinary and extraordinary needs of the state, which surplus equals zero, and second, the revenues from the heavenly domains of original sin and redemption, which likewise equal zero. These two zeroes provide a splendid basis for the one-third of the people which has no basis for its existence, a powerful support for other third which is on the decline. Imaginary surpluses, original sin and redemption will undoubtedly satisfy the people's hunger in quite another way than the long speeches of liberal deputies! It is further stated:

> "We also pray, in the Lord's prayer: 'Lead us not into temptation.' And what we supplicate for ourselves we ought to practice with general regard to our fellow human beings. Our social conditions undoubtedly tempt man, and the excess of poverty incites to crime."

And *we*, gentlemen, we bureaucrats, judges, and Consistorial

Counsellors of the Prussian state, practice this consideration by having people broken on the wheel, beheaded, locked up, and flogged to our heart's content, thereby "leading" the proletariat "into the temptation" to have us later similarly broken on the wheel, beheaded, locked up and flogged. Which will not fail to occur.

"Such conditions," declares the Consistorial Counsellor, "must not be tolerated by a Christian state, it must remedy them."

Indeed, with absurd blusterings about society's duties of solidarity, with imaginary surpluses and unacceptable bills of exchange on God the Father, Son and Company.

"We can also save ourselves all this tedious talk of communism," opines our observing Consistorial Counsellor. "If only those who have the vocation for it develop the social principles of Christianity, then the Communists will soon fall silent."

The social principles of Christianity have now had eighteen hundred years to be developed, and need no further development by Prussian Consistorial Counsellors.

The social principles of Christianity justified the slavery of antiquity, glorified the serfdom of the Middle Ages and are capable, in case of need, of defending the oppression of the proletariat, even if with somewhat doleful grimaces.

The social principles of Christianity preach the necessity of a ruling and an oppressed class, and for the latter all they have to offer is the pious wish that the former may be charitable.

The social principles of Christianity place the Consistorial Counsellor's compensation for all infamies in heaven, and thereby justify the continuation of these infamies on earth.

The social principles of Christianity declare all the vile acts of the oppressors against the oppressed to be either a just punishment for original sin and other sins, or trials which the Lord, in his infinite wisdom, ordains for the redeemed.

The social principles of Christianity preach cowardice, self-contempt, abasement, submissiveness and humbleness, in short, all the qualities of the rabble, and the proletariat, which will not permit itself to be treated like rabble, needs its courage, its self-confidence, its pride and its sense of independence even more than its bread.

The social principles of Christianity are sneaking and hypocritical, and the proletariat is revolutionary.

So much for the social principles of Christianity.

Further:

"We have acknowledged social reform to be the most distinguished vocation of the monarchy."

Have we? There has not been a single word of this hitherto. However, let it stand. And what does the social reform of the monarchy consist in? In promulgating an Income Tax stolen from the liberal press, which is to provide surpluses the Minister of Finance knows nothing about, in the abortive Land Annuity Banks, in the Prussian Eastern Railway, and in particular the profits from a vast capital of original sin and redemption!

"The interests of the monarchy itself makes this advisable"— how low, then, the monarchy must have sunk!

"The distress in society demands this"—for the moment it demands protective tariffs far more than dogmas.

"The gospel recommends this"—this is recommended by everything in general, only not by the terrifyingly barren condition of the Prussian State treasury, this abyss, which, within three years, will irrevocably have swallowed up the 15 Russian millions. The gospel recommends a great deal besides, among other things also castration as the beginning of social reform with oneself (Matth[ew] 19:12).

"The monarchy," declares our Consistorial Counsellor, "is one with the people."

This pronouncement is only another form of the old "*l'état c'est moi*" ["I am the state"], and precisely the same form, in fact, as was used by Louis XVI against his rebellious states on June 23, 1789: "If you do not obey, then I shall send you back home"—"*et seul je ferai le bonheur de mon people*" [and alone I shall make my people happy].

The monarchy must indeed be very hard-pressed if it decides to make any use of this formula, and our learned Consistorial Counsellor certainly knows how the French people thanked Louis XVI for its use on that occasion.

"The throne," the Consistorial Counsellor assures us further, "must rest on the broad foundation of the people, there it stands best."

So long, that is, as those broad shoulders do not, with one powerful heave, throw this burdensome superstructure into the gutter.

"The *aristocracy*," thus concludes the Herr Consistorial Counsellor, "leaves the monarchy its dignity and gives it a poetical adornment, but removes real power from it. The *bourgeoisie* robs it both of its power and its dignity, and only gives it a civil list. The *people* preserves to the monarchy its power, its dignity and its poetry."

In this passage the Herr Consistorial Counsellor has unfortunately taken the boastful appeal *to His People*, made by Frederick William in his Speech from the Throne, too seriously.[1] Its last word is—overthrow of the aristocracy, overthrow of the bourgeoisie, creation of a monarchy drawing its support from the people.

If these demands were not pure fantasies they would contain in themselves a complete revolution.

We have not the slightest wish to argue in detail that the aristocracy cannot be overthrown in any other manner than by the bourgeoisie and the people together, that rule of the people in a country where the aristocracy and the bourgeoisie still exist side by side is a piece of sheer nonsense. One cannot reply to such yarn-spinnings from one of Eichhorn's Consistorial Counsellors with any serious development of ideas.

We merely wish to make some well-intentioned comments to those gentlemen who would like to rescue the apprehensive Prussian monarchy by means of a somersault into the people.

Of all political elements the people is by far the most dangerous for a king. Not the people of which Frederick William speaks, which offers thanks with moist eyes for a kick and a silver penny; this people is completely harmless, for it only exists in the king's imagination. But the real people, the proletarians, the small peasants and the plebs—this is, as Hobbes says, *puer robustus, sed malitiosus,*[2] a robust, but ill-natured youth, which permits no kings, be they lean or fat, to get the better of him.

The people would above all extort from His Majesty a constitution, together with a universal franchise, freedom of association, freedom of the press and other unpleasant things.

And if it had all this, it would use it to pronounce as rapidly as possible on the *power*, the *dignity* and the *poetry* of the monarchy.

The current worthy occupant of this monarchy could count himself fortunate if the people employed him as a public barker of the Berlin Artisans' Association with a civil list of 250 talers and a cool pale ale daily.

If the Consistorial gentlemen now directing the destiny of the Prussian monarchy and the *Rhein[ischer] Beobachter* should doubt this,

---

[1] The same cannot be said of E in his commentary on "The Prussian Constitution" and his cartoon of the king delivering his address. See MECW 6.65–71.

[2] Thomas Hobbes, *Elementa philosophica de cive*, Praefatio Ad Lectores, i3. Hobbes's Latin is compacted for maximum emphasis by M.

then let them merely cast a glance at history. History provides a quite different horoscopes [sic] for kings who appealed to their people.

Charles I of England also appealed *to His People* against his estates. He called his people to arms against parliament. The people, however, declared itself to be against the king, threw all the members who did not represent the people out of parliament and finally caused parliament, which had thus become the real representative of the people, to behead the king. Thus ended the appeal of Charles I to his people. This occurred on January 30, 1649, and has its bicentenary in the year 1849.

Louis XVI of France likewise appealed *to His People*. Three years long he appealed from one section of the people to another, he sought His people, the true people, the people filled with enthusiasm for him, and found it nowhere. Finally he found it in the encampment of Koblenz, behind the ranks of the Prussian and Austrian army. This, however, was too much of a good thing for his people in France.[1] On August 10, 1792 it locked up the appellant in the Temple and summoned the National Convention, which represented it in every respect.

This convention declared itself competent to judge the *appeal* of the ex-king, and after some consultation the appellant was taken to the Place de la Révolution, where he was guillotined on January 21, 1793.

That is what happens when the kings *appeal to Their People*. Just what happens, however, when Consistorial Counsellors wish to found a democratic monarchy, we shall have to wait and see.

First published in the
Deutsche-Brusseler-Zeitung No.73,
September 12, 1847

(MECW: 6.220-34)

---

[1] See Appendices L.1 and 2.

Appendix E: Communist Journal, No. 1, September 1847

[In fairness to the leading members of the League of the Just, they were certainly dependent on the intellect and expressive powers of Marx and Engels but they were not entirely lacking in those capacities themselves. This first and only number of their new publication recognizes the challenge facing those who wish to get a revolutionary message out. But they are compelled to try one more time because of the promise of the newly formed Communist League and a growing sense of emergency and opportunity. Both pieces here are well written and cogently argued, with a strong proletarian emphasis and a resolve to pursue the struggle in Europe where the oppressor is best known and most firmly entrenched. The political potential of general literacy is well understood, the blights of militarization and the sexual harvesting of proletarian women powerfully conveyed. The anti-romantic, anti-utopian emphasis of the first piece is effectively elaborated via an assessment of Cabet's Icarianism.[1] There is no factionalism for its own sake, but rather the push for a solidarity that eschews emigration as an unfortunate echo of colonialism. The power of "public opinion" is plainly admitted and shrewdly accessed via sober analysis and the promising of the impending statement of a new political program. This is an important preparing of the ground for the *Manifesto,* showing not only the influence on Schapper and the others of the ideas of Marx and Engels but an ability to apply and translate them convincingly. This too is scholarship.]

(*Translated from the German original*)
[TRIAL NUMBER]

Communist Journal

"PROLETARIANS OF ALL LANDS, UNITE!"
- No. 1 -   London, September, 1847.   Price 2d.

---

[1]   Etienne Cabet (1788–1856), a leading French utopian socialist whose *Journey to Icaria* (1840) attracted self-styled Icarians eager to turn his fictional community into fact in places like Illinois.

We request all those who sympathise with our undertaking and who are living abroad to send articles and subscriptions to this journal to The Workers' Educational Society, 191 Drury Lane, High Holborn, London. Subscription rates: for Germany, 2 Silbergroschen or 6 Kreuzer; for France and Belgium, 4 sous; for Switzerland, 1½ batzen.

CONTENTS:—Introduction—Cabet's Scheme of Emigration.— The Prussian Diet and the Proletariat in Prussia in particular and in Germany in general.—The German Refugees.—Political and Social Survey.

Introduction

THERE are thousands of newspapers run off the presses day by day; every political party, every religious sect has its mouthpieces; the proletariat alone, that vast multitude of persons who possess nothing, has hitherto found it impossible to run a permanent organ of its own, one that shall defend the interests of the working class, one that can serve the workers as a guide in their endeavour to educate themselves. Not that the need for such an organ has not been felt by proletarians. Indeed, attempts have been made in one place or the other to establish suitable newspapers of the kind. Always in vain. In Switzerland, following close upon one another's heels came the "Junge Generation," the "Fröhliche Botschaft" [The Gospel or Good News] the "Blätter der Gegenwart" [Current News]; in France we had "Vorwaerts" and "Blätter der Zukunft" [News of the Future]; in Prussian Rhineland, the "Gesellschaftsspiegel" [Mirror of Society]; and so on. All of them were ephemeral. Either the police took a hand and scattered the staff; or the necessary money was not forthcoming, for the proletariat had not the wherewithal and the bourgeoisie would not help. In spite of these misadventures, we have been asked again and again to make a further venture into the realm of newspaper production, seeing that here in England freedom of the press prevails and that we need have no fear of police interference.

Both intellectuals and manual workers promised their collaboration. Yet we hesitated, for we dreaded lest after a very short period of activity, publication would cease for lack of funds. It was finally suggested that we acquire a printing press of our own so as to give the venture a more stable foundation. A subscription list was opened, and the members of both the workers' educational societies in

London did everything in their power to swell the fund. Nay, they did even more than seemed possible, and in a short time the sum of £25 was collected. The money permitted us to have the necessary type brought over from Germany; our compositor members have set up this issue gratuitously; and here in actual fact is the first number of our paper, whose existence is assured if we can get a little further help from the Continent. We still lack a printing press, but as soon as we have the money we intend to purchase one. Then our printing establishment will be in a position, not only to run off our newspaper, but likewise to print the pamphlets necessary for the defence of the proletariat. Since we are determined to be cautious, we shall content ourselves for the present with sending out this trial number, and shall await the response from abroad before proceeding to print any thing more. We hope that towards the close of the year a satisfactory response will be forthcoming. Then we shall have to decide whether the journal is to be issued weekly or fortnightly. The London readers alone are almost sufficient to guarantee a monthly issue. Provisionally the price of each copy is fixed at twopence, four sous, two silbergroschen, or six kreuzers, as the case may be. As soon as we have two thousand subscribers, we shall be able to reduce the price.

And now, Proletarians, the matter is in your hands. Send us articles, become subscribers if you possibly can, win over readers for the paper wherever an opportunity presents itself. The journal is to champion a holy, a righteous cause, the cause of justice against injustice, the cause of the oppressed against the oppressors. We stand for truth and against superstition and falsehood. We work for no recompense, for no pay: we are merely acting as in duty bound. Proletarians, do you wish to be free? Then rouse up from your slumbers and join hands one with another! Mankind expects every man to do his duty.

PROLETARIANS!

Since the origin and meaning of the word we apostrophise you with may not be known to many among you, we will prelude our articles by a short explanation.

When the Roman State was at the zenith of its power, when it had reached the climax of its civilisation, its citizens were divided into two classes: owners and non-owners. The owners paid direct taxes to the State; the non-owners gave the State their children. The latter were made use of to protect the wealthy and were condemned to drench in-numerable battlegrounds with their blood, in order to increase the power and the property of the owning class. "Proles" is the Latin for children, for offspring. Proletarians, therefore, constituted that class of citizens who owned nothing but the arms of their body and the children of their loins.

Contemporary society is approaching the highest point of its civilisation, machines have been invented, great factories have been erected, property is more and more becoming concentrated into the hands of a few individuals, and, consequently, the proletariat has likewise developed and increased in numbers. A few privileged individuals own all the property there is to own, whilst the broad masses of the people possess nothing but their hands and their children.

Just as of old in the Roman State so now do we see proletarians and their sons thrust into military uniforms, trained to become automata which protect the very persons who oppress them, the persons at whose nod their blood is to be shed. Just as of old, so now, must the sisters and the daughters of the proletariat be sacrificed to the bestial lusts of rich voluptuaries. Just as of old, so now, is hatred ri[f]e against the oppressors. Nevertheless, the proletarian of our own day is in a much better position than was his Roman brother. The Roman proletariat had neither the means whereby it could win to freedom, nor the education that could guide it on its way; nothing remained for it but to rise in revolt, to revenge itself, and to die defeated. Many a proletarian to-day has attained a high degree of education thanks to the development of book printing; others, by endeavour and by uniting their forces, are daily acquiring knowledge. Whilst the proletariat is ever aspiring to loftier altitudes, is ever seeking for greater solidarity, the privileged class is setting an example of the most flagrant selfishness and most detestable immorality. Civilisation to-day has at its command enough means wherewith to make all members of society happy. The aim of the modern proletariat is, therefore, not merely to destroy, to wreak revenge, to find freedom in death. On the contrary, the proletariat must act in such a way that a society shall be established wherein all mankind can live as free and happy creatures. In contemporary society, the proletarians are those who can have no capital to live on, worker and professor, artist and petty bourgeois alike. Even though the petty bourgeois may still possess a little property, nevertheless he soon falls into the ranks of the proletariat, a victim of the fierce competition of large-scale capital. He can, therefore, already be counted as one of ourselves, for it is quite as much to his better interest to guard against a condition of complete destitution as it is for us to rise out of this condition. Let us unite; unity cannot fail to advantage us both.

The aim of this journal is to work on behalf of the emancipation of the proletariat, and to make it possible for the proletariat to call upon all the oppressed to close their ranks in solidarity.

We have christened our paper the "Communist Journal," because we are convinced and know that this emancipation can be secured in no other way than by a complete trans-formation of extant property relations. In a word, the liberation of the oppressed can only be achieved in a society based upon common ownership. We had contemplated introducing into this issue a short and easily comprehensible profession of communist faith. Indeed, the draft is already written. But since this profession of faith will have to serve as a guide in our future propaganda activities and is, therefore, of the utmost importance, we considered it our duty to submit the draft to our friends abroad in order to profit by their views in the matter. As soon as we receive replies we shall make the necessary emendations and additions, and shall print it in our next issue.

The communist movement is so universally misunderstood, when it is not intentionally calumniated and its teaching distorted, that we may suitably say a few words about it, in so far as we know its aims, and ourselves are taking part in its activities. Here it beho[o]ves us mainly to state what communism is not if we are to put an end to the libellous accusations which might be uttered against us.

We are no quack-mongers advocating a system that shall be a cure-all. Experience has taught what folly it is to discuss and elaborate the details of a future society, and to ignore all the means which might help us to achieve our aims. That philosophers and professors should spend time upon excogitating the organisation of a future society is a good thing and has its uses; but if we were to set ourselves in full earnest to discuss with our fellow proletarians as to how the workshops of the future State were to be inaugurated, how the future community of goods was to be administered, what was the best cut for the wearing apparel of the future, and how we should most conveniently clean the closets, we should make ourselves a laughing-stock and should quite justly deserve to be called unpractical dreamers—a name so often applied to us without reason. Our generation has its task to perform, which is to find and to assemble the building materials needed for the erection of the new edifice. It will be up to the next generation to do the work of construction, and we may rest easy that when the time comes master builders will not be lacking.

We are not among those communists who believe that our goal can be won by the exercise of love alone. No salt sad tears are wept by us in the moonlight deploring the misery of mankind, our profound depression being followed by an ecstasy of delight at the thought of a golden future. Our day is one of earnest endeavour, it needs the whole of each man's exertions. This love-and-sob stuff is nothing more than a kind of mental self-enervation which deprives those addicted to it of all capacity for energetic action.

We are not among those communists who preach everlasting peace here and now at a time our opponents in every land are girding their loins for battle. We know only too well that, with the possible exceptions of Britain and the United States, we shall not be able to enter our better world unless we have previously and by the exercise of force won our political rights. Should there still be persons to condemn us and to call us revolutionists, we can only shrug our shoulders in disdain. No dust is going to be thrown in the eyes of the people by us. We mean to tell the people the truth, to warn the people of the approaching storm, so that all preparations can be made in advance. We are not conspirators who have determined to begin the revolution on such and such a day or who are plotting the assassination of princes. But neither are we patient sheep who shoulder their cross uncomplainingly. We know that, on the continent of Europe, the discord between aristocrat and democrat cannot be resolved without a clash of arms—indeed, our enemies are well aware of this, too, and are making warlike preparations. It is incumbent on each and every one of us to make ready so that we may not be taken by surprise and destroyed. A final and serious struggle lies ahead of us. If our party comes out of it victorious then will the day have dawned when we can for ever lay our weapons on the shelf.

We are not among those communists who believe that a community in goods can be established, as if by magic, on the morrow of a victory. We know that mankind advances, not by leaps, but only step by step. We cannot pass from an inharmonious society to a harmonious one betwixt night and morning. A transitional period will be needed, longer or shorter as circumstances may dictate. Only by degrees can private property be transformed into social property.

We are not among those communists who are out to destroy

personal liberty, who wish to turn the world into one huge barrack or into a gigantic workhouse. There certainly are some communists who, with an easy conscience, refuse to countenance personal liberty and would like to shuffle it out of the world because they consider that it is a hindrance to complete harmony. But we have no desire to exchange freedom for equality.[1] We are convinced, and we intend to return to the matter in subsequent issues, that in no social order will personal freedom be so assured as in a society based upon communal ownership.

Thus far what we are not. In our profession of faith we shall declare what we are and what we aim at achieving. Here we have only to address a few words to those proletarians who belong to other political or social parties. We are all of us out to fight extant society, because it oppresses us and allows us to rot in poverty and wretchedness. Instead of realising this and uniting our ranks, we are prone, alas, to squabble among ourselves, to fight with one another— much to the delight of our oppressors. Instead of, like one man, putting our hands to the work in order to establish a democratic State wherein each party would be able by word or in writing to win a majority over to its ideas, we wrangle one with another as to what will or what will not happen when once we have been victorious. We cannot help but recall in this connection the fable of the bear hunters, who, before ever they had caught sight of a bear, came to fisticuffs as to who should become owner of the bear-skin! It is more than time that we should lay aside our enmities and join hands in mutual protection. If we are to achieve solidarity, the spokesmen of the various parties must cease their bitter attacks upon those who hold other views and must put an end to the abuse showered upon the adherents of opposing theories. We respect all, even aristocrats and pietists, who have opinions of their own; and are prepared to defend, persistently and resolutely, what they believe to be right. But those who, behind the mask of this or that religion or of this or that political or social party, have no other object in view than the advantage of their own filthy selves, will receive no quarter from us. All men of honour are in duty bound to unmask such hypocrites, to expose them in all their loathsome nakedness to the world. Any one can make a mistake and champion false doctrines. But we must think no worse of him for that, if he himself believes in them and is true

---

[1] Compare Appendix L.3.

to his colours. Hence Carl Heinzen[1] is exceeding his rights when he attacks the communists as he does in the second issue of the "Tribun." Either Carl Heinzen is completely ignorant of the meaning of communism, or he has allowed his personal antagonism to certain communists to prejudice his judgment of a party which stands in the front ranks of the armies fighting for democracy. When we read his attack on the communists we were filled with amazement. His accusations did not touch us on the raw because such communists as he describes simply do not exist. They have probably been created by Heinzen's vivid imagination in order that he may then proceed to take cock-shies at them. When we say we were amazed at his article we mean that it was hard for us to believe that a democrat could have been guilty of throwing the apple of discord into the midst of his own comrades-in-arms. But our astonishment waxed even greater when, at the close of the article we read his 9 points which were to form the bases of the new social order. These points are almost identical with the demands put forward by the communists! The only difference would appear to be that Citizen Carl Heinzen looks upon his nine points as the bases of the new social order, whereas we would look upon them merely as a foundation for the transitional period which shall prelude the inauguration of a fully communised society. It is, therefore, reasonable to hope that we shall become united in order to achieve what Carl Heinzen proposes. Once having got so far, if we find that the people is content, is so perfectly satisfied that it would fain go no farther, we shall have to submit to the popular will. But should the people wish to go forward until communism is established, we do not suppose that Citizen Heinzen would raise any objections. We are well aware that Citizen Heinzen is the object of attack and calumny on the part of our common oppressors, and is, therefore, in a state of acute irritability. We, ourselves, will in no way molest him. On the contrary, we will not refuse to extend the hand of solidarity towards him. Unity is strength; unity alone can lead us to the goal.

Therefore proletarians of all lands unite—openly where the laws permit, for our activities need not fear the light of day—secretly where the arbitrary will of tyrants imposes secrecy upon us. So-called

---

[1] Karl Heinzen (1809–80), sometime German ally of M in his attacks on Prussian bureaucracy, but by 1847 anti-communist and anti-socialist. He spent the last 30 years of his life in the US.

laws which forbid men to meet together in order to discuss the problems of the day and to demand their rights are not laws in the true sense, they are no more than the peremptory decisions of tyrants. He who pays heed to such laws and observes them is a coward and acts dishonourably; but he who scorns them and breaks them is a man of courage and honour.

A word in conclusion. The columns of our journal are not open for the ventilation of personal grievances or for the commendation of those who perform their duty. When, however, a proletarian is oppressed and ill-used, he need but turn to us and we shall wholeheartedly rally to his aid, and make widely known the name of the oppressor so that public opinion may curse the miscreant as he deserves. Even the most stiff-necked tyrant trembles before public opinion.

Citizen Cabet's Emigration Scheme

Citizen Cabet has issued an appeal to the French communists wherein we read: "Since we are persecuted not only by the government, the priests, and the bourgeoisie, but even by the revolutionary republicans as well, since we are calumniated and driven from pillar to post in so irksome a manner as to make it difficult for us to gain a livelihood or to maintain our physical and moral integrity, let us shake the dust of France from off our feet and journey to Icaria." Cabet imagines that from twenty to thirty thousand communists are ready to follow his call, and, in another continent, to found a communist colony. He has not yet made it clear what destination he has in view, but we may assume that his choice will single out one or other of the free states of North America. Maybe he has Texas in mind; or perhaps California, so recently conquered by the Americans, is the land of his predilection.

We are glad to recognise, as all communists must recognise, the indefatigable zeal, the amazing persistence with which Cabet fights in the cause of suffering humanity; nor do we fail to give him credit for the successful issue of his work. Further, he has done inestimable service by his warnings in respect of those who plot and scheme against the proletariat. Nevertheless we cannot allow matters to pass unnoticed when, in our view, Cabet enters upon a false path. We respect Citizen Cabet personally, but we feel it essential to oppose his emigration plan. Nay more; we are convinced that should his plan ever materialise it would bring contumely upon the principles of communism and serve as a triumph for the government, so that Cabet's last days would be embittered by a terrible disappointment [and they were, with acrimonious collapse of the Illinois colony].

Here are the grounds for our opinion.

I. We believe that when in any country the most shameless corruption comes to be looked upon as a matter of course, when the people is basely exploited and oppressed, when right and justice are no longer held in honour, when society is disappearing in anarchy as is the case in France at the present day, it is up to every champion of justice and of truth to remain in that country, to enlighten the people, to inspire the weak with fresh courage, to lay the foundations of a new social order, and to face the foe with a bold heart. If decent, honest men, fighters for a better world, leave the country and abandon the field to obscurantists, cheats, and rogues, then will Europe inevitably fall upon evil days, and poor humanity will have to go through another century of suffering by fire and sword. Yet Europe is precisely that quarter of the earth's surface where the community of goods could most easily be introduced.

2. We are convinced that such a scheme as Cabet proposes, *i.e.*, the founding of a colony, an Icaria, in America, wherein community of goods shall be in force, is impossible of accomplishment at the present time.

(a) In the first place, because those who, together with Cabet, would emigrate to the new settlement, though they be zealous communists, are nevertheless tainted by their upbringing with all the faults and prejudices of contemporary society, and will not be able suddenly to discard these failings on arriving in Icaria.

(b) Secondly, at the very outset, quarrels and friction will inevitably arise among the members of the colony precisely on account of these educational blemishes. Such mis-understandings will be utilised by the members of society at large, which is powerful and antagonistic to the experiment and likewise by the European governments through the intermediation of their spies; these inimical forces will foment the trouble until the whole little communistic society becomes completely disintegrated.

(c) Thirdly, most of the emigrants are likely to be artisans, whereas what is needed out there above all are sturdy men of the plough, men who shall furrow the soil and make it fruitful. It is not so easy a task as some seem to fancy, to convert an industrial worker into a land worker.

(d) Fourthly, the privations and the sicknesses which a change of climate entail will discourage many and prompt them to back out of the experiment. At the moment, many favour the plan because they can only see its rosy side, they have accepted it with enthusiasm. But when they are faced with rude reality, when privations of every sort fall to their lot, when all the little amenities of civilisation are withdrawn (amenities which even the poorest European worker sometimes has at his command), then many who are now so keen will find their enthusiasm replaced by overwhelming discouragement.

(e) Fifthly, it is impossible for a communist to envisage the inauguration of a society based on the community of goods without its having first passed through a period of transition, and indeed a democratic period of transition, during which personal property would gradually become merged into social property; for communists recognise the principle of personal freedom (as, probably, do the Icarians likewise). A leap, such as Cabet contemplates, in the sequence of events is as impossible from a communist outlook as, from a farmer's outlook, would be a harvest when there has been no seed-time.

3. The failure of a scheme such as Cabet has in mind, although it would not annul the communist principle or make the practical inauguration of communism impossible, nevertheless would sap the courage of many communists, causing them to leave our ranks, and thereby in all probability dooming the proletariat to yet further decades of wretchedness and poverty.

4. Lastly, the community of goods cannot be established and maintained among a few hundred or a few thousand persons, without the little society becoming exclusivist or sectarian in character. An example is furnished us by Rapp's experiment in America.[1] It is certainly not our intention, nor do we

---

[1] German born George Rapp (1757–1847) established a "primitive" Christian Harmony Society of some six hundred souls near Pittsburgh in 1804. The community prospered and then moved to New Harmony in Indiana, to a property purchased by Robert Owen in 1824. The largely celibate and communitarian Harmonists then moved back to Pennsylvania to establish the village of Economy which endured until 1905.

believe the intention of the Icarians, to set up any community on Rapp's lines.

Nor have we yet had to suffer persecutions such as the Icarians, if they keep up intercourse with the outer world, will probably have to suffer at the hands of their American neighbours. We would advise every one who is contemplating emigration with Cabet to America to read a report of the persecutions which the Mormons, a religious sect based upon communist principles, have had to endure and are still enduring.

Such are the reasons why we consider Cabet's emigration plan a harmful undertaking. We appeal to the communists in every land: Brothers, let us man the breach here, in old Europe; let us remain here to work and to fight; for in Europe alone are all the elements ready for the establish of a society based on the community of goods. Such a society will be inaugurated here if it is ever going to be inaugurated anywhere at all.

(Translation by Eden and Cedar Paul from *The Communist Manifesto of Karl Marx and Friedrich Engels*, edited, with an Introduction, Explanatory Notes and Appendices by D. Ryazanoff. New York: Russell and Russell, 1930. 286–97).

Appendix F: Engels, "Principles of Communism," late October 1847

[This iteration of a communist program retains the catechetical form of the earlier "Draft" (Appendix C) but establishes its difference in its bold revision of the first six points of the "Draft" and in the addition of 12 new questions. The form has yet to shift to that of a manifesto, but Engels strengthens the emphasis on the historical specificity and growing revolutionary power of the proletariat. Now that Moses Hess's vision has been effectively discredited, there is less and less need for conciliation of moderate opinion in the residues of the League of the Just, and more need to underscore the recurrent crises in capitalism and the opportunities and obligations they represent.]

Frederick Engels

PRINCIPLES OF COMMUNISM

Question 1: *What is communism?*
Answer: Communism is the doctrine of the conditions for the emancipation of the proletariat.

Question 2: *What is the proletariat?*
Answer: The proletariat is that class of society which procures its means of livelihood entirely and solely from the sale of its labour and not from the profit derived from any capital; whose weal and woe, whose life and death, whose whole existence depend on the demand for labour, hence, on the alternation of times of good and bad business, on the fluctuations resulting from unbridled competition. The proletariat, or class of proletarians, is, in a word, the working class of the nineteenth century.

Question 3: *Then there have not always been proletarians?*
Answer: No. Poor folk and working classes have always existed, and the working classes have for the most part been poor. But such poor, such workers who live under the

conditions just stated, that is, proletarians, have not always existed, any more than competition has always been free and unbridled.

Question 4: *How did the proletariat arise?*

Answer: The proletariat arose as a result of the industrial revolution which took place in England in the latter half of the last century and which has repeated itself since then in all the civilised countries of the world. This industrial revolution was brought about by the invention of the steam-engine, of various spinning machines, of the power-loom, and of a great number of other mechanical devices. These machines which were very expensive and, consequently, could only be purchased by big capitalists, changed the entire hitherto existing mode of production and supplanted the former workers because machines produced cheaper and better commodities than could the workers with their imperfect spinning-wheels and hand-looms. Thus, these machines delivered industry entirely into the hands of the big capitalists and rendered the workers' scanty property (tools, looms, etc.) quite worthless, so that the capitalists soon had their hands on everything and the workers were left with nothing. In this way the factory system was introduced into the manufacture of clothing materials.—Once the impetus had been given to the introduction of machinery and the factory system, this system was soon applied to all the other branches of industry, notably the calico and book-printing trades, pottery, and hardware industry. There was more and more division of labour among the individual workers, so that the worker who formerly had made a whole article now produced only a part of it. This division of labour made it possible to supply products more speedily and therefore more cheaply. It reduced the activity of each worker to a very simple, constantly repeated mechanical operation, which could be performed not only just as well but even much better by a machine. In this way, all these branches of industry came one after another under the domination of steam-power, machinery, and the factory-system, just like spinning and weaving. But they thus fell at the same time completely into the hands of the big capitalists, and here too the workers were deprived of the last shred of independence. Gradually, in addition to actual manufacture, the handicrafts likewise fell increasingly under the domination of the factory system, for here also the big capitalists more and more supplanted the small craftsmen by the establishment of large workshops, in which many savings on costs can be made and there can be a very high division of labour. Thus we have now reached the point when in the civilised countries almost all branches of labour are carried on under the factory system, and in almost all branches handicraft and manufacture have been ousted by large-scale industry.—As a result, the former middle classes, especially the smaller master handicraftsmen, have been increasingly ruined, the former position of the workers has been completely changed, and two new classes which gradually swallowing up all other classes have come into being, namely:

I. The class of big capitalists who already now in all civilised countries almost exclusively own all the means of subsistence and the raw materials and instruments (machinery, factories, etc.), needed for the production of these means of subsistence. This class is the bourgeois class or bourgeoisie.

II. The class of the completely propertyless, who are compelled therefore to sell their labour to the bourgeois in order to obtain the necessary means of subsistence in exchange. This class is called the class of the proletarians or the proletariat.

Question 5: *Under what conditions does this sale of the labour of the proletarians to the bourgeois take place?*

Answer: Labour is a commodity like any other and its price is determined by the same laws as that of any other commodity. The price of a commodity under the domination of large-scale industry or of free competition, which, as we shall see, comes to the same thing, is on the average always equal to the cost of production of that commodity. The price of labour is, therefore, likewise equal to the cost of production of labour. The cost of production of labour consists precisely of the amount of the means of subsistence required for the worker to maintain himself in a condition in which he is capable of working and to prevent the working class from dying out. Therefore, the worker will not receive for his labour any more than is necessary for that purpose; the price of labour, or wages, will be the lowest, the minimum required for subsistence. Since business is now worse, now better, the worker will receive now more, now less for his commodity. But just as on the average between good times and bad the factory owner receives for his commodity neither more nor less than the cost of its production, so also the worker will on the average receive neither more nor less than this minimum. This economic law of wages will come to be more stringently applied the more all branches of labour are taken over by large-scale industry.

Question 6: *What working classes existed before the industrial revolution?*

Answer: Depending on the different stages of the development of society, the working classes lived in different conditions and stood in different relations to the possessing and ruling classes. In ancient times the working people were the *slaves* of their owners, just as they still are in many backward countries and even in the southern part of the United States. In the Middle Ages they were the *serfs* of the landowning nobility, just as they still are in Hungary, Poland, and Russia. In the Middle Ages and up to the industrial revolution there were in the towns also journeymen in the service of the petty-bourgeois craftsmen, and with the development of manufacture there gradually emerged manufactory workers, who were already employed by the big capitalists.

Question 7: *In what way does the proletariat differ from the slave?*

Answer: The slave is sold once and for all, the proletarian has to sell himself by the day and by the hour. Being the property of *one* master, the individual slave has, since it is in the interest of this master, a guaranteed subsistence, however wretched it may be; the individual proletarian, the property, so to speak, of the whole bourgeois *class*, whose labour is only bought from him when somebody needs it, has no guaranteed subsistence. This subsistence is guaranteed only to the proletarian *class* as a whole. The slave stands outside the competition; the proletarian stands within it and feels all its fluctuations. The slave is accounted a thing, not a member of civil society; the proletarian is recognised as a person, as a member of civil society. Thus, the slave may have a better subsistence than the proletarian, but the proletarian belongs to a higher stage than the slave. The slave frees himself by abolishing, among all the private property relationships, only the relationship of slavery and thereby only then himself becomes a proletarian; the proletarian can free himself only by abolishing private property in general.

Question 8: *In what way does the proletarian differ from the serf?*

Answer: The serf has the possession and use of an instrument of production, a piece of land, in return for handing over a portion of the yield or for the performance of work. The proletarian works with instruments of production belonging to another person for the benefit of this other person in return for receiving a portion of this yield. The serf gives, to the proletarian is given. The serf has a guaranteed subsistence, the proletarian has not. The serf stands outside competition, the proletarian stands within it. The serf frees himself either by running away to the town and there becoming a handicraftsman or by giving his landlord money instead of labour and products and becoming a free tenant; or by driving out his feudal lord and himself becoming a proprietor, in short, by entering in one way or another into the possessing class and competition. The proletarian frees himself by doing away with competition, private property and all class distinctions.

Question 9:   *In what way does the proletarian differ from the handi-craftsman?*

[Answer: left missing here. Engels had already given it in his Draft Confession.]

Question 10:   *In what way does the proletarian differ from the manufactory worker?*

Answer: The manufactory worker of the sixteenth to eighteenth centuries almost everywhere still owned an instrument of production, his loom, the family spinning-wheels, and a little plot of land which he cultivated in his leisure hours. The proletarian has none of these things. The manufactory worker lives almost always in the country and in more or less patriarchal relations with his landlord or his employer; the proletarian lives mostly in large towns, and stands to his employer in a purely money relationship. The manufactory worker is torn up from his patriarchal relations by large-scale industry, loses the property he still has and thereby only then himself becomes a proletarian.

Question 11:   *What were the immediate results of the industrial revolution and the division of society into bourgeois and proletarians?*

Answer: *Firstly*, owing to the continual cheapening of the price of industrial products as a result of machine labour, the old system of manufacture or industry founded upon manual labour was completely destroyed in all countries of the world. All semi-barbarian countries, which until now had been more or less outside historical development and whose industry had until now been based on manufacture, were thus forcibly torn out of their isolation. They bought the cheaper commodities of the English and let their own manufactory workers go to ruin. The countries that for thousands of years had made no progress, for example India, were revolutionized through and through, and even China is now marching towards a revolution. It has reached the point that a new machine invented today in England, throws millions of workers in China out of work within a year. Large-scale industry has thus brought all the peoples of the earth into a relationship with one another, thrown all the small local markets into the world market, prepared the way everywhere for civilisation and progress, and brought it about that everything that happens in the civilised countries must have its repercussions on all other countries. So if now in England or France the workers liberate themselves, this must lead to revolutions in all other countries, which sooner or later will also bring about the liberation of the workers in those countries.

Secondly, wherever large-scale industry replaced manufacture, the industrial revolution developed the bourgeoisie, its wealth and its power, to the highest degree and made it the first class in the land. The result was that wherever this happened, the bourgeoisie obtained political power and ousted the hitherto ruling classes—the aristocracy, the guild-burghers and the absolute monarchy representing both. The bourgeoisie annihilated the power of the aristocracy, the nobility, by abolishing entails or the ban on the sale of landed property, and all privileges of the nobility. It destroyed the power of the guild-burghers by abolishing all guilds and craft privileges. In place of both it put free competition, that is, a state of society in which everyone has the right to engage in any branch of industry he likes, and where nothing can hinder him in carrying it on except lack of the necessary capital. The introduction of free competition is therefore the public declaration that henceforward the members of society are only unequal in so far as their capital is unequal, that capital has become the decisive power and therefore the capitalists, the bourgeois, have become the first class in society. But free competition is necessary for the beginning of large-scale industry since it is the only state of society in which large-scale industry can grow. The bourgeoisie having thus anni-

hilated the social power of the nobility and the guild-
burghers, annihilated their political power as well.
Having become the first class in society, the bourgeoisie proclaimed itself also the first class in the political sphere. It did this by establishing the representative
system, which rests upon bourgeois equality before the
law and the legal recognition of free competition, and
which in European countries was introduced in the
form of constitutional monarchy. Under these constitutional monarchies those only are electors who
possess a certain amount of capital, that is to say, the
bourgeois; these bourgeois electors elect the deputies,
and these bourgeois deputies, by means of the right to
refuse taxes, elect a bourgeois government.

Thirdly, the industrial revolution built up the proletariat in the same measure in which it built up the bourgeoisie. In the same proportion in which the bourgeois
became wealthier, the proletarians became more
numerous. For since proletarians can only be employed
by capital and since capital only increases when it
employs labour, the growth of the proletariat keeps
exact pace with the growth of capital. At the same time
it concentrates the bourgeois as well as the proletarians
in large cities, in which industry can most profitably be
carried on, and through this throwing together of great
masses in *one* place it makes the proletarians conscious
of their power. Further, the more it develops, the more
machines are invented which displace manual labour,
the more large-scale industry, as we already said,
depresses wages to their minimum, and thereby makes
the condition of the proletariat more and more unbear-
able. Thus, through the growing discontent of the
proletariat, on the one hand, and through its growing
power, on the other, the industrial revolution prepares
a social revolution by the proletariat.

Question 12: *What were the further results of the industrial revolution?*
Answer: In the steam-engine and the other machines large-scale
                industry created the means of increasing industrial
                production in a short time and at slight expense to an

unlimited extent. With this facility of production the free competition necessarily resulting from large-scale industry very soon assumed an extremely intense character; numbers of capitalists launched into industry, and very soon more was being produced than could be used. The result was that the goods manufactured could not be sold, and a so-called trade crisis ensued. Factories had to stand idle, factory owners went bankrupt, and the workers lost their bread. Everywhere there was the greatest misery. After a while the surplus products were sold, the factories started working again, wages went up, and gradually business was more brisk than ever. But before long too many commodities were again produced, another crisis ensued, and ran the same course as the previous one. Thus since the beginning of this century the state of industry has continually fluctuated between periods of prosperity and periods of crisis, and almost regularly every five to seven years a similar crisis has occurred, and every time it has entailed the greatest misery for the workers, general revolutionary ferment, and the greatest danger to the entire existing system.

Question 13: *What conclusions can be drawn from these regularly recurring trade crises?*

Answer: *Firstly,* that although in the initial stages of its development large-scale industry itself created free competition, it has now nevertheless outgrown free competition; that competition and in general the carrying on of industrial competition by individuals have become a fetter upon large-scale industry, so long as it is conducted on its present basis, can only survive though a general confusion repeating itself every seven years which each time threatens all civilization, not merely plunging the proletarians into misery but also ruining a great number of bourgeois; therefore that either large-scale industry must itself be given up, which is utterly impossible, or that it absolutely necessitates a completely new organisation of society, in which industrial production is no longer directed by individual factory owners, competing one against the other, but by the whole of society according to a fixed plan and according to the needs of all. *Secondly*, that large-scale industry and the unlimited expansion of production which it makes possible can bring into being a social order in which so much of all the necessities of life will be produced that every member of society will thereby be enabled to develop and exercise all his powers and abilities in perfect freedom. Thus, precisely that quality of large-scale industry which in present society produces all misery and all trade crises is the very quality which under a different social organisation will destroy the same misery and these disastrous fluctuations.

Thus it is most clearly proved:

1. that from now on all these ills are to be attributed only to the social order which no longer corresponds to the existing conditions;
2. that the means are available to abolish these ills completely through a new social order.

Question 14: *What kind of new social order will this have to be?*

Answer: Above all, it will have to take the running of industry and all branches of production in general out of the hands of separate individuals competing with each other and instead will have to ensure that all the branches of production are run by society as a whole, i.e., for the social good, according to a social plan and with the participation of all members of society. It will therefore do away with competition and replace it by association. Since the running of industry by individuals had private ownership as its necessary consequence and since competition is nothing but the manner in which industry is run by individual private owners, private ownership cannot be separated from the individual running of industry and competition. Hence, private ownership will also have to be abolished, and in its stead there will be common use of all the instruments of production and the distribution of all products by common agreement, or the so-called community of property. The abolition of private ownership is indeed the most succinct and characteristic summary of the transformation of the entire social system necessarily following from the development of industry, and it is therefore rightly put forward by the Communists as their main demand.

Question 15: *The abolition of private property was therefore not possible earlier?*

Answer: No. Every change in the social order, every revolution in property relations, has been the necessary result of the creation of new productive forces which would no longer conform to the old property relations. Private property itself arose in this way. For private property has not always existed, but when towards the end of the Middle Ages a new mode of production appeared in the form of manufacture which could not be subordinated to the then existing feudal and guild property, manufacture, having outgrown the old property relations, created a new form of ownership—private ownership. For manufacture and the first stage of development of large-scale industry, no other form of ownership was possible than private ownership and no other order of society than that founded the cause of the proletarians by deed just as well as we do now by word.

Question 17: *Will it be possible to abolish private property at one stroke?*

Answer: No, such a thing would be just as impossible as at *one* stroke to increase the existing productive forces to the degree necessary for instituting community of property. Hence, the proletarian revolution, which in all probability is impending, will transform existing society only gradually, and be able to abolish private property only when the necessary quantity of the means of production has been created.

Question 18: *What will be the course of this revolution?*

Answer: In the first place it will inaugurate a *democratic constitution* and thereby, directly or indirectly, the political rule of the proletariat. Directly in England, where the proletariat already constitutes the majority of the people. Indirectly in France and in Germany, where the majority of the people consists not only of proletarians but also of small peasants and urban petty bourgeois, who are only now being proletarianised and in all their political interests are becoming more and more dependent on the proletariat and therefore soon will have to conform to the demands of the proletariat. This will perhaps involve a second fight, but one that can end only in the victory of the proletariat.

Democracy would be quite useless to the proletariat if it were not immediately used as a means of carrying through further measures directly attacking private ownership and securing the means of subsistence of the proletariat. Chief among these measures, already made necessary by the existing conditions, are the following:

1. Limitation of private ownership by means of progressive taxation, high inheritance taxes, abolition of inheritance collateral lines (brothers, nephews, etc.), compulsory loans and so forth.

2. Gradual expropriation of landed proprietors, factory owners, railway and shipping magnates, partly through competition of state industry and partly directly through compensation in assignations.

3. Confiscation of the property of all emigrants and rebels against the majority of the people.

4. Organisation of the labour or employment of the proletarians on national estates, in national factories and workshops, thereby putting an end to competition among the workers themselves and compelling the factory owners, as long as they still exist, to pay the same increased wages as the state.

5. Equal liability to work for all members of society until complete abolition of private ownership. Formation of industrial armies, especially for agriculture.

6. Centralisation of the credit and banking systems in the hands of the State by means of a national bank

with state capital and the suppression of all private banks and bankers.

7. Increase of national factories, workshops, railways, and ships, cultivation of all uncultivated land and improvement of land already cultivated in the same proportion in which the capital and workers at the disposal of the nation increase.

8. Education of all children, as soon as they are old enough to do without the first maternal care, in national institutions and at the expense of the nation. Education combined with production.

9. The erection of large palaces on national estates as common dwellings for communities of citizens engaged in industry as well as agriculture, and combining the advantages of both urban and rural life without the one-sidedness and disadvantages of either.

10. The demolition of all insanitary and badly built dwellings and town districts.

11. Equal right of inheritance to be enjoyed by illegitimate and legitimate children.

12. Concentration of all means of transport in the hands of the nation.

Of course, all these measures cannot be carried out at once. But one will always lead on to the other. Once the first radical onslaught upon private ownership has been made, the proletariat will see itself compelled to go always further, to concentrate all capital, all agriculture, all industry, all transport, and all exchange more and more in the hands of the State. All these measures work towards such results; and they will become reliable and will develop their centralising consequences in the same proportion in which the productive forces of the country will be manipulated by the labour of the proletariat. Finally, when all capital, all production, and all exchange are concentrated in the hands of the nation, private ownership will automatically have ceased to exist, money will have become superfluous, and production will have so increased and men will be so much changed that the last forms of the old social relations will also be able to fall away.

Question 19: *Will it be possible for this revolution to take place in one country alone?*

Answer: No. Large-scale industry, already by creating the world market, has so linked up all the peoples of the earth, and especially the civilised peoples, that each people is dependent on what happens to another. Further, in all civilised countries large-scale industry has so leveled social development that in all these countries the bourgeoisie and the proletariat have been the two decisive classes of society and the struggle between them the main struggle of the day. The communist revolution will therefore be no merely national one; it will be a revolution taking place simultaneously in all civilised countries, that is, at least in England, America, France, and Germany. In each of these countries it will develop more quickly or more slowly according to whether the country has a more developed industry, more wealth, and a more considerable mass of productive forces. It will therefore be slowest and most difficult to carry out in Germany, quickest and easiest in England. It will also have an important effect upon the other countries of the world, and will completely change and greatly accelerate their previous manner of development. It is a worldwide revolution and will therefore be worldwide in scope.

Question 20: *What will be the consequences of the final abolition of private ownership?*

Answer: Above all, through society's taking out of the hands of the private capitalists the use of all the productive forces and means of communication as well as the exchange and distribution of products and managing them according to a plan corresponding to the means available and the needs of the whole of society, all the evil consequences of the present running of large-scale industry will be done away with. There will be an end to crises; the extended production, which under the present system of society means overproduction and is such a great cause of misery, will then not even be adequate and will have to be expanded much further. Instead of creating misery, overproduction beyond the immediate needs of society will mean the satisfaction of the needs of all, create new needs and at the same time the means to satisfy them. It will be the condition and the cause of new advances, and it will achieve these advances without thereby, as always hitherto, bringing the order of society into confusion. Once liberated from the pressure of private ownership, large-scale industry will develop on a scale that will make its present level of development seem as paltry as seems the manufacturing system compared with the large-scale industry of our time. This development of industry will provide society with a sufficient quantity of products to satisfy the needs of all. Similarly agriculture, which is also hindered by the pressure of private ownership and the parceling of land from introducing the improvements already available and scientific advancements, will be given a quite new impulse, and place at society's disposal an ample quantity of products. Thus society will produce enough products to be able so to arrange distribution that the needs of all its members will be satisfied. The division of society into various antagonistic classes will thereby become superfluous. Not only will it become superfluous, it is even incompatible with the new social order. Classes came into existence through the division of labour and the division of labour in its hitherto existing form will entirely disappear. For in order to bring industrial and agricultural production to the level described, mechanical and chemical aids alone are not enough; the abilities of the people who set these aids in motion must also be developed to a corresponding degree. Just as in the last century the peasants and the manufactory workers changed their entire way of life, and themselves became quite different people when they were drawn into large-scale industry, so also will the common management of production by the whole of society and the resulting new development of production require and also produce quite different people. The common management of production cannot be effected by people as they are today, each one being assigned to a single branch of production, shackled to it, exploited by it, each having developed only one of his abilities at the cost of all the others and knowing only one branch, or only a branch of a branch of the total production. Even present-day industry finds less and less use for such people. Industry carried on in common and according to plan by the whole of society presupposes moreover people of all-round development, capable of surveying the entire system of production. Thus the division of labour making one man a peasant, another a shoemaker, a third a factory worker, a fourth a stockjobber, which has already been undermined by machines, will completely disappear. Education will enable young people quickly to go through the whole system of production, it will enable them to pass from one branch of industry to another according to the needs of society or their own inclinations. It will therefore free them from that one-sidedness which the present division of labour stamps on each one of them. Thus the communist organization of society will give its members the chance of an all-round exercise of abilities that have received all-round development. With this, the various classes will necessarily disappear. Thus the communist organisation of society is, on the one hand, incompatible with the existence of classes and, on the other, the very establishment of this society furnishes the means to do away with these class differences.

It follows from this that the antagonism between town and country will likewise disappear. The carrying on of agriculture and industrial production by the same people, instead of by two different classes is already for the purely material reasons an essential condition of communist association. The scattering of the agricultural population over the countryside, along with the crowding of the industrial population into the big towns, is a state which corresponds only to an underdeveloped stage of agriculture and industry, an obstacle to all further development which is already now making itself very keenly felt.

The general association of all members of society for the common and planned exploitation of the productive forces, the expansion of production to a degree where it will satisfy the needs of all, the termination of the condition where the needs of some are satisfied at the expense of others, the complete annihilation of the classes and their antagonisms, the all-round development of the abilities of all the members of society through doing away with the hitherto existing division of labour, through industrial education, through change of activity, through the participation of all in the enjoyments provided by all, through the merging of town and country—such are the main results of the abolition of private property.

Question 21: *What influence will the communist order of society have upon the family?*

Answer: It will make the relation between the sexes a purely private relation which concerns only the persons involved, and in which society has no call to interfere. It is able to do this because it abolishes private property and educates children communally, thus destroying the twin foundation of hitherto existing marriage—the dependence through private property of the wife upon the husband and of the children upon the parents. Here is also the answer to the outcry of moralising philistines against the communist community of women. Community of women is a relationship that belongs altogether to bourgeois society and is completely realised today in prostitution. But prostitution is rooted in private property and falls with it. Thus instead of introducing the community of women, communist organisation puts an end to it.

Question 22: *What will be the attitude of the communist organisation towards existing nationalities?*

—remains [the same answer as to question 21 of the earlier "draft"]

Question 23: *What will be its attitude towards existing religions?*
—remains [the same answer as to question 22 of the earlier "draft"]

Question 24: *In what way do Communists differ from socialists?*
Answer: The so-called socialists fall into three groups.

The first group consists of adherents of the feudal and patriarchal society which has been or is still being daily destroyed by large-scale industry, world trade and the bourgeois society they have both brought into existence. From the ills of present-day society this group draws the conclusion that feudal and patriarchy society should be restored because it was free from these ills. Directly or deviously, all its proposals make for this goal. Despite all its professions of sympathy and its bewailing the misery of the proletariat, this group of *reactionary* socialists will be strongly opposed by the Communists, because

1. it is striving after something utterly impossible;
2. it seeks to establish the rule of the aristocracy, the guild-masters and the manufacturers, with the retinue of absolute or feudal monarchs, officials, soldiers and priests, a society which was indeed free from the vices of present society, but brought at least as many other evils in its train and did not even hold out the prospect of the emancipation of the oppressed workers through a communist organisation;
3. it always gives away its real intentions every time the proletariat becomes revolutionary and communist, when it immediately allies itself with the bourgeoisie against the proletarians.

The second group consists of adherents of present society in whom the evils inseparable from it have awakened fears for its survival. They therefore endeavour to preserve present society but to remove the evils bound up with it. With this end in view, some of them propose measures of mere charity, and other grandiose systems of reform which, under the pretext of reorganising society, would retain the foundations of present society, and thus prevent society itself. These *bourgeois socialists* will also have to be continuously fought by the Communists, since they work for the enemies of the Communists and defend the society which it is the Communists' aim to destroy. Finally, the third group consists of democratic socialists, who in the same way as the Communists desire part of the measures listed in Question [left blank in ms.] not, however, as a means of transition to communism but as measures sufficient to abolish the misery of present society and to cause its evils to disappear. These *democratic socialists* are either proletarians who are not yet sufficiently enlightened regarding the conditions of the emancipation of their class, or they are members of the petty bourgeoisie, a class which, until the winning of democracy and the realisation of the socialist measures following upon it, has in many respects the same interest as the proletariat. At moments of action the Communists will, therefore, have to reach an understanding with these democratic socialists, and in general for the time being pursue as much as possible a common policy with them, insofar as these democratic socialists do not enter the service of the ruling bourgeoisie and attack the Communists. It is obvious that this common action does not exclude the discussion of differences with them.

Question 25: *What is the attitude of the Communists towards the other political parties of our day?*

Answer: This attitude differs from country to country.—In England, France, and Belgium, where the bourgeoisie rules, the Communists still have for the time being a common interest with the various democratic parties, which is all the greater the more in the socialist measures they are now everywhere advocating the democrats approach the aims of the Communists, that is, the more clearly and definitely they uphold the interests of the proletariat and the more they rely on the proletariat. In *England*, for instance, the Chartists, who are all workers, are incalculably nearer to the Communists than are the democratic petty bourgeois or so-called radicals.

In *America*, where a democratic constitution has been introduced, the Communists must make common cause with the party that will turn this constitution against the bourgeoisie and use it in the interest of the proletariat, that is, with the national agrarian reformers.

In *Switzerland* the radicals, although still a very mixed party, are yet the only people with whom the Communists can have anything to do, and, further, among these radicals those in the cantons of Vaud and of Geneva are the most advanced.

Finally, in *Germany* the decisive struggle between the bourgeoisie and the absolute monarchy is still to come. Since, however, the Communists cannot count on the decisive struggle between themselves and the bourgeoisie until the bourgeoisie rules, it is in the interests of the Communists to help bring the bourgeoisie to power as soon as possible to overthrow them again. The Communists must therefore always take the side of the liberal bourgeoisie against the governments but they must ever be on their guard against sharing the self-deceptions of the bourgeois or believing their false assurances about the benefits which the victory of the bourgeoisie will bring to the proletariat. The only advantages which the victory of the bourgeoisie will provide for the Communists will be: 1. various concessions which make easier for the Communists defense, discussion and spreading of their principles and thus the unification of the proletariat into a closely knit, militant and organised class, and 2. the certainty that from the day when the absolute governments fall, comes the turn for the fight between bourgeois and proletarians. From that day onwards the party policy of the Communists will be the same as in the countries where the bourgeoisie already rules.

(First published separately in 1914)

(MECW 6: 341–57)

Appendix G: Letter from Engels to Marx, 23–24 November 1847

[In this letter we witness how carefully the two friends were preparing for the crucial meeting that would give Marx responsibility for completing the *Manifesto*. Engels' confidence that they will control the agenda of the second Congress derives from preparations such as this. His determination that this has to happen intensifies as he complains that other messages are out there and that only Marx can squash them. Engels reports on his latest networking efforts in Paris among the leading French radicals while urging Marx to do likewise in Brussels. The turn to history from catechism is a decisive recommendation modestly advanced by Engels in the right terms at the right time.]

ENGELS TO MARX
IN BRUSSELS
[Paris, 23–24 November 1847]

Dear Marx,

Not until this evening was it decided that I should be coming. Saturday evening, then, in Ostend, Hôtel de la Couronne, just opposite the railway station beside the harbour, AND SUNDAY MORNING ACROSS THE WATER. If you take the train that leaves between 4 and 5, you'll arrive at about the same time as I do.

If, contrary to expectations, there is no packet-boat to Dover on Sundays, write and tell me by return. I.e., since you will receive this letter on Thursday morning, you must make inquiries at once and, should a letter be necessary, it must be posted the same evening—before five o'clock, I think—at the main post office. So if you want to make any changes as regards the meeting place there is still time. If I haven't heard by Friday morning I shall count on meeting you and Tedesco[1] on Saturday evening at the Couronne. We shall then have time enough to talk things over; this congress must be a decisive one, AS THIS TIME WE SHALL HAVE IT ALL OUR OWN WAY.

---

[1]   Victor Tedesco (1821–97), Belgian lawyer, activist, and member of the CL.

For a long time now I have been completely at a loss to understand why you have not put a stop to Moses'[1] gossip. It's been giving rise to the most devilish confusion for me here and the most tedious contradictory speeches to the workers. Entire district sittings have been wasted over it, nor is there any possibility of effectively combating this "vapid" nonsense in the communities; particularly before the elections there could be no question of it.

I expect to see L[ouis] Blanc again tomorrow. If not, I shall in any case see him the day after tomorrow. If I have nothing to add at the end of this letter, you will hear the sequel on Saturday.

By the way, Reinhardt[2] talked nonsense to me about the number of copies sold [of *The Poverty of Philosophy*]—not 37, but 96 had been sold a week ago today. That same day I myself took your book to L. Blanc. All the copies had been despatched save to [Alphonse de] Lamartine (not here), L. Blanc and Vidal,[3] whose address cannot be found. I have had it taken to the *Presse*.

By the way, Frank's despatch arrangements have been truly appalling.

At least see that Moses doesn't get up to any nonsense during our absence! *Au revoir*, then

Your

E.

Tuesday evening

Verte [Over]

Give a little thought to the Confession of Faith. I think we would do best to abandon the catachetical form and call the thing Communist *Manifesto*. Since a certain amount of history has to be narrated in it, the form hitherto adopted is quite unsuitable. I shall be bringing with me the one from here, which I did ["Principles of Communism"]; it is in simple narrative form, but wretchedly worded, in a tearing hurry. I start off by asking: What is communism?

---

[1] Moses Hess (1812–75), pioneering German socialist, journalist, and theorist whose allegiance to "True Socialism" was weakened by M in the 1840s, but not enough to please M and E.

[2] Richard Reinhardt (1829–98), German poet who corresponded regularly with M from Paris, became a friend of the family, and was for several years secretary to Heinrich Heine.

[3] François Vidal (1812–72), French lawyer and eclectic socialist.

and then straight on to the proletariat—the history of its origins, how it differs from earlier workers, development of the antithesis between the proletariat and the bourgeoisie, crises, conclusions. In between, all kinds of secondary matter and, finally, the communists' party policy, in so far as it should be made public. The one here has not yet been submitted in its entirety for endorsement but, save for a few quite minor points, I think I can get it through in such a form that at least there is nothing in it which conflicts with our views.

Wednesday morning

Have just received your letter to which the above is an answer. I went to see L. Blanc. I'm remarkably unlucky with him—*il est en voyage, il reviendra peut-être aujourd'hui* [he is travelling, returning perhaps today]. I shall go there again tomorrow and, if necessary, the day after.

I can't be in Ostend by Friday evening because the money won't have been got together until Friday.

This morning your cousin [Karl, son of uncle Lion] Philips came to see me.

[Stephan] Born should make quite a good speech [to the Democratic Association in Brussels in Marx's absence] if you drum something into him. It's good that the Germans are represented by a working man. But Lupus [Wilhelm Wolff] must be purged of all trace of his excessive modesty. The good fellow is one of those rare people who have to be *thrust* into the foreground. Not Weerth,[1] for heaven's sake, as representative! A man who was always too lazy, until pitchforked by his *succès d'un jour* [being a one-day wonder] at the Congress. And who, to boot, wishes to be AN INDEPENDENT MEMBER. *Il faut le retenir dans sa sphère* [He must be kept in his place].

(MECW 38: 146-50)

---

[1] Georg Weerth (1822–56), German poet and revolutionary whose "real job," like E's, took him from the German textile industry to its counterpart on the north of England.

Appendix H: Engels, "On the History of the Communist League," 1885

[In 1885 Engels took the chance of a third German edition of Marx's *Revelations Concerning the Communist Trial in Cologne* (1853; MECW 11. 395–457) to counter neglect and distortion of the history of rivalries, negotiations, mergers, and secessions that marked the first phase of the "independent German workers' movement" and included the writing of the *Manifesto*. Dispersal is not necessarily defeat, and several decades later Engels is able to disclose and celebrate personal details about the leaders of the League of the Just and claim the internationalizing of the workers movement as a direct result of the setbacks of the early 1850s and the translatability of the *Manifesto*'s "theoretical principles." Engels as usual plays up his own limitations and plays down the importance of his own writing, seeing it as necessary background to Marx's authoritative exposure of Prussian government and police corruption. The political "instinct" of a pre-proletarian bourgeois class "appendage" is treated generously within an evolutionary narrative that will gain in clarity and inevitability only with the spread of industrialization and the application of Marx's methods of socio-economic analysis. The "Demands" reprinted here underscore how the *Manifesto* was put rapidly to work within the German-speaking diaspora. Engels is blunt in his criticism of residual and resurgent sentimental socialism, firm in his insistence on revolution deriving from conflict between the social and economic relations of production, and consistently ironic in his use of religious categories (including "a kind of communist Islam") to distinguish well-meaning enthusiasm and optimism from scientific analysis of the reactionary intensity of the early 1850s.]

ON THE HISTORY OF THE COMMUNIST LEAGUE

With the sentence of the Cologne Communists in 1852,[1] the curtain falls on the first period of the independent German workers'

---

[1] Ten of the communists were sentenced to prison terms ranging from 3 to 6 years, while four were acquitted. The bourgeois media in Germany and Britain made special efforts to represent the trial as the inevitable death of communism.

movement. Today this period is almost forgotten. Yet it lasted from 1836 to 1852 and, with the spread of German workers abroad, the movement developed in almost all civilised countries. Nor is that all. The present-day international workers' movement is in substance a direct continuation of the German movement of that time, which was the *first international workers' movement* ever, and which brought forth many of those who took on the leading role in the International Working Men's Association. And the theoretical principles that the Communist League had inscribed on its banner in the *Communist Manifesto* of 1847 [sic] constitute today the strongest international bond of the entire proletarian movement in both Europe and America.

Up to now there has been only one main source for a coherent history of that movement. This is the so-called Black Book, *Die Communisten-Verschwörungen des neunzehnten Jahrhunderts*, by Wermuth and Stieber, Berlin, two parts, 1853 and 1854. This sorry effort fabricated by two of the most contemptible police scoundrels of our century, which bristles with deliberate falsifications, still today serves as the final source for all non-communist writings about that period.

What I am able to give here is only a sketch, and even this only in so far as the League itself is concerned; only what is absolutely necessary to understand the *Revelations*. I hope that some day I shall have the opportunity to work on the rich material collected by Marx and myself on the history of that glorious period of the youth of the international workers' movement. In 1836 the most extreme, chiefly proletarian elements of the secret democratic-republican Outlaws' League, which had been founded by German refugees in Paris in 1834, split off and formed the new secret *League of the Just*. The parent League, in which only the most sleepy-headed elements à la Jakob Venedey[1] remained, soon fell asleep altogether: when in 1840 the police scented out a few sections in Germany, it was hardly a shadow of its former self. The new League, on the contrary, developed comparatively rapidly. Originally it was a German offshoot of the French worker-communism reminiscent of Babouvism that was taking shape in Paris at about the same time; community of goods was demanded as the necessary consequence of "equality." The aims were those of the Parisian secret societies of the time: half propaganda association, half conspiracy, Paris, however, always being

---

[1] Jakob Venedey (1805–71), refused the call to communism before supporting suppression of German radicals in 1848.

regarded as the focus of revolutionary action, although preparation for occasional *putsches* in Germany was by no means excluded. But as Paris remained the decisive battleground, the League was at that time actually not much more than the German branch of the French secret societies, notably the *Société des saisons* led by Blanqui and Barbès,[1] with which close links were maintained. The French went into action on May 12, 1839; the sections of the League marched with them and were thus embroiled in the common defeat.

Of the Germans, *Karl Schapper* and *Heinrich Bauer* were arrested; Louis Philippe's government contented itself with deporting them after a fairly long term of imprisonment. Both went to London. Schapper came from Weilburg in Nassau and while a student of forestry at Giessen in 1832 had joined in the conspiracy organised by Georg Büchner;[2] he had taken part in the storming of the Frankfurt constable station on April 3, 1833, had escaped abroad and in February 1834 joined Mazzini's[3] march on Savoy. Of gigantic stature, resolute and energetic, always ready to risk civil existence and life, he was a model of the professional revolutionary with the role he played in the thirties. In spite of a certain sluggishness of thought, he was by no means incapable of superior theoretical understanding, as is proved by his development from "demagogue" to Communist, and he then held all the more rigidly to what he had come to recognise. Precisely on that account his revolutionary passion sometimes got the better of his understanding, but he always realised his mistake in hindsight and openly acknowledged it. He was a true man and what he did for the founding of the German workers' movement will not be forgotten.

Heinrich Bauer [1813–?], from Franconia, was a shoemaker; a lively, alert, witty little fellow, in whose little body, however, also lay hidden much shrewdness and determination.

Having arrived in London, where Schapper, who had been a compositor in Paris, now tried to earn his living as a language teacher, the two of them again joined together the broken threads

---

1   Auguste Blanqui (1805–81) and Armand Barbès (1809–70), co-conspirators in events leading up to the failed insurgency in Paris in 1839.

2   Georg Büchner (1813–37), radical dramatist best known for *Danton's Death* and *Woyzeck*, the source of Alban Berg's 1920 opera of the same name.

3   Giuseppe Mazzini (1805–72), active in Italian secret societies working for Italy as an independent republic, and in exile in London in the 1840s. For M, Mazzini was incurably, insufferably bourgeois.

of alliance and made London the centre of the League. They were joined here, if not already earlier in Paris, by *Joseph Moll* [1813–49], a watchmaker from Cologne, a medium-sized Hercules—how often did Schapper and he victoriously defend the entrance to a hall against hundreds of onrushing opponents—a man who was at least the equal of his two comrades in energy and determination, and intellectually superior to both of them. Not only was he a born diplomat, as the success of his numerous trips on various missions proved; he was also more capable of theoretical insight. I came to know all three of them in London in 1843. They were the first revolutionary proletarians whom I had seen, and however far apart our views were at that time in details—for I still bore, as against their narrow-minded egalitarian communism, a goodly dose of just as narrow-minded philosophical arrogance—I shall never forget the deep impression that these three real men made upon me, who was still to become a man at that time.

In London, as to a lesser degree in Switzerland, they had the benefit of freedom of association and assembly. The legally functioning German Workers' Educational Society, which still exists, was founded as early as February 7, 1840. The Society served the League as a recruiting ground for new members, and since, as always, the Communists were the most active and intelligent members of the Society, it was a matter of course that its leadership lay entirely in the hands of the League. The League soon had several communities, or, as they were then still called, "lodges," in London. The same obvious tactics were followed in Switzerland and elsewhere. Where workers' associations could be founded, they were utilised in like manner. Where this was forbidden by law, one joined choral societies, gymnastics societies and the like. Contacts were to a large extent maintained by members who were continually traveling back and forth; they also, when required, served as emissaries. In both respects the League obtained lively support through the wisdom of the governments which, by resorting to deportation, converted any objectionable worker—and in nine cases out of ten he was a member of the League—into an emissary.

The spread of the restored League was considerable. Notably in Switzerland, *Weitling, August Becker* (a highly gifted man who, however, like so many Germans, came to grief through his innate instability of character) and others created a strong organisation more or less pledged to Weitling's communist system. This is not the place to criticise the communism of Weitling. But as regards its significance as the first independent theoretical stirring of the German proletariat, I still today subscribe to Marx's words in the Paris *Vorwärts!* of 1844: "Where among the" (German) "bourgeoisie—including its philosophers and learned writers—is to be found a book *about the emancipation of the bourgeoisie*—political emancipation—similar to Weitling's work: *Garantien der Harmonie und Freiheit?*[1] It is enough to compare the petty, faint-hearted mediocrity of German political literature with this vehement and brilliant literary début of the German workers, it is enough to compare these *gigantic infant shoes of the proletariat* with the dwarfish, worn-out political shoes of the bourgeoisie, and one is bound with the prophesy that the *German Cinderella* will one day have the figure of an athlete." This athlete's figure confronts us today, although still far from being fully grown.

Numerous sections existed in Germany too; by the nature of things they were of a transient character, but those coming into existence more than made up for those folding up. Only after seven years, in late 1846, did the police discover traces of the League in Berlin (Mentel) and Magdeburg (Beck), without being in a position to follow them further.

In Paris, Weitling, still there in 1840, likewise gathered the scattered elements together again before he left for Switzerland.

The tailors formed the central force of the League. German tailors were everywhere: in Switzerland, in London, in Paris. In the last-named city, German was so much the prevailing tongue in this trade that I was acquainted there in 1846 with a Norwegian tailor who had traveled directly by sea from Drontheim to France and in the space of eighteen months had learned hardly a word of French but had acquired an excellent knowledge of German. Two of the Paris communities in 1847 consisted predominantly of tailors, one of cabinet makers.

After the centre of gravity had shifted from Paris to London, a new feature came to the fore: from being German, the League gradually became *international*. In the Workers' Society there were, besides Germans and Swiss, also members of all those nationalities for whom German served as the chief means of communication with foreigners, notably, therefore, Scandinavians, Dutch, Hungarians, Czechs,

---

[1]   *Guarantees of Harmony and Freedom* (1842).

Southern Slavs, also Russians and Alsatians. In 1847 the regular attendants even included an English grenadier of the Guards in uniform. The Society soon called itself the *Communist* Workers' Education Society, and the membership cards bore the inscription "All Men are Brothers," in at least twenty languages, though not without mistakes here and there. Like the open Society, so also the secret League soon took on a more international character; at first in a restricted sense, practically through the varied nationalities of its members, theoretically through the realisation that any revolution, to be victorious, must be a European one. It did not go any further as yet; but the foundations were there.

Close contact was maintained with the French revolutionaries through the London refugees, comrades-in-arms of May 12, 1839. Similarly with the more radical Poles. The official Polish *émigrés*, as also Mazzini, were, of course, opponents rather than allies. The English Chartists, on account of the specific English character of their movement, were disregarded as not revolutionary. The London leaders of the League came into contact with them only later, through me.

In other ways, too, the character of the League had altered with events. Although the League still looked upon Paris—and at that time quite rightly—as the mother city of the revolution, it had nevertheless cast off the dependence of the Paris conspirators. The spread of the League raised its self-confidence. There was a feeling that more and more roots were being struck in the German working class and that these German workers were historically destined to be the standard-bearers of the workers of the North and East of Europe. In Weitling there was to be found a communist theoretician who could be boldly placed at the side of his contemporary French rivals. Finally, the experience of May 12 had taught them that for the time being there was nothing more to be gained by attempted *putsches*. And if every event was still explained as a sign of the approaching storm, if the old, semi-conspiratorial rules were still preserved intact, that was mainly the fault of the old revolutionary defiance, which was already beginning to collide with the sounder views that were gaining headway.

However, the social doctrine of the League, no matter how poorly defined it was, contained a very great defect, but one that had its roots in the conditions themselves. The members, insofar as they were workers at all, were almost exclusively real artisans. Even in the big metropolises, the man who exploited them was usually only a small master. The exploitation of tailoring on a large scale, of what is now called the manufacture of off-the-peg clothing, by the conversion of handicraft tailoring into a domestic industry working for a big capitalist, was at that time only just making its appearance even in London. On the one hand, the exploiter of these artisans was a small master; on the other hand, they all hoped ultimately to become small masters themselves. And besides, a host of inherited guild notions still clung to the German artisan at that time. The greatest honour is due to them, in that they, who themselves were not yet full proletarians but only an appendage of the petty bourgeoisie, an appendage which was in the transition to becoming the modern proletariat and which did not yet stand in direct conflict with the bourgeoisie, that is, with big capital—in that these artisans were capable of instinctively anticipating their future development and of constituting themselves, even if not yet with full consciousness, as the party of the proletariat. But it was also inevitable that their old handicraft prejudices were a stumbling block to them at every moment, whenever it was a question of criticising existing society in detail, that is, of investigating economical facts. And I do not believe there was a single man in the whole League at that time who had ever read a book on political economy. But that mattered little; for the time being "equality," "brotherhood" and "justice" helped them to surmount every theoretical obstacle.

Meanwhile a second, essentially different communism had developed alongside that of the League and of Weitling. In Manchester it had tangibly been brought home to me that the economic facts which have so far played no role or only a contemptible one in historiography are, at least in the modern world, a decisive historical force; that they form the basis for the emergence of the present-day class antagonisms; that these class antagonisms, in the countries where they have become fully developed by a dint of large-scale industry, hence especially in England, are in their turn the basis of the formation of political parties, party struggles, and thus of all political history. Marx had not only arrived at the same view, but had already, in the *Deutsch-Französische Jahrbücher* (1844), generalised it to the effect that it is not the state which conditions and regulates civil society at all, but civil society which conditions and regulates the state, and, consequently, that policy and its history are to be explained from the economic relations and their development, and not the other way round. When I visited Marx in Paris in the summer of 1844, our complete agreement in all theoretical fields became evident and our joint work dates from that time. When, in the spring of 1845, we met again in Brussels, Marx had already fully developed his materialist theory of history in its main features from the above-mentioned foundations, and we now applied ourselves to the detailed elaboration of the newly won outlook in the most varied directions.

This discovery, which revolutionised the science of history and, as we have seen, is essentially the work of Marx—a discovery in which I can claim for myself only a very small share—was, however, of immediate importance for the workers' movement of the time. Communism among the French and the Germans, Chartism among the English, now no longer appeared as something accidental which could just as well not have occurred. These movements now presented themselves as a movement of the modern oppressed class, the proletariat, as more or less developed forms of its historically necessary struggle against the ruling class, the bourgeoisie; as forms of class struggle, but distinguished from all earlier class struggles by this one thing: that the present-day oppressed class, the proletariat, cannot achieve its emancipation without at the same time emancipating society as a whole from division into classes and, therefore, from class struggles. And communism now no longer meant the concoction, by means of the imagination, of a social ideal as perfect as possible, but insight into the nature, the conditions and the consequent general aims of the struggle waged by the proletariat.

Now, we were by no means of the opinion that the new scientific results should be confided in large tomes exclusively to the "learned" world. Quite the contrary. We were both of us already following in the educated world, especially of Western Germany, and abundant contact with the organised proletariat. It was our duty to provide a scientific substantiation for our view, but it was equally important for us to win over the European, and in the first place the German, proletariat to our conviction. As soon as we had become clear in our own minds, we set to work. We founded a German Workers' Society in Brussels and took over the *Deutsche-Brüssler-Zeitung*, which served us as an organ up to the February Revolution. We kept in touch with the revolutionary section of the English Chartists through Julian Harney, the editor of the movement's central organ, *The Northern Star*, to which I was a contributor. We entered likewise into a sort of cartel with the Brussels democrats (Marx was vice-president of the Democratic Association) and with the French Social-Democrats of the *Réforme*, which I supplied with news of the English and German movements. In short, our connections with the radical and proletarian organisations and press organs were quite what one could wish.

Our relations with the League of the Just were as follows: The existence of the League was, of course, known to us; in 1843 Schapper had suggested that I join it, which I at that time naturally refused to do. However, we not only kept up our continuous correspondence with the Londoners, but remained on still closer terms with Dr. Ewerbeck, the then leader of the Paris communities. Without occupying ourselves with the League's internal affairs, we nevertheless learnt of every important happening. On the other hand, we influenced the theoretical views of the most important members of the League by word of mouth, by letter and through the press. For this purpose we also made use of various lithographed circulars, which we dispatched to our friends and correspondents throughout the world on particular occasions when we were concerned with the internal affairs of the Communist Party that was in the process of formation. In these, the League itself was sometimes involved. Thus, a young Westphalian student, Hermann Kriege [1820-50], who went to America, posed there as an emissary of the League and associated himself with the crazy Harro Harring[1] for the purpose of using the League to turn South America upside down. He founded a paper [*Der Volks-Tribun*], 1846 in which, in the name of the League, he preached an effusive communism of starry-eyed love, based on "love" and overflowing with love. Against this we let fly a circular that did not fail to have its effect. Kriege vanished from the League scene [and died insane].

Later, Weitling came to Brussels. But he was no longer the naïve young journeyman-tailor who, astonished at his own talents, was trying to clarify in his own mind just what a communist society would look like. He was now the great man, persecuted by the envious on account of his superiority, who scented rivals, secret enemies and traps everywhere—the prophet, driven from country to country, who carried a prescription for the realization of heaven on earth ready-made in his pocket, and who imagined that everybody was out to steal it from him. He had already fallen out with members of the League in London; and even in Brussels, where particularly

---

[1]   Harro Harring (1798–1870), poet, painter, and romantic revolutionary.

Marx and his wife treated him with almost superhuman forbearance, he could get along with nobody. So he soon went to America to try out his role of prophet there.

All these circumstances contributed to the quiet revolution that was taking place in the League, and especially among the leaders in London. The inadequacy of the conception of communism held hitherto, both the simplistic French egalitarian communism and that of Weitling, became more and more clear to them. The tracing of communism back to early Christianity introduced by Weitling— no matter how brilliant certain details to be found in his *Evangelium eines armen Sünders* [Gospel of a Poor Sinner]—had resulted in the movement of Switzerland being delivered to a large extent into the hands, first of fools like Albrecht, and then of exploiting fake prophets like Kuhlmann. The "true socialism" dealt in by a few writers of fiction—a translation of French socialist phraseology into corrupt Hegelian German, and sentimental starry-eyed love (see the section on German or "true," socialism in the *Communist Manifesto*)—that Kriege and the study of said literature introduced in the League was bound to disgust the old revolutionaries of the League, if only because of its slobbering feebleness. In contrast to the untenability of the previous theoretical views, and in contrast to the practical aberrations resulting therefrom, it was realised more and more in London that Marx and I were right in our new theory. This understanding was undoubtedly promoted by the fact that among the London leaders there were now two men who were considerably superior in their capacity for theoretical perception to those previously mentioned: the miniature painter Karl Pfänder[1] from Heilbronn and the tailor Georg Eccarius from Thuringia.

Suffice it to say that in the spring of 1847 Moll visited Marx in Brussels and immediately afterwards myself in Paris, and invited us repeatedly, in the name of his comrades, to join the League. He reported that they were as much convinced of the general correctness of our views as of the need to free the League from the old conspiratorial traditions and forms. Should we join, we would be

---

[1] Pfänder died about eight years ago in London. He was a man of peculiarly fine intelligence, witty, ironical and dialectical. Eccarius, as we know, was later for many years General Secretary of the International Working Men's Association, in the General Council of which the following old League members were to be found, among others: Eccarius, Pfänder, Lessner, Lochner, Marx and myself. Eccarius subsequently devoted himself exclusively to the English trade-union movement. [Engels' note]

given an opportunity of expounding our critical communism before a congress of the League in a manifesto, which would then be published as the manifesto of the League; we would likewise be able to contribute our quota towards the replacement of the obsolete League organisation by one in keeping with the new times and aims.

We entertained no doubt that an organisation within the German working class was necessary, if only for propaganda purposes, and that this organisation, in so far as it were not merely local in character, could only be a secret one, even outside Germany. Now, there already existed exactly such an organisation in the shape of the League. What we previously objected to in this League was now relinquished as erroneous by the representatives of the League themselves; we were even invited to cooperate in the work of the reorganisation. Could we say no? Certainly not. Therefore, we joined the League; Marx founded a League community in Brussels from among our close friends, while I attended the three Paris communities.

In the summer of 1847, the first League congress took place in London, at which W. Wolff represented the Brussels and I the Paris communities. First of all the congress carried out the reorganisation of the League. Whatever remained of the old mystical names dating back to the conspiratorial period was now also abolished; the League now consisted of communities, circles, leading circles, a Central Authority and a Congress, and henceforth called itself the "Communist League." "The aim of the League is the overthrow of the bourgeoisie, the rule of the proletariat, the abolition of the old bourgeois society which rests on the antagonism of classes, and the foundation of a new society without classes and without private property"—thus ran the first article. The organization itself was thoroughly democratic, with elective and removable authorities. This alone barred all hankering after conspiracy, which requires dictatorship, and the League was converted—for ordinary peacetime at least—into a pure propaganda society. These new Rules were submitted to the communities for discussion—so democratic was the procedure now followed—then once again debated at the Second Congress and finally adopted by the latter on December 8, 1847. They are to be found printed in Wermuth and Stieber, Part I, 239, Appendix X.

The Second Congress took place in late November and early December of the same year. Marx too attended this time and expounded the new theory in a lengthy debate—the congress lasted at least ten days. All contradiction and doubt were finally over and done with, the new basic principles were adopted unanimously, and Marx and I were commissioned to draw up the Manifesto. This was done immediately afterwards. A few weeks before the February Revolution it was sent to London to be printed. Since then it has traveled round the world, has been translated into almost all languages and still today serves in numerous countries as a guide for the proletariat movement. In place of the old League motto, "All Men Are Brothers," appeared the new battle cry, "Working Men of All Countries, Unite!" which openly proclaimed the international character of the struggle. Seventeen years later this battle cry resounded throughout the world as the motto of the International Working Men's Association, and today the valiant proletariat of all countries has inscribed it on its banner.

The February Revolution broke out. The London Central Authority functioning hitherto immediately transferred its powers to the Brussels leading circle. But this decision came at a time when an actual state of siege already existed in Brussels, and the Germans in particular could no longer assemble anywhere. We were all of us just on the point of going to Paris, and so the new Central Authority decided likewise to dissolve, to hand over all its powers to Marx and to empower him immediately to constitute a new Central Authority in Paris. Hardly had the five persons who adopted this decision (March 3, 1848) separated, when the police forced their way into Marx's home, arrested him and compelled him to leave for France the following day, which was just where he wanted to go.

In Paris we all soon came together again. It was there that the following document was drawn up and signed by the members of the new Central Authority. It was distributed throughout Germany and quite a few can still learn something from it even today [in the following selection]:

DEMANDS OF THE COMMUNIST PARTY IN GERMANY

1. The whole of Germany shall be declared a single and indivisible republic.

[...]

3. Representatives of the people shall receive payment so that workers, too, shall be able to become members of the German parliament.

4. Universal arming of the people.

[...]

7. Princely and other feudal estates, together with mines, pits, and so forth, shall become the property of the state. The estates shall be cultivated on a larger scale and with the most up-to-date scientific devices in the interests of the whole of society.

8. Mortgages on peasant lands shall be declared the property of the state. Interest on such mortgages shall be paid by the peasants to the state.

9. In localities where the tenant system is developed, the land rent or the quit-rent shall be paid to the state as a tax.

[...]

11. All the means of transport, railways, canals, steamships, roads, the posts, etc. shall be taken over by the state. They shall become the property of the state and shall be placed free at the disposal of the impecunious classes.

[...]

14. The right of inheritance to be curtailed.

15. The introduction of steeply graduated taxes, and the abolition of taxes on articles of consumption.

16. Inauguration of national workshops. The state guarantees a livelihood to all workers and provides for those who are incapacitated for work.

17. Universal and free education of the people.

It is to the interest of the German proletariat, the petty bourgeoisie and the small peasants to support these demands with all possible energy. Only by the realisation of these demands will the millions in Germany, who have hitherto been exploited by a handful of persons and whom the exploiters would like to keep in further subjection, win the rights and attain to that power to which they are entitled as the producers of all wealth.

The Committee
Karl Marx, Karl Schapper, H. Bauer,
F. Engels, J. Moll, W. Wolff

At that time the craze for revolutionary legions prevailed in Paris. Spaniards, Italians, Belgians, Dutchmen, Poles, and Germans flocked together in crowds to liberate their respective fatherlands. The German legion was led by [poet and journalist, Georg] Herwegh, [sometime Prussian army officer and undercover spy,[1] Adalbert von] Bornstedt, [Austrian journalist and man of the theatre, Heinrich] Börnstein. Since immediately after the revolution all foreign workers not only lost their jobs but in addition were harassed by the public, the influx into these legions was very great. The new government saw in them a means of getting rid of foreign workers and granted them *l'étape du soldat,* that is, quarters along their line of march and a marching allowance of fifty centimes per day up to the frontier, whereupon the eloquent Lamartine, the Foreign Minister who was so readily moved to tears, found an opportunity of betraying them to their perspective governments.

We opposed this playing with revolution most decisively. To carry an invasion, which was to import the revolution forcibly from outside, into the midst of the ferment then going on in Germany, meant to undermine the revolution in Germany itself, to strengthen the governments and to deliver the legionaries—Lamartine stood as guarantor for that—defenceless into the hands of the German troops. When subsequently the revolution was victorious in Vienna and Berlin, the legion became all the more pointless; but once begun, the game was continued.

We founded a German communist club in which we advised the workers to keep away from the legion and to return instead to their homelands singly and work there for the movement. Our old friend [radical journalist, Ferdinand] Flocon, who had a seat in the Provisional Government, obtained for the workers sent by us the same travel concessions as had been granted to the legionaries. In this way we returned three or four hundred workers to Germany, including the great majority of the League members.

As could easily be foreseen, the League proved to be much too weak a lever by comparison with the popular mass movement that had now broken out. Three quarters of the League members who had previously lived abroad had changed their domicile by returning to their homeland; their previous communities were thus to a great extent dissolved and they lost all contact with the League. Some of the more ambitious among them did not even try to resume this contact, but each one began a small separate movement on his own account in his own locality. Finally, the conditions in each separate

---

[1] Georg Herwegh (1817–75), radical Swiss poet and journalist, and a leading figure in the German Democratic Association in Paris in the later 1840s.

small state, each province and each town were so different that the League would have been incapable of giving more than the most general directives; such directives were, however, much better disseminated through the press. In short, from the moment when the causes which had made the secret League necessary ceased to exist, the secret League lost all significance as such. But this could least of all surprise the persons who had just stripped this same secret League of the last vestige of its conspiratorial character.

That, however, the League had been an excellent school for revolutionary activity was now demonstrated. On the Rhine, where the *Neue Rheinische Zeitung* provided a firm centre, in Nassau, in Rheinish Hesse, etc., everywhere members of the League stood at the head of the extreme democratic movement. The same was the case in Hamburg. In Southern Germany the predominance of petty-bourgeois democracy stood in the way. In Breslau, Wilhelm Wolff was active with great success until the summer of 1848; in addition he received a Silesian mandate as an alternate deputy to the Frankfurt parliament. Finally, the composer Stephan Born, who had worked in Brussels and Paris as an active member of the League, founded a Workers' Fraternity in Berlin which became fairly widespread and existed until 1850. Born, a very talented young man, who, however, was a bit too much in a hurry to become a political figure, "fraternised" with the most motley Cherethites and Pelethites [Old Testament religious sects expressive of undue narrowness] just to get a crowd together, and was not at all the man who could bring unity into the conflicting tendencies, light into chaos. Consequently, in the official publications of the association the views represented in the *Communist Manifesto* were mingled hodge-podge with guild recollections and guild aspirations, fragments of Louis Blanc and Proudhon, protectionism, etc.; in short, they wanted to please everybody. In particular, strikes, trade unions and producers' co-operatives were set going and it was forgotten that above it all was a question of first conquering, by means of political victories, the field in which alone such things could be realised on a lasting basis. When, afterwards, the victories of the reactionaries made the leaders of the Fraternity realise the necessity of taking a direct part in the revolutionary struggle, they were naturally left in the lurch by the confused mass which they had grouped around themselves. Born took part in the Dresden uprising of May 1849 and had a lucky escape. But, in contrast to the great political movement of the proletariat, the Workers' Fraternity proved to be a pure *Sonderbund* [or collection of reactionary separatists], which to a large extent existed only on paper and played such a subordinate role that the reactionaries did not find it necessary to suppress it until 1850, and its surviving offshoots until several years later. Born, whose real name was Buttermilch, has become not a big political figure but an insignificant Swiss professor, who no longer translates Marx into guild language but the meek [historian, Hebraist and critic, Ernest] Renan into his own fulsome German.

With June 13, 1849, in Paris, the defeat of the May insurrections in Germany and the suppression of the Hungarian revolution by the Russians, a great period of the 1848 Revolution came to a close. But the victory of the reactionaries was as yet by no means final. A reorganisation of the scattered revolutionary forces was required, and hence also of the League. The situation again forbade, as in 1848, any open organisation of the proletariat; hence one had to organise again in secret.

In the Autumn of 1849 most of the members of the former central authorities and congress gathered again in London. The only ones still missing were Schapper, who was imprisoned in Wiesbaden but came after his acquittal in the spring of 1850, and Moll, who, after he had accomplished a series of most dangerous missions and agitational journeys—eventually he recruited mounted gunners for the Palatinate artillery right under the noses of the Prussian army in the Rhine Province—joined the Besançon workers' company of Willich's corps and was killed by a shot [in the stomach] during the battle at the Murg in front of the Rothenfels Bridge. On the other hand Willich now entered upon the scene. Willich was one of those sentimental Communists so common in Western Germany since 1845, who on that account alone was instinctively, furtively antagonistic to our critical tendency. More than that, he was entirely the prophet, convinced of his personal mission as the predestined liberator of the German proletariat and as such a direct claimant as much to political as to military dictatorship. Thus, to the early Christian communism previously preached by Weitling was added a kind of communist Islam. However, propaganda for this new religion was for the time being restricted to the refugee barracks under Willich's command.

Hence, the League was organised afresh; the Address of March 1850, published in an appendix (IX, No. 1), was put into effect and Heinrich Bauer sent as an emissary to Germany. The Address, edited by Marx and myself, is still of interest today, because petty-bourgeois democracy is even now the party which must certainly be the first to take the helm in Germany as the saviour of society from the communist workers on the occasion of the next European upheaval now soon due (the European revolutions, 1815, 1830, 1848-52, 1870, have occurred at intervals of fifteen to eighteen years in our century). Much of what is said there is, therefore, still applicable today. Heinrich Bauer's mission was crowned with complete success. The jolly little shoemaker was a born diplomat. He brought the former members of the League, some who had become laggards and some who were acting on their own account, back into the active organisation, particularly the then leaders of the Workers' Fraternity. The League began to play the dominant role in the workers', peasants' and gymnastic associations to a far greater extent than before 1848, so that the next quarterly address to the communities, in June 1850, could already report that the student Schurz from Bonn (later on American ex-minister), who was touring Germany in the interest of petty-bourgeois democracy, had "found that the League already controlled all useful forces" (see Appendix IX, No. 2). The League was undoubtedly the only revolutionary organisation that had any significance in Germany.

But what purpose this organisation should serve depended very substantially on whether the prospects of a renewed upsurge of the revolution materialised. And in the course of the year 1850 this became more and more improbable, indeed impossible. The industrial crisis of 1847, which had paved the way for the Revolution of 1848, had been overcome; a new, unprecedented period of industrial prosperity had set in; whoever had eyes to see and used them must have clearly perceived that the revolutionary storm of 1848 was gradually declining.

"With this general prosperity, in which the productive forces of bourgeois society develop as luxuriantly as is at all possible within bourgeois relationships, *there can be no talk of a real revolution*. Such a revolution is only possible in the periods when both these factors, the modern productive forces and the bourgeois forms of production, come in collision with each other. The various quarrels in which the representatives of the individual factions of the Continental Party of Order [an alliance of French monarchists] now indulge and mutually compromise themselves, far from providing the occasion for new revolutions, are, on the contrary, possible only because the basis of the relationship is momentarily so secure and, what the reaction does not know, so *bourgeois*. All reactionary attempts to hold up bourgeois development *will rebound off it just as certainly as all moral indignation and all enthusiastic proclamations of the democrats.*" Thus Marx and I wrote in the "Review. May to October 1850" in the *Neue Rheinische Zeitung. Politisch-ökonomische Revue*, No. V-VI, Hamburg, 1850, p.153.

This cool estimation of the situation, however, was regarded as heresy by many persons, at a time when Ledru-Rollin, Louis Blanc, Mazzini, Kossuth and, among the lesser German lights, Ruge, Kinkel, Goegg and the rest of them were flocking together in London to form provisional governments of the future not only for their respective fatherlands but for the whole of Europe, and when it only remained a matter of obtaining the requisite money from America as a revolutionary loan to consummate at a moment's notice the European revolution and the various republics which went with it as a matter of course. Can anyone be surprised that a man like Willich was taken in by this, that Schapper, acting on his old revolutionary impulse, also allowed himself to be fooled, and that the majority of London workers, to a large extent refugees themselves, followed them into the camp of the bourgeois-democratic artificers of revolution? Suffice it to say that the reverse maintained by us was not to the liking of these people; one was to enter into the game of making revolutions. We most decisively refused to do so. A split ensued; more about this is to be read in the *Revelations*. Then came the arrest of Nothjung, followed by that of Haupt, in Hamburg. The latter turned traitor by divulging the names of the Cologne Central Authority and being envisioned as the chief witness in the trial; but his relatives had no desire to be thus disgraced and bundled him off to Rio de Janeiro, where he later established himself as a merchant and in recognition of his services was appointed first Prussian and then German Consul General. He is now back in Europe.[1]

For a better understanding of what follows, I give the list of the Cologne accused: 1) P. G. Röser, cigarmaker; 2) Heinrich Bürgers, who

---

[1] Schapper died in London at the end of the sixties. Willich took part in the American Civil War with distinction; he became Brigadier-General and was shot in the chest during the battle of Murfreesboro (Tennessee) but recovered and died about ten years ago in America.—Of the other persons mentioned above, I shall only remark that all trace was lost of Heinrich Bauer in Australia, and that Weitling and Ewerbeck died in America. [Engels' note]

later died, a Party of Progress deputy to the provincial Diet; 3) Peter Nothjung, tailor, who died a few years ago as a photographer in Breslau; 4) W.J. Reiff; 5) Dr. Hermann Becker, now chief burgomaster of Cologne and member of the Upper Chamber; 6) Dr. Roland Daniels, medical practitioner, who died a few years after the trial of tuberculosis contracted in prison; 7) Karl Otto, chemist; 8) Dr. Abraham Jacobi, now medical practitioner in New York; 9) Dr. J.J. Klein, now medical practitioner and town councillor in Cologne; 10) Ferdinand Freiligrath, who, however, was at that time already in London; 11) J.L. Erhard, clerk; 12) Friedrich Lessner, tailor, now in London. Of these, after a public trial before a jury lasting from October 4 to November 12, 1852, the following were sentenced for attempted high treason: Röser, Bürgers, and Nothjung to six, Reiff, Otto and Becker to five and Lessner to three years' confinement in a fortress; Daniels, Klein, Jacobi and Erhard were acquitted.

With the Cologne trial this first period of the German communist workers' movement comes to an end. Immediately after the sentence we dissolved our League; a few months later the Willich-Schapper Sonderbund was also laid to eternal rest.

★ ★ ★

A whole generation lies between then and now. At that time Germany was a country of handicraft and of domestic industry based on manual labour; now it is a big industrial country still undergoing continual industrial transformation. At that time one had to seek out one by one the workers who had an understanding of their position as workers and of their historico-economic antagonism to capital, because this antagonism was itself in the process of taking more shape. Today the entire German proletariat has to be placed under exceptional [explicitly anti-socialist] laws, merely in order to slow down a little the process of its development to full consciousness of its position as an oppressed class. At that time the few persons who reached an understanding of the historical role of the proletariat had to gather in secret, to assemble clandestinely in small communities of 3 to 20 persons. Today the German proletariat no longer needs any official organisation, either public or secret. The simple self-evident interconnection of like-minded class comrades suffices, without any rules, authorities, resolutions or other tangible forms, to shake the whole German Empire. [Prussian Prime Minister, Prince

Otto von] Bismarck is the arbiter of Europe beyond the frontiers of Germany, but within them there grows daily more threateningly the athletic figure of the German proletariat that Marx foresaw back in 1844, the giant for whom the cramped imperial edifice designed to fit the philistine is already becoming too small and whose mighty stature and broad shoulders grow until the moment comes when by merely rising from his seat he will blast the whole structure of the imperial constitution to rubble. And still more. The international movement of the European and American proletariat has so grown in strength that not only its first narrow form—the secret League—but even its second, infinitely broader form—the open International Working Men's Association—has become a fetter for it, and that the simple feeling of solidarity based on the understanding of the identity of class position suffices to create and to hold together one and the same great party of the proletariat among the workers of all countries and tongues. The doctrine which the League represented from 1847 to 1852, and which at that time was treated by the wise philistines with the shrug of the shoulders as the hallucinations of utter madcaps, as the secret doctrine of a few scattered sectarians, has now innumerable adherents in all civilised countries of the world, among those condemned to the Siberian mines as much as among the gold diggers of California; and the founder of this doctrine, the most hated, most slandered man of his time, Karl Marx, was when he died, the ever-sought-after and ever-willing counsellor of the proletariat of the old and the new world.

London, October 8, 1885
Frederick Engels

(MECW 26: 312–30)

Appendix I: Engels, "The Labour Movement in America." Preface to the American Edition of The Condition of the Working Class in England, 26 January 1887

[As a note to the 1887 offprint of this preface attests, Engels' work of 1844 needed translation into English and dissemination in America because industrial conditions there now "coincide" with those in Britain four decades earlier, and are producing America's own radical calendar and martyrs. Engels reads American rawness and apparent lack of historical baggage as a basis for accelerated progress towards revolution. Abolition of slavery and the growth of manufacturing industries mean that the formation of an American proletariat is not only thinkable at last but achievable at once. Engels treats the United States as *terra nullius*, a kind of unoccupied land (no mention of indigenous inhabitants) in which development is happening in freebooting style, but only at the price of creating three strains of resistance: one associated with progressive journalist Henry George in New York City, another with the co-operative and mutualist "assemblies" of the Knights of Labor, and a third with the Socialist labor party dominated by German-speaking immigrants. Only the latter is sufficiently clear about what is to be done, but for this to happen it must happen in and through the English rather than the German language. Engels practices what he preaches in the translation of his own single-authored works and via his substantial citation here from the *Manifesto*, and shows a shrewd sense of the importance of communication in a country as large as the United States and of the growing reality that world revolution will have to occur in significant part in a world language like English. His commitment to the transformative power of the *Manifesto*, to the living nature of Marx's legacy, and to recent proletarian mobilization in America's industrial centers and across Europe leads him in conclusion to hype Socialist unity and "victory everywhere."]

THE LABOUR MOVEMENT IN AMERICA

PREFACE TO THE AMERICAN EDITION OF
THE CONDITION OF THE WORKING CLASS IN ENGLAND

Ten months have elapsed since, at the translator's [Florence Kelley-Wischnewetzky's] wish, I wrote the Appendix to this book; and during these ten months, a revolution has been accomplished in American society such as, in any other country, would have taken at least ten years. In February 188[6], American public opinion was almost unanimous on this one point; that there was no working class, in the European sense of the word, in America; that consequently no class struggle between workmen and capitalists, such as tore European society to pieces, was possible in the American Republic; and that, therefore, Socialism was a thing of foreign importation which could never take root on American soil. And yet, at that moment, the coming class struggle was casting its gigantic shadow [more than ten thousand strong] before it in the strikes of the Pennsylvania coal miners, and of many other trades, and especially in the preparations, all over the country, for the great Eight Hours' movement which was to come off, and did come off, in the May following [only to be followed by brutal reprisals and the execution of 4 "ringleaders" in Chicago]. That I then duly appreciated these symptoms, that I anticipated a working class movement on a national scale, my "Appendix" shows; but no one could then foresee that in such a short time the movement would burst out with such irresistible force, would spread with the rapidity of a prairie-fire, would shake American society to its very foundations.

The fact is there, stubborn and indisputable. To what an extent it had struck with terror the American ruling classes, was revealed to me, in an amusing way, by American journalists who did me the honor of calling on me last summer; the "new departure" had put them into a state of helpless fright and perplexity. But at that time the movement was only just on the start; there was but a series of confused and apparently disconnected upheavals of that class which, by the suppression of negro slavery and the rapid development of manufactures, had become the lowest stratum of American society. Before the year closed, these bewildering social convulsions began to take a definite direction. The spontaneous, instinctive movements of these vast masses of working people, over a vast extent of country, the simultaneous outburst of their common discontent with a miserable social condition, the same everywhere and due to the same causes, made them conscious of the fact, that they formed a new and distinct class of American society; a class of—practically speaking—more or less hereditary wage-workers, proletarians. And with the true American instinct this consciousness led them at once to take the next step towards their deliverance: the formation of a political working-man's party, with a platform of its own, and with the conquest of the Capitol and the White House for its goal. In May the struggle for the Eight Hours' working-day, the troubles in Chicago, Milwaukee, etc., the attempts of the ruling class to crush the nascent uprising of Labor by brute force and brutal class-justice; in November the new [United] Labor Party organized in all great centers, and the New York, Chicago and Milwaukee elections. May and November have hitherto reminded the American bourgeoisie only of the payment of coupons of U.S. bonds; henceforth May and November will remind them, too, of the dates on which the American working class presented *their* coupons for payment.

In European countries, it took the working class years and years before they fully realized the fact that they formed a distinct and, under the existing social conditions, a permanent class of modern society; and it took years again until this class-consciousness led them to form themselves into a distinct political party, independent of, and opposed to, all the old political parties formed by the various sections of the ruling classes. On the more favored soil of America, where no mediaeval ruins bar the way, where history begins [sic] with the elements of the modern bourgeois society as evolved in the seventeenth century, the working class passed through these two stages of its development within ten months.

Still, all this is but a beginning. That the laboring masses should feel their community of grievances and of interests, their solidarity as a class in opposition to all other classes; that in order to give expression and effect to this feeling, they should set in motion the political machinery provided for that purpose in every free country—that is the first step only. The next step is to find the common remedy for these common grievances, and to embody it in the platform of the new Labor Party. And this—the most important and the most difficult step in the movement—has yet to be taken in America.

A new party must have a distinct platform; a platform which may vary in details as circumstances vary and as the party itself develops, but still one upon which the party, for the time being, is agreed. So long as such a platform has not been worked out, or exists but in a rudimentary form, so long the new party, too, will have but a rudimentary existence; it may exist locally but not yet nationally; it will be a party potentially but not actually.

That platform, whatever may be its first initial shape, must develop in a direction which may be determined beforehand. The causes that brought into existence the abyss between the working class and the Capitalist class are the same in America as in Europe; the means of filling up that abyss, are equally the same everywhere. Consequently, the platform of the American proletariat will in the long run coincide as to the ultimate end, the conquest of political supremacy by the working class, in order to effect the direct appropriation of all means of production—land, railways, mines, machinery, etc.—by society at large, to be worked in common by all for the account and benefit of all.

But if the new American party, like all political parties everywhere, by the very fact of its formation aspires to the conquest of political power, it is as yet far from agreed upon what to do with that power when once attained. In New York and the other great cities of the East, the organization of the working class has proceeded upon the lines of Trades' Societies, forming in each city a powerful Central Labor Union. In New York the Central Labor Union, last November, chose for its standard bearer Henry George,[1] and consequently its temporary electoral platform has been largely imbued with his principles. In the great cities of the North West the electoral battle was fought upon a rather indefinite labor platform, and the influence of Henry George's theories was scarcely, if at all, visible. And while in these great centers of population and of industry the new class movement came to a political head, we find all over the country two wide spread labor organizations: the "Knights of Labor"[2] and the "Socialist Labor Party,"[3] of which only the latter has a platform harmony with the modern European standpoint as summarized above.

---

[1]   Henry George (1839–97), developed in California his theory that industry should be taxed while land became immune from taxation. He took his social-reforming journalism to New York where he refined his self-taught political economy and, with working-class support, made a solid bid in 1886 to be mayor of New York.

[2]   Founded in 1809 in Philadelphia as a secret society, the Knights rapidly became a national organization welcoming all workers but appealing most to the unskilled. They preferred mutualism to class struggle and opposed the general strike of 1886.

[3]   Founded in Philadelphia in 1876 as the Working Men's Party, it was sectarian in the manner of Ferdinand Lasalle and consequently unappealing to M and E.

Of the three more or less definite forms under which the American labor movement thus presents itself, the first, the Henry George movement in New York, is for the moment of a chiefly local significance. No doubt New York is by far the most important city of the states; but New York is not Paris and the United States are not France. And it seems to me that the Henry George platform, in its present shape, is too narrow to form the basis for anything but a local movement, or at best for a short-lived phase of the general movement. To Henry George, the expropriation of the mass of the people from the land is the great and universal cause of the splitting up of the people into Rich and Poor. Now this is not quite correct historically. In Asiatic and classical antiquity, the predominant form of class-oppression was slavery, that is to say, not so much the expropriation of the masses from the land as the appropriation of their persons. When, in the decline of the Roman Republic, the free Italian peasants were expropriated from their farms, they formed a class of "poor whites" similar to that of the Southern Slave States before 1861; and between slaves and poor whites, two classes equally unfit for self-emancipation, the old world went to pieces. In the middle ages, it was not the expropriation of the people *from*, but on the contrary, their appropriation *to* the land which became the source of feudal oppression. The peasant retained his land, but was attached to it as a serf or villain, and made liable to tribute to the lord in labor and in produce. It was only at the dawn of modern times, towards the end of the fifteenth century, that the expropriation of the peasantry on a large scale laid the foundation for the modern class of wage-workers who possess nothing but their labor-power and can live only by the selling of that labor power to others. But if the expropriation from the land brought this class into existence, it was the development of capitalist production, of modern industry and agriculture on a large scale which perpetuated it, increased it, and shaped it into a distinct class with distinct interests and a distinct historical mission. All this has been fully expounded by Marx ("Capital," Part VIII: "The so-called primitive Accumulation.") According to Marx, the cause of the present antagonism of the classes and of the social degradation of the working class is their expropriation from *all* means of production, in which the land is of course included.

If Henry George declares land-monopolization to be the sole cause of poverty and misery, he naturally finds the remedy in the resumption of the land by society at large. Now, the Socialists of the school of Marx, too, demand the resumption, by society, of the land, and not only of the land but of all other means of production likewise. But even if we leave these out of the question, there is another difference. What is to be done with the land? Modern Socialists, as represented by Marx, demand that it should be held and worked in common and for common account, and the same with all other means of social production, mines, railways, factories, etc.; Henry George would confine himself to letting it out to individuals as at present, merely regulating its distribution and applying the rents for public, instead of, as at present, for private purposes. What the Socialists demand, implies a total revolution of the whole system of social production; what Henry George demands, leaves the present mode of social production untouched, and has, in fact, been anticipated by the extreme section of Ricardian[1] bourgeois economists who, too, demanded the confiscation of the rent of land by the State.

It would of course be unfair to suppose that Henry George has said his last word once for all. But I am bound to take this theory as I find it.

The second great section of the American movement is formed by the Knights of Labor. And that seems to be the section most typical of the present state of the movement, as it is undoubtedly by far the strongest. An immense association spread over an immense extent of country in innumerable "assemblies," representing all shades of individual and local opinion within the working class; the whole of them sheltered under a platform of corresponding indistinctness and held together much less by their impracticable constitution than by the instinctive feeling that the very fact of clubbing together for their common aspiration makes them a greater power in the country; a truly American paradox clothing the most modern tendencies in the most mediaeval mummeries, and hiding the most democratic and even rebellious spirit behind an apparent, but really powerful despotism—such is the picture the Knights of Labor offer to a European observer. But if we are not arrested by mere outside whimsicalities, we cannot help seeing in this vast agglomeration an immense amount of potential energy evolving slowly but surely into actual force. The Knights of Labor are the first national organization created by the American Working Class as a whole; whatever be

---

[1]   David Ricardo (1772–1823), English political economist whom M relied on even more than on Adam Smith in the development of his own economic theories.

their origin and history, whatever their shortcomings and little absurdities, whatever their platform and their constitution, here they are, the work of practically the whole class of American wage-workers, the only national bond that holds them together, that makes their strength felt to themselves not less than to their enemies, and that fills them with the proud hope of future victories. For it would not be exact to say that the Knights of Labor are liable to development. They are constantly in full process of development and revolution; a heaving, fermenting mass of plastic material seeking the shape and form appropriate to its inherent nature. That form will be attained as surely as historical evolution has, like natural evolution, its own immanent laws. Whether the Knights of Labor will then retain their present name or not, makes no difference, but to an outsider it appears evident that here is the raw material out of which the future of the American working class movement, and along with it, the figure of American society at large, has to be shaped.

The third section consists of the Socialist Labor Party. This section is a party but in name, for nowhere in America has it, up to now, been able actually to take its stand as a political party. It is, moreover, to a certain extent foreign to America, having until lately been made up almost exclusively by German immigrants, using their own language and for the most part little conversant with the common language of the country. But if it came from a foreign stock, it came, at the same time, armed with the experience earned during long years of class-struggle in Europe, and with an insight into the general conditions of working class emancipation, far superior to that hitherto gained by American workingmen. This is a fortunate circumstance for the American proletarians who thus are enabled to appropriate, and to take advantage of, the intellectual and moral fruits of the forty years' struggle of their European classmates, and thus to hasten on the time of their own victory. For, as I said before, there cannot be any doubt that the ultimate platform of the American working class must and will be essentially the same as that now adopted by the whole militant working class of Europe, the same as that of the German-American Socialist Labor Party. In so far [sic] this party is called upon to play a very important part in the movement. But in order to do so they will have to doff every remnant of their foreign garb. They will have to become out and out American. They cannot expect the Americans to come to them; they, the minority and the immigrants, must go to the

Americans, who are the vast majority and the natives. And to do that, they must above all learn English.

The process of fusing together these various elements of the vast moving mass—elements not really discordant, but indeed mutually isolated by their various starting points—will take some time and will not come off without a deal of friction, such as is visible at different points even now. The Knights of Labor, for instance, are here and there, in the Eastern cities, locally at war with the organized Trades Unions. But then this same friction exists within the Knights of Labor themselves, where there is anything but peace and harmony. These are not symptoms of decay, for capitalists to crow over. They are merely signs that the innumerable hosts of workers, for the first time set in motion in a common direction, have as yet found out neither the adequate expression for their common interests, nor the form of organization best adapted to the struggle, nor the discipline required to insure victory. They are as yet the first levies *en masse* of the great revolutionary war, and equipped locally and independently, all converging to form one common army, but as yet without regular organization and common plan of campaign. The converging columns cross each other here and there; confusion, angry disputes, even threats of conflict arise. But the community of ultimate purpose in the end overcomes all minor troubles; ere long the straggling and squabbling battalions will be formed in a long line of battle array, presenting to the enemy a well-ordered front, ominously silent under their glittering arms, supported by bold skirmishers in front and by unshakeable reserves in the rear.

To bring about this result, the unification of the various independent bodies into one national labor Army, with no matter how inadequate a provisional platform, provided it be a truly working-class platform—that is the next great step to be accomplished in America. To effect this, and to make that platform worthy of the cause, the Socialist Labor Party can contribute a great deal, if they will only act in the same way as the European Socialists have acted at the time when they were but a small minority of the working class. That line of action was first laid down in the "Communist Manifesto" of 1847 [sic] in the following words:

"The Communists"—that was the name we took at the time which even now we are far from repudiating—"the Communists do not form a separate party opposed to other working class parties.

"They have no interests separate and apart from the interests of the whole working class.

"They do not set up any sectarian principles of their own, by which to shape and model the proletarian movement.

"The Communists are distinguished from the other working class parties by this only: 1. In the national struggles of the proletarians of the different countries they point out, and bring to the front, the common interests of the whole proletariat, interests independent of all nationality; 2. In the various stages of development which the struggle of the working class against the capitalist class has to pass through, they always and everywhere represent the interests of the movement as a whole.

"The Communists, therefore, are on the one hand, practically, the most advanced and resolute section of the working class parties of all countries, that section which ever pushes forward all others; on the other hand, theoretically, they have, over the great mass of the proletarians, the advantage of clearly understanding the line of march, the conditions, and the ultimate general results of the proletarian movement.

"Thus they fight for the attainment of the immediate ends, for the enforcement of the momentary interests of the working class; but in the movement of the present, they represent and take care of the future of the movement."

That is the line of action which the great founder of Modern Socialism, Karl Marx, and with him, I and the Socialists of all nations who worked along with us, have followed for more than forty years, with the result that it has led to victory everywhere, and that at this moment the mass of European Socialists, in Germany and in France, in Belgium, Holland and Switzerland, in Denmark and Sweden as well as in Spain and Portugal, are fighting as one common army under one and the same flag.

London, January 26, 1887
Frederick Engels

(MECW 26: 434–42)

Appendix J: Engels, "Notes on My Journey Through America and Canada," late September 1888

[These notes are based on a visit to North America in August and September 1888, when Engels was accompanied by Eleanor Marx-Aveling, her husband Edward, and Carl Schorlemmer, a German-born communist and professor of organic chemistry at the University of Manchester. Engels never lost his talent for observation, and these notes give a specially clear indication of a marxist reading for contradiction beneath the veneer of prosperity. However, the dangers of the flying visit to a small portion of a vast area are evident in the ascription of "feudal" characteristics to Canada, "bourgeois" ones to the United States. The remarks on French Canadians are a little more astute. The idea of profit coming before all else in America struck many European visitors of this period. Engels resists the presentism of commerce via historical allusion and comparison with French revolutionary traditions.]

[NOTES ON MY JOURNEY THROUGH AMERICA AND CANADA]

Primitiveness. "CIVILISED COUNTRY."

Furniture.—Manners—Boston cabs. Hotel organisation, stage coaches, 17th-century travel. Alongside hypermodern features—even in rooms. Window fastenings—roller blinds—keys—double locks.

Country of unexpected contrasts: more railways than roads and the latter appalling—GOOD PLANK ROAD—ELEVATED RAILWAYS above and dreadful pavement below—log cabins but carpets and pianos inside—indeed, even the bourgeois Yankees and the feudal Canadians alongside them—the idyllic Hoboken and insects close to New York.

Publicness of life, in contrast to England. Only bedrooms private, and even these scarcely so (fanlights, ventilation).—Hall, OFFICE, WRITING ROOM, LADIES' PARLORS; heaters make it unnecessary to keep rooms closed even in winter, and so it does not exist. LOAFING ABOUT in the hotels.

Greeks in Rome in the last days of the republic.

Religion—*their* theory, to be grasped historically. GO-AHEAD NATION—pushing past, not being able to see anyone walking or standing in front of them. Even in Boston, and worst there on account of the narrow streets—women too.

Spitting—privies—hypocrisy about drink not only in PROHIBITION STATES—nobody drinks in public—prudery—ROOSTER and ROACHES.

Opposite to Canada.—French Canadians really detached from France by the Revolution and have preserved the feudalism guaranteed by the conquest—they are going to ruin—Falls opposite Niagara—empty houses, bridges, etc.—Emigration to New England, where they replace the Chinese.—English Canadians also slow, even in Toronto much dilapidation.

The Americans *unable to enjoy.*

The Americans unable to walk—either rush or loaf.

Provincials.

Foundation the old solid petty bourgeois, small townsman and small peasant of the 17th–18th centuries. He is everywhere unmistakable with his unmistakable wooden fashion, but also forms the solid foundation amidst wild speculation, just like the Swiss, to whom a certain resemblance.

Obtrusiveness of American manners: Doctor, *City of Berlin* [steamship on which Engels' party crossed the Atlantic to New York].

Get up early.

New York—harbour—beauty.—Natural setting for the centre of capitalist production—and how this destiny is fulfilled. First evening impression, dazzling, pavements, dirt, noise, horrible. By day even more ugliness—telegraph poles, overhead railways, signs crossways, company signs, architecture hidden, throngs of people, carriages, TRAMS and ELEVATED far above London, ugly, disfigured, everywhere *advertisements*, obtrusiveness. Croupier type. Haggard appearance of the people, even the women. Shops dazzling compared with London, and in greater numbers. This the *gateway* to the promised land. Ghastly noises at sea and on land. Noise from the carts, one makes more than ten in Europe. All aesthetics trampled underfoot as soon as momentary profit comes in view.

Horses like the people: elements of a good stock, not yet ready. Mostly lighter than in England—in Canada, on the other hand, thoroughly English type.

Résumé: capitalist production is overexploitation. Adirondacks forest devastation—nowhere else timber forest either (Isle of Gnats perhaps excepted).

Railways poor, slow, stopping train, delay and wait in Buffalo, incomprehensively long halt at the stations; *few* trains per day; long bends, hence the long carriages (cf. street corner tracks in New York—ELEVATED), rolling, due to elasticity of the beams and the trembling, sea-sickness.

Americans no nation. 5–6 different types, held together by the need for cohesion forged in the Civil War, and the feeling that they have in them the making *of the greatest nation of the 20th century.*

Genuinely capitalist:

Business is concluded in a strictly businesslike manner. No tips. Anyone who gives them in situations where we would consider them unavoidable is then thoroughly exploited as a GREENHORN.

———————————

The parvenu—national character.

Educated persons commonly display great self-possession, others at least show confidence and ASSURANCE to the point of importunity.

(Written in the latter half of September 1888)

(MECW 26: 581–4)

Appendix K: Engels, "Impressions of a Journey Round America," late September 1888

[It is interesting to compare Engels' Notes to this fragment in continuous prose dealing with the same trip. He never completed and published the article he proposed on this topic of America first imagined and then experienced. Engels focuses on newness once again, recycling the Eurocentric trope of "discovery" and the idea of the fledgeling American state while resisting those of that state's illusions about itself more plainly resting on the claims of free enterprise and meritocracy. He overdraws the opposition between Europe and the United States before entering the specifics of encounter, first on the journey across the Atlantic and via a favourite theme, "younger ladies." The reduction of American distinctiveness and self-confidence to a particular type of the petty-bourgeoisie allows Engels to return Americans from the vanguard to the provincial rearguard, an outcome undoubtedly gratifying to "we Europeans" whom he sees himself as representing and addressing. Women, furniture, carriages, inns, are alike read for signs of country bumpkins inside the *nouveaux riches*. Sound construction is not the same as good taste, while to move outside an American city is to travel back more than two centuries in time. In reclaiming cutting edge modernity for quaint outmodedness, Engels challenges a widespread triumphalism in and about the United States, but in doing so he gives further support to the notion of "virgin" territory energetically developed which is integral to that very triumphalism. It is a cautionary instance of blindness and insight.]

[IMPRESSIONS OF A JOURNEY ROUND AMERICA]

We generally imagine America to be a new world—new not merely with regard to the time of its discovery, but also in all its institutions, far ahead of us old-worlde sleepy Europeans in its scorn for everything hereditary and traditional, a world, newly built from scratch on virgin soil, by modern men on purely modern, practical, rational principles. And the Americans do their part in strengthening this view of ours. They look down with contempt on us as dubious, impractical people, enmeshed in all sorts of received prejudices, who go in fear of everything new, whereas they, THE MOST GO-AHEAD NATION, examine every new proposal for improvement simply for its practical utility and, having once recognised it as possible, introduce it immediately, indeed almost overnight. But in America everything ought to be new, rational, practical—that is, everything ought to be different from what it is with us.

I first met a large number of Americans on the steamer *City of Berlin*. They were mostly very nice people, ladies and gentlemen, more accessible than the English, at times somewhat blunt in their speech, but otherwise rather like the better dressed people anywhere else. What, however, set them apart was a strangely petty-bourgeois bearing—not that of the timid, uncertain German petty bourgeois, nor that of the English; a bearing which, by virtue of the great assurance with which it presented itself as if it were quite natural, showed itself to be an inherited quality. The younger ladies, in particular, left the impression of a certain naivety such as is found in Europe only in smaller towns; when striding resolutely, almost fiercely across the deck, arm in arm, or on the arm of a man, they had the very same springy gait and held down their skirts when threatened by the wind with the same demure grip as innocent young things from the country back home. They reminded me mostly of Swedish girls—they were big and robust like them, too—and I expected them to curtsey at any moment, as Swedish women do. My American fellow travelers had also received their share of the physical and intellectual clumsiness which is the universal hereditary trait of the Germanic race and had not shaken it off at all. In short, my initial impression of the Americans was by no means one of national superiority over the Europeans, by no means that of a totally new, modern national type, but on the contrary that they were people who still clung on to inherited petty-bourgeois habits which are considered outdated in Europe, that we Europeans contrast with them in this connection as the Parisians with the provincials.

When I entered my first bedroom in New York, what did I find? Furniture of the quaintest old style imaginable, chests of drawers with brass rings or hoops as handles on the drawers, such as was the fashion in the early years of the century, and in Europe are still found only in the country; alongside them, more recent styles after the English or French pattern, but even these were also outdated enough and mostly in the wrong place; nothing new since the huge rocking chair, which described an arc of 240 degrees, went out of fashion again. And thus everywhere, the chairs, tables and cupboards mostly look like the heirlooms of past generations. The carriages on the New York streets have such an outdated appearance that at first glance one believes no European farm would still have in its possession a hand-cart of such a model. True, on closer observation one finds that these carriages are much improved and most expediently equipped, furnished with excellent suspension and extremely lightly built out of very strong wood; but for all these improvements the old-fashioned model remained intact. In London, right up to the early 40s, there were cabs which people boarded from the rear and where they sat on the right and the left opposite one another, as in an omnibus; since 1850 they have disappeared; yet in Boston, as far as I know the only American city where cabs are in common use, these boneshakers still flourish to this day. The American inns of today, with their luxurious furnishings and their hundreds of rooms, show in their entire AMERICAN PLAN that they have grown out of the remote farmhouses in sparsely populated areas, which even today occasionally offer travellers board and lodging for payment—I shall return to this point—and hence display peculiarities which appear to us to be not simply strange, but downright quaint. And so on.

But anyone who wishes to savour the pleasure of a journey such as one had to endure in Europe at the time of the Thirty Years' War [1618–48] should head for an American mountain district and travel to the end of the last railway line and take the stagecoach further out into the wilderness. The four of us made such a trip to the Adirondacks and have seldom laughed as much as we did on the roof of that coach. An old boneshaker of an indescribable model, compared with which the famous Prussian carriages from the year dot seem the height of splendour, with seats—quite in keeping—for six to nine people up on the roof and the box that was the conveyance. As for the road, I beg your pardon, it wasn't a road, one could hardly even call it a path; two deeply rutted tracks in the sandy soil, uphill, downhill.

(Written in late September 1888)

(MECW 26: 584–86)

Appendix L: Manifestoes

1. The Brunswick Manifesto, 25 July 1792

[The manifesto form rose to new prominence during the French Revolution. An event which was in important respects a war of ideas was clearly receptive to statements designed to win converts and mobilize opinion on behalf of one political position or another. The genre has no natural or exclusive association with radical politics, though it seems fair to say that established authority in the later eighteenth century tried to reach a wider audience than its own elites only when challenged from below and feeling itself obliged to react to the novelty and impudence (or worse) of that challenge. The following example was published under the signature of the Duke of Brunswick, and under intense pressure from the French *émigrés* who wanted the clock turned back and the royal family and themselves restored. It is a good example of reactionary rhetoric and the networks of sovereignty that would be vanquished and substantially replaced by Napoleon, only to restore and reassert themselves in 1815. The French and German monarchies and the Austro-Hungarian empire felt the winds of revolutionary change most directly, and were most resolute in maintaining the alliance which Marx and Engels describe so caustically in the opening of their *Manifesto* in 1848. The predicament for reactionaries is conveyed well in the 1792 document's hierarchical forms of naming and modes of address, its blending of disbelief and threats, of elitist solidarity and truculent populism, its attachment to nobility as a product of social class while implying that it was a moral condition accessible to all right-thinking French citizens. The claim to exclusive legitimacy is undermined by characterizations of the revolutionary government in terms that are powerful reminders of the arbitrary excesses and the abusive proprieties of the Old Regime. Such effusions could be only too readily deconstructed by revolutionary intellectuals like Robespierre.]

Their Majesties, the Emperor [Leopold II] and the King [Frederick William II] of Prussia, having entrusted me with the command of the combined armies which they have assembled on the frontiers of France, I have resolved to announce to the inhabitants of that kingdom the motives that have determined the actions of the two sovereigns and the intentions that guide them.

After having arbitrarily suppressed the rights and possessions of the German princes in Alsace and Lorraine, disturbed and overthrown good order and legitimate government, committed against the sacred person of the King and his august family outrages and violence which are still continued and repeated daily, those who have usurped the reins of administration have finally filled the cup to overflowing by causing an unjust war to be declared [April 20] against His majesty the Emperor, and by attacking his provinces situated in the Low Countries. Some of the possessions of the Germanic Empire have been involved in this oppression, and several others have escaped the same danger only by yielding to the imperious threats of the dominant party and its emissaries. His Prussian Majesty, united with His Imperial Majesty by the bonds of a close and defensive alliance [since February 1792], and himself a preponderant member of the Germanic body, could not, therefore, absolve himself from marching to the aid of his ally and co-state; and it is in this dual relationship that he assumes the defence of this monarch and of Germany.

To these noble interests is added still another aim, equally important and very dear to the hearts of the two sovereigns: to terminate anarchy in the interior of France, to check attacks on the Throne and the Church, to re-establish legal power, to give the king the security and liberty of which he is deprived, and to enable him to exercise the legitimate authority which is his due.

Convinced that the sound part of the French nation abhors the excesses of a faction which subjugates it, and that the majority of the inhabitants impatiently awaits the moment of relief in order to declare openly against the odious enterprises of its oppressors, His Majesty the Emperor and His Majesty the King of Prussia summon and invite them to return without delay to the ways of reason, justice, order, and peace. It is in accordance with these views that I, the undersigned, general commander of the two armies declare:

1st   That drawn into the present war by irresistible circumstances, the two allied courts propose no other aim than the welfare of France, and do not intend to enrich themselves by conquests;

2nd   That they do not intend to interfere in the internal government of France, but only wish to deliver the King, the Queen, and the Royal Family from their captivity, and to procure for His Most

Christian Majesty the necessary security to enable him, without danger or hindrance, to hold whatever convocations he deems suitable, and to labour to assure the welfare of his subjects, according to his promises and in so far as it is within his power;

3rd   That the combined armies will protect the cities, towns, and villages, and the persons and property of all who submit to the King, and that they will co-operate in the immediate re-establishment of order and police throughout France;

4th   That the National Guards[1] are called upon to supervise provisionally the peace of the cities and rural districts, the security of the persons and property of all Frenchmen, until the arrival of the troops of their Imperial and Royal Majesties, or until otherwise ordered, under penalty of being personally responsible therefor; that, on the contrary, those National Guards who have fought against the troops of the two allied courts, and who are captured bearing arms, will be treated as enemies and punished as rebels against their King and as disturbers of the public peace;

5th   That the generals, officers, noncommissioned officers, and soldiers of the French troops of the line likewise are summoned to return to their former fidelity, and to submit immediately to the King, their legitimate sovereign;

6th   That the members of the departments, districts, and municipalities likewise shall be responsible with their lives and property for all offences, fires, murders, pillaging, and acts of violence which they permit or which they manifestly have not exerted themselves to prevent within their territory; that they likewise shall be required to continue in office provisionally, until His Most Christian Majesty, restored to full liberty, has subsequently provided therefor, or until otherwise ordered in his name in the meantime;

7th   That inhabitants of the cities, towns, and villages who dare defend themselves against the troops of their Imperial and Royal Majesties, and fire on them either in the open country or through the windows, doors, and openings of their houses, shall be punished immediately, according to the rigour of the law of war, and their houses demolished or burned. On the other hand, all inhabitants of the said cities, towns, and villages who hasten to submit to their King by opening their doors to the troops of Their Majesties, shall be

---

[1]   Established in 1789 and comprising prosperous citizens, this militia both took the French royal family into custody and protected them from would-be assassins.

placed at once under their immediate protection; their persons, property, and effects shall be under the protection of the laws, and the general security of each and every one of them shall be provided for;

8th   The city of Paris and all its inhabitants, without distinction, shall be required to submit at once and without delay to the King, to place that Prince fully at liberty, and to assure him, as well as all Royal personages, the inviolability and respect which the law of nature and nations requires of subjects towards their sovereigns; their Imperial and Royal Majesties hold all the members of the National Assembly,[1] of the department, district, municipality, and National Guard of Paris, the justices of the peace, and all others concerned personally responsible with their lives for whatever may happen, to be punished by military law, without hope of pardon. Their said Majesties further declare, on their faith and word as Emperor and King, that if the Palace of the Tuileries is entered by force or attacked, if the least violence, the least outrage be done Their Majesties, the King, the Queen, and the Royal Family, if their security, preservation, and liberty be not provided for immediately, they will exact an exemplary and ever-memorable vengeance thereon by delivering the city of Paris to military punishment and total destruction, and the rebels who are guilty of outrages, to the punishments they deserve. On the other hand, Their Imperial and Royal Majesties promise the inhabitants of the city of Paris to use their good offices with His Most Christian Majesty to obtain pardon for their misdeeds and errors, and to take the most vigorous measures to assure their persons and property if they obey the above injunction promptly and exactly.

Finally, Their Majesties, recognizing in France only those laws which emanate from the King, in the full enjoyment of liberty, repudiate in advance the authenticity of all declarations made in the name of His Most Christian Majesty; so long as his sacred person, that of the Queen, and all the Royal Family are not really secure; to which end their Imperial and Royal Majesties invite and solicit His Most Christian Majesty to designate the city in his kingdom, nearest the frontiers, to which he deems it fitting to retire with the Queen and his family, under a proper and trustworthy escort, which

---

[1]   The body by which the third estate and its aristocratic and clerical allies challenged the monarchy and proceeded to devise a new national constitution. The Assembly had 745 deputies from across France.

will be sent him for such a purpose, in order that His Most Christian Majesty may in all security summon about him such ministers and councillors as it pleases him to designate, hold such convocations as appear to him suitable, provide for the re-establishment of good order, and regulate the administration of his kingdom.

Finally, I declare and obligate myself, moreover, in my own private name and in my aforementioned capacity, to have the troops under my command observe proper and correct discipline everywhere, promising to treat with kindness and moderation those well-intentioned subjects who show themselves peaceable and submissive, and to use force only against those who render themselves guilty of resistance or ill will.

For these reasons I require and exhort all inhabitants of the kingdom, in the most forceful and urgent manner, not to oppose the progress and operations of the troops which I command, but rather to grant them everywhere a free entry and all the good will, aid, and assistance which circumstances may require.

Given at headquarters at Coblenz, 25 July, 1792.

Signed Charles-William-Ferdinand,
Duke of Brunswick-Lunebourg

(Reprinted and translated from the *Moniteur,* 3 August, 1792, in John Hall Stewart, *A Documentary Survey of the French Revolution.* New York: Macmillan, 1951. 306–11)

2a. Report on the Manifestoes of the Allied Kings Against the Republic, 5 December 1793

[Maximilien Robespierre (1758–94) uses his formidable intellect and command of language to show how all manifestoes, including the Brunswick one reprinted above, are vulnerable to critique. It is important always to attend to the reception history of such works and to remember that manifestoes do not monopolize forceful intervention and advocacy but are part of much larger struggles, within and beyond print culture, for authority and legitimacy. *Propaganda,* in the sense of propagating the tenets of Roman Catholicism, had been the concern of a committee of cardinals so entitled since 1622, when they were charged with the care and oversight of overseas missions. In the age of revolutions, when secular intellectuals across Europe were questioning or openly contesting the status and practices of the Church, *propaganda* takes on the wider set of applications familiar to readers today. For an "incorruptible" revolutionary like Robespierre, the claims of sovereigns ("the masterpieces of human corruption") and degenerate aristocrats are part of a systematic propaganda campaign that misrepresents privilege to itself as well as to those it subordinates. This travesty of representation warrants response at the highest republican level, in this case under the aegis of the National Convention which now incarnates popular sovereignty after the execution of Louis XVI in January of 1793. The following Report and Reply abound in trenchant analysis, radical classicism, devastating comparisons and rhetorical questions, open and oblique mockery, virulent sexism, and a list of grievances affirming the unfinished business of restorative justice after the iniquities of the Old Regime. Sterile or complicit "philosophism," like bourgeois English commercialism, is given as short shrift by Robespierre as by Marx. Learning fuels praxis on behalf of the Revolution and a radically redefined national interest. The *Brunswick Manifesto* both disdained and feared to name the new institutions and governing bodies of Republican France. Robespierre shows no such compunction. His commitment to inclusive Revolution concludes with a fitting call for unity.]

The kings combining against the Republic make war against us with armies, with intrigues and with libels. We oppose their armies with more courageous armies; their intrigues with vigilance and the terror of national justice; their libels with truth.

Ever eager to reknot the strands of their lethal web to the extent that they have been broken by the hand of patriotism; always adept at turning the arms of liberty against liberty itself, the emissaries of the enemies of France are currently at work overthrowing the Republic via republicanism, and rekindling civil war via philosophism. This great programme of subversion and hypocrisy coincides marvellously with a perfidious plan to defame the National Convention and the nation itself.

So long as treachery or imprudence detract so much from the energy of the revolutionary measures commanded by national security, leave others unexecuted, others maliciously exaggerated or applied in ways contrary to initial intention; so long as in the midst of these embarrassments the agents of foreign powers put to work the volatile elements in the populace, diverting our attention from the authentic dangers and pressing needs of the Republic in order to emphasize religious ideas; so long as they strive to substitute for a political revolution a new revolution in order to replace public reason and the energy of patriotism; so long as the same men openly attack all cults while secretly encouraging fanaticism; so long as at the same time they make the whole of France resound with their senseless declamations, and dare to abuse the name of the National Convention in order to justify the deliberate excesses of the aristocracy disguised under the mantle of stupidity; the enemies of France were once again haggling over your ports, your generals, your armies, reassured a terrified federalism, intrigued with all foreign peoples in order to multiply your enemies. They armed against you the priests of all nations; they opposed the empire of religious opinions against the natural ascendancy of your moral and political principles, and the manifestoes of all governments in the world denounced us as a nation of fools and atheists.

It is up to the National Convention to intervene between a reviving fanaticism and the patriotism some wish to lead astray, and to rally all the citizens round the principles of liberty, reason and justice. Legislators who love our country and have the courage to save it must not again come together as reeds ceaselessly swaying to the breath of foreign factions. It is part of the duty of the Committee of Public Safety to unveil them for you and to propose to you the measures necessary to extinguish them: it will undoubtedly fulfil it. Meanwhile it has charged me to present you with an apt project whose goal is to confound the woolly impostures of the tyrants leagued against the Republic, and to unveil for the eyes of the world their hideous hypocrisy.

In this combat between tyranny and liberty, we enjoy such an advantage that it would be folly for us to avoid it, and since the oppressors of the human race have the temerity to wish to plead their case before it, let us make haste and follow them before this formidable tribunal in order to speed up the inevitable arrest which awaits them.

b. Reply of the National Convention to the Manifestoes of the Kings leagued against the Republic (1793)

Will the National Convention reply to the manifestoes of the tyrants leagued against the French Republic? It is natural to disdain them, but it is useful to confound them and just to punish them.

A manifesto of despotism against liberty! What a bizarre

phenomenon! How have they dared to take some men to be judges between them and us? Why do they not fear that the subject of the quarrel will reactivate the memory of their crimes and hasten their ruin?

Of what do they accuse us? Of their own crimes.

They accuse us of rebellion. Slaves revolting against the sovereignty of peoples, do you not know that this blasphemy can be justified only by victory? But regard then the gallows of the last of our tyrants [Louis XVI], and behold the French people armed to punish its peers. This is our reply.

The kings accuse the French people of immorality. Peoples, lend an attentive ear to these worthy preceptors of the human race. The morality of kings, just heaven! And the virtue of courtesans! Peoples, celebrate the good faith of Tiberius [a Roman emperor famous for duplicity and vice] and the candour of Louis XVI; admire the good sense of Claude and the wisdom of Georges; extol the justice and temperance of William and of Leopold; exalt the chastity of Messalina [licentious wife of the emperor Claudius], the marital fidelity of Catherine [the Great of Russia] and the modesty of [Marie] Antoinette [executed in October 1793]; praise the invincible horror of all the despots past, present and future, for usurpations and tyranny, their tender regard for oppressed innocence, their religious respect for the rights of humanity.

They accuse us of being irreligious; they broadcast that we have declared war on Divinity itself. How edifying it is, the piety of tyrants! And how agreeable to heaven must be the virtues which scintillate at court, the benefits they spread across the earth! About which God are they talking to us? Are they familiar with anything other than pride, debauchery and all the vices? They style themselves the image of Divinity! Is this so as to force the world to abandon their altars? They claim that their authority is its creation! No, God created tigers, but monarchs are the masterpieces of human corruption. If they invoke heaven, it is but to usurp the earth; if they speak to us of the Deity, it is but to take His place themselves. They direct to Him the prayers of the poor and the wailing of the wretched: they are themselves the gods of the wealthy, of the oppressors and assassins of the people. To honour the Deity and punish kings is the same thing. And which people ever produced a purer cult than ours for this great Being, under the auspices of which we have proclaimed the immutable principles of all human society? The laws of eternal justice were disdainfully termed the dreams of honest folk; from this we have created imposing realities. Morality was in the books of the philosophers; we have infused it into the governments of nations. The death sentence for tyrants slept forgotten in the vanquished hearts of timid mortals; we have implemented it. The world belonged to several races of tyrants, as the wastes of Africa did to tigers and snakes; we have restored it to the human race.

Peoples, if you lack the strength to take back your share of this common heritage, if it has not been given to you to make valuable the titles which we have made available to you, restrain yourselves at least from breaking our laws, or from impugning our courage. The French are not at all afflicted with the mania that allows no nation happy and free except itself. All kings would have been able to vegetate or die unpunished on their bloody thrones, if they had known how to respect the independence of the French people. We wish only to enlighten you about their impudent calumnies.

Your masters tell you that the French nation has forbidden all religions; that it has substituted a cult of some men for worship of the Deity; they depict us to you as an idolatrous or insane people. They are lying. The French people and their representatives respect freedom of religion and prohibit none. They honour the virtue of humanity's martyrs without infatuation or idolatry; they abhor intolerance and persecution, no matter how they conceal themselves under pretexts; they condemn the extravagances of philosophism as they do the follies of superstition and the crimes of fanaticism. Your tyrants impute to us some of the irregularities inseparable from the tempestuous movements of a great revolution; they impute to us the effects of their own intrigues and the outrages of their emissaries. Everything wise and sublime produced by the French Revolution is the work of the people. Everything of a different character derives from our enemies. All reasonable and generous men support the Republic. All the treacherous and corrupt belong to your tyrants' faction. Does one slander the star that animates nature just for some light clouds which slip across its dazzling disk? Does august liberty lose her divine charms because the vile agents of tyranny seek to profane her? Your misfortunes and ours are the crimes of the common enemies of humanity. Is this a reason for you to hate us? No; it is reason to punish them!

Cowards dare to denounce to you the founders of the French Republic. The modern Tarquins [doomed for their arrogance like the last of the kings of Rome] have dared to say that the Roman

Senate was a gathering of brigands. Even the servants of [the last Roman king, Lars] Porsenna treated Scaevola [a man principled and brave enough to defy tyranny and then hold his own hand in fire] as insane. Following the manifestoes of Xerxes [after the Battle of Marathon], Aristides pillaged the treasure of Greece. The hands experienced in plunder and stained with Roman blood, Octavius and Antony, commanded the whole world to believe them the only merciful ones, the only ones just and virtuous. Tiberius and Sejanus [whom he appointed Prefect of his Praetorian Guard] saw Brutus and Cassius as only murderers or even knaves.

Frenchmen, men of all lands, it is you who are violated by insults to liberty in the person of your representatives or defenders; several members of the Convention have been reproached for weaknesses, others for crimes. Well! in common with the whole French nation! What does the national representation have in common with these particular facts, if not the strength they impart to the weak and the pain they inflict on the guilty? All the armies of the European tyrants repulsed, in spite of five years of betrayal, conspiracy and internal strife; the gallows for disloyal representatives erected beside the one for the last of the French tyrants; the immortal tablets where the hands of the peoples' representatives engraved midst raging storms the social compact of the French people; all men equal before the law; all the guilty great ones trembling in face of justice; unsupported innocence heartened to have found at last a refuge in the tribunals; love of homeland triumphant; in spite of all the vices of slaves, despite all the treachery of our enemies; the people, energetic and wise, formidable and just, rallies to the voice of wisdom and learns to distinguish its enemies even under the mask of patriotism; the French people hastening to arms to defend the magnificent achievement of its courage and virtue; here is the penance we present to the world, both for our own errors and for the crimes of our enemies!

If necessary, we can present still further claims. Our blood too has been shed for the homeland. The National Convention can show to the friends and foes of France honourable scars and glorious mutilations.

Here, two of tyranny's illustrious adversaries [Lepelletier de Saint Fargeau (1760–93), former President of the Constituent Assembly, and the more notorious Jean Paul Marat (1743–93), theorist and provocateur of terror] have fallen before the parricidal blows of what they regarded as a criminal faction; there, a worthy rival in republican virtue [Jean Baptiste Drouet (1763–1824)], trapped in a besieged village, dares to form the generous resolve to make his way with several companions through the ranks of the enemy; noble victim of hateful betrayal, he falls into the hands of followers of the Austrians, and under protracted torture his sublime devotion to the cause of liberty is extinguished! Other representatives penetrate across the rebel territory of the Midi [i.e. the south of France], escape with difficulty the fury of the traitors, save the French army caused to surrender by its perfidious leaders, and report the terror and flight to the followers of the Austrian, Spanish, and Piedmontese tyrants.

In this wretched city [Toulon], itself a blight on the French name, [Pierre Marie] Baille and [Charles Nicolas] Beauvais [de Préau], sated with tyranny's outrages, died for the homeland and its sacred laws. Before the wall of this sacrilegious city, [Thomas Augustin de] Gasparin, directing the thunderbolt that must punish him, Gasparin, inflaming the republican valour of our soldiers, fell victim to his courage and to the most cowardly knavery of all our enemies [namely poison].

The North, and the Midi, the Alps and the Pyrénées, the Rhone and the Scheldt, the Rhine and the Loire, the Moselle and the Sambre, witnessed our battalions rally to the voice of the people's representatives, under the flags of liberty and victory: some perished, others triumphed.

The Convention in its entirety confronted death and braved the fury of all the tyrants.

Illustrious defenders of the cause of kings, princes, ministers, generals, courtesans, tell us about your civic virtues; recount for us the important services you have rendered humanity; speak to us of the fortresses conquered by the force of your guineas; boast to us of the talent of your emissaries and the readiness of your soldiers to fly before the defenders of the Republic; boast to us of your noble contempt for the rights of men and for humanity; our prisoners stuffed with calm, our womenfolk mutilated by your janissaries, children massacred on the bosoms of their mothers, and the murderous teeth of the Austrian tigers ripping apart their bloody limbs; boast to us of your exploits in America, in Genoa and Toulon; boast to us especially of supreme skill in the arts of poisoning and assassination; tyrants, behold your virtues!

Sublime Parliament of Great Britain recite for us your heroes. You have an opposition party.

With you, patriotism is opposed so that despotism triumphs; the minority is opposed, thus the majority is corrupted. Insolent and vile people, your simulated representation is venal, according to your witness and opinion; you yourself adopt their favourite maxim: That the talent of its representatives are an object of industry like the wool of your sheep and the steel of your manufactures; and you will dare to speak of morality and liberty! What then is this strange privilege to act irrationally, without modesty or restraint, which the stolid patience of the people seems to grant to tyrants! What! These little men whose principal merit consists in knowing the price of British consciences; which labours to transplant into France the vices and corruptions of their country; who wage war, not with arms but with crimes, daring to accuse the National Convention of corruption and to insult the virtues of the French people! Generous people, we swear by you that you will be avenged! Before waging war ourselves, we will exterminate all our enemies; the House of Austria will perish rather than France; London will be free before Paris is again enslaved; the destiny of the Republic and of the tyrants of the earth have been weighed in the eternal balance: the tyrants have proven lighter.

People of France, let us forget our quarrels and march against the tyrants; tame thou them with your arms and with our laws. May the traitors tremble, may the last of the cowardly emissaries of our enemies disappear, may patriotism triumph and innocence find assurance. People of France, to battle; your cause is holy, your courage invincible; your representatives know how to die; they can do more, knowing how to vanquish!

(H. Morse Stephens, *The Principal Speeches of the Statesmen and Orators of the French Revolution 1789–1805*. 2 vols. Oxford: Clarendon Press, 1892. 2.374–83. My translation.)

3. Manifesto of the Equals (1796)

[Among the supporters of the French Revolution there were many factions beyond the main Jacobin/Girondin split. These factions attempted various purges, including the one that cost Robespierre his life in 1794. Most factions espoused bourgeois values and tendencies very apparent (and unattractive) to Marx and Engels. However, there was one markedly proto-communist group, the Society of

Equals, who called for the abolition of the constitution of 1795 and a return to the 1793 version. The manifesto produced here was drawn up by the radical poet, librarian, journalist, and atheist, Sylvain Maréchal (1750–1803), on behalf of a group which included the most uncompromising opponent of private property, François Noel ["Gracchus"] Babeuf (1760–97). This manifesto proved too radical even for its sponsors—most notably in its willingness to sacrifice art to politics, and its anticipation of the one great and final revolution still to come—though these sponsors shared the view that true equality was as yet easier to apostrophize than to enjoy, and that the Revolution remained in important respects incomplete. Maréchal shares Babeuf's sense of agrarian reform as key to distributive justice, and of the authority of nature and reason in educating the people of France about their rights and how to attain them. This document became one of the "justificatory pieces" accompanying Filippo Michele Buonarroti's (1828) account of the Babeuf Conspiracy and of the trial in 1797, instigated by the Directory, which cost Babeuf his life—though only after providing him with a stage from which to deliver a most searching and memorable critique of anti-democratic betrayals of the Revolution and a vision of its communistic realization. Buonarotti's work was translated into English in 1836 by the leading Chartist and radical journalist, James ["Bronterre"] O'Brien (1804–64), and functioned as an inspiration or warning, depending on the views of its readers on the property question and the social relations it shapes and is shaped by.]

People of France!—During fifteen ages you have lived slaves, and consequently unhappy. During six years you breathe with difficulty in the expectation of independence, of prosperity, and of equality.

Equality!—first vow of nature, first want of man, and chief bond of all legitimate association! People of France! You have not been more favoured than the other nations which vegetate on this ill-fated globe! Always and everywhere does the unfortunate human species, delivered over to cannibals more or less artful, serve for a plaything to all ambitions—for pasture to all tyrannies. Always and everywhere have men been fooled by fine words; never and nowhere have they obtained the *thing* with the word. From time immemorial we have been hypocritically told—*men are equal*; and from time immemorial does the most degrading and monstrous inequality insolently oppress the human race. Ever since the first existence of civil societies has the finest apanage of man been uncontradictedly *acknowledged*; but never, up to this moment, has it been once *realized*. Equality has never been other than a beautiful and barren fiction of law. Even now, when it is claimed with a stronger voice, we are answered, "Be silent miserables!—absolute equali[t]y is but a chimaera; be content with conditional equality; you are all equal before the law. Rabble! What more do we want? Legislators, governors, rich proprietors—listen in your turn.

We are all equal, are we not? This principle remains uncontested, because, without being self-convicted of folly, one cannot seriously say that it is night when it is day.

Well! We pretend henceforward to live and die equal, as we are born so. We desire real equality or death; behold what we want. And we shall have this real equality, no matter at what price. Woe to them who will interpose themselves between it and us! Woe to him who will offer resistance to so determined a resolve!

The French Revolution is but the forerunner of another revolution far more grand, far more solemn, and which will be the last. The people has marched over dead bodies against the kings and priests coalesced against it; it will do the same against the new tyrants—against the new political Tartuffes[1] who have usurped the places of the old.

"What do we want," you ask, "more than equality of rights?" We want that equality but not merely written in the "Declaration of the Rights of Man and of the Citizen";[2] we want it in the midst of us— under the roofs of our houses. We consent to everything for it—to become as *pliable as wax, in order to have its characters engraven upon us.* Perish, if needs be, all the arts, provided real equality abides with us!

Legislators and governors, who are as destitute of genius as of honesty—you rich proprietors, without bowels of pity—in vain do you essay to neutralize our holy enterprise, by saying, "They are only re-producing the old Agrarian law, so often demanded already before them."

Calumniators! Be silent in your turn; and in the silence of confusion hearken to our pretensions, dictated by nature herself, and based upon eternal justice. The Agrarian law, or partition of lands,

---

[1]   Tartuffe is a famous hypocritical character in one of Molière's plays. [Bronterre's note].

[2]   The provisions of this foundational document were debated for two years before being published as the preface to the Constitution in 1791.

was only the instantaneous wish of certain soldiers without princi-ples—of certain small tribes, moved by instinct rather than by reason. We aim at something more sublime, and more equitable; we look to *common property*, or the *community of goods!* No more indi-vidual property in lands. *The earth belongs to no one.* We claim—we demand—we *will* the communal enjoyment of the fruits of the earth; *the fruits belong to all.*

We declare that we can no longer suffer that the great majority of men shall labour and sweat to serve and pamper the extreme minority. Long enough, and too long, have less than a million of individuals disposed of what belongs to more than twenty millions of men like themselves—of men in every respect their equals. Let there be at length an end to this enormous scandal, which poster-ity will scarcely credit. Away for ever with the revolting distinctions of rich and poor, of great and little, of masters and servants, of *gover-nors* and *governed.*

Let there be no longer any other differences in mankind than those of age and sex. Since all have the same wants, and the same faculties, let all have accordingly the same education—the same nourishment. They are content with one sun, and the same air for all; why should not the like portion, and the same quality of food, suffice for each according to his wants?

But already do the enemies of an order of things the most natu-ral that can be imagined, declaim against us,——Disorganizers, and seditionists," they exclaim, "you want but massacres and plunder."

People of France! We will not waste our time to answer them; but we will tell you,——the holy enterprise we are organizing has no other object in view than to put an end to civil dissensions and to public disorder. Never was a more vast design conceived and put in execution. At distant intervals in the history of the world, it has been talked of by some men of genius "by a few philosophers" but they spoke it with a low and trembling voice. Not one of them has had the courage to speak the entire truth.

The moment for great measures has arrived. Evil is at its height; it has reached its *maximum*, and covers the face of the earth. Chaos, under the name of politics, has too long reigned over it. Let every-thing revert to order, and resume its proper place. At the voice of equality, let the elements of justice and felicity be organized. The moment is come to found the Republic of Equals—that grand asylum open to all human kind. The days of general restitution are come. Weeping families, come and seat yourselves at the common table provided by nature for all her children.

People of France! The purest of all earthly glories has been reserved for you—yes, 'tis you who are first destined to present the world with this touching spectacle.

Old habits, old prejudices, will again seek to oppose obstacles to the establishment of the Republic of Equals. The organization of real equality—the only one which satisfies all wants, without making victims, without costing sacrifices—will not, perhaps, at first please everybody. The egotist, the ambitious, will yell with rage. Those who possess unjustly, will raise the cry of injustice. Exclusive enjoyments, solitary pleasures, personal ease and privileges, will cause poignant regrets to some few individuals who are dead or callous to the pangs of others. The lovers of absolute power, the vile instruments of arbitrary authority, will feel it hard that their haughty chiefs should bend to the level of equality. Their short-sightedness will, with difficulty, penetrate into the future of public happiness, however near; but what can avail a few thousand malcontents against such a mass of human beings, all happy, and astonished at having been so long in quest of a felicity which they had within hands' reach. On the day that follows this real revolution, they will say to one another in amazement—"What—universal happiness depended on so little! We had but to will it. Ah, why had we not willed it sooner? Was it then necessary to have it told to us so often? Yes, no doubt, a single man on the earth, more rich, more powerful, than his fellow men, than his equals, destroys the equilibrium, and crime and misfortune come on the world.

People of France! By what sign then ought you henceforward to recognise the excellence of a constitution? .... That which altogether reposes on actual, absolute equality, is the only one that can be suitable to you, and satisfy all your desires.

The aristocratic charters of 1791 and 1795 rivetted your chains, instead of breaking them. That of 1793 was a great practical step towards real equality; never before was equality so nearly approached; but that Constitution did not yet touch the end, nor was it fully competent to attain general happiness, of which, however, it has solemnly consecrated the great principle.

People of France! Open your eyes and hearts to the fulness of felicity; recognize and proclaim with us the

REPUBLIC OF EQUALS!

(*Buonarroti's History of Babeuf's Conspiracy for Equality; with the Author's Reflections on the Causes and Character of the French Revolution, and his estimate of the Leading Men and Events of that Epoch. Also, his views of Democratic Government, Community of Property, and Political and Social Equality.* Translated by Bronterre [O'Brien], Editor of the Poor Man's Guardian, Hetherington's Twopenny dispatch, etc. etc. London: H. Hetherington, 1836. 314–17.)

4. Manifesto of the Delegates to their Countrymen, 6 June 1797

[We have seen in the manifestoes reproduced above varying concern about the loyalty of the French military. Here we see the capacity of seamen to blend mutiny and worker solidarity in an unprecedented way in a nation at war that had authorities fearing the reconstitution of the British Navy as a "floating republic." Most notably at Spithead and the Nore, Portsmouth, and Yarmouth discontent erupted among the much brutalized, irregularly and inadequately paid sailors in His Majesty's senior service. The sailors showed themselves better educated and better organized than the Government and the Lords of the Admiralty anticipated, and they soon won important concessions on matters of discipline, conditions of service, and compensation, and also a Royal Pardon for their mutinous actions on 27 May, 1797. All this happened too late to quell insurgency on board 26 vessels on the Nore in the Thames estuary, and, under the leadership of former officer Richard Parker, the crews there were still issuing communications in June. The more publicly oriented of these missives, like the manifesto reproduced here, were part of a communications strategy that included bands and parades, the running of the red flag up the masthead, and rituals of intimidation and self-discipline. However, this particular manifesto had to depend for its publication on assistance from an American ship, and that proved unreliable. A version was presented to Lord Southesk as part of a collection of communications from the delegates to George III, but the seamen were by now losing the battle for public opinion and the capacity to militarily exploit or escape from their increasingly encircled situation. The mélange here of French, American, and United Irish sentiments, rhetorically overwrought heroism and apologetic patriotism, suggests something of the confusion among the mutineers and the vulnerability underlying their bravado. By the end of June Parker had been hanged, and four hundred of his mates sent to trial. By the end of October a number of the disrupted vessels and crews were being hailed as heroes of the Battle of Camperdown where the Dutch were defeated in a fierce and costly struggle.]

COUNTRYMEN,

It is to you particularly that we owe an explanation of our conduct. His Majesty's Ministers too well know of our intentions, which are founded on the laws of humanity, honour, and national safety—long since trampled underfoot by those who ought to have been friends to us—the sole protectors of your laws and property. The public prints teem with falsehoods and misrepresentations to induce you to credit things as far from our design as the conduct of those at the helm of national affairs is from honesty or common decorum.

Shall we have who endured the toils of a tedious disgraceful war, be the victims of tyranny and oppression which vile, gilded, pampered knaves, wallowing in the lap of luxury, choose to load us with? Shall we, who amid the rage of the tempest and the war of jarring elements, undaunted climb the unsteady cordage and totter on the topmast's dreadful height, suffer ourselves to be treated worse than the dogs of London Streets? Shall we, who in the battle's sanguinary rage, confound, terrify and subdue your proudest foe, guard your coasts from invasion, your children from slaughter, and your lands from pillage—be the footballs and shuttlecocks of a set of tyrants who derive from us alone their honours, their titles and their fortunes? No, the Age of Reason [as recently described by Tom Paine in his book of that name] has at length revolved. Long have we been endeavouring to find ourselves men. We now find ourselves so. We will be treated as such. Far, very far, from us is the idea of subverting the government of our beloved country. We have the highest opinion of our Most Gracious Sovereign, and we hope none of those measures taken to deprive us of the common rights of men have been instigated by him.

You cannot, countrymen, form the most distant idea of the slavery under which we have for many years laboured. Rome had her Neros and Caligulas, but how many characters of their description might we not mention in the British Fleet—men without the least tincture of humanity, without the faintest spark of virtue, education or abilities, exercising the most wanton acts of cruelty over those

whom dire misfortune or patriotic zeal may have placed in their power—basking in the sunshine of prosperity, whilst we (need we repeat who we are?) labour under every distress which the breast of inhumanity can suggest? The British seaman has often with justice been compared to the lion—gentle, generous and humane—no one would certainly wish to hurt such an animal. Hitherto we have laboured for our sovereign and you. We are now obliged to think for ourselves, for there are many (nay, most of us) in the Fleet who have been prisoners since the commencement of the War, without receiving a single farthing. Have we not a right to complain? Let His Majesty but order us to be paid and the little grievances we have made known redressed, we shall enter with alacrity upon any employment for the defence of our country; but until that is complied with we are determined to stop all commerce and intercept all provisions, for our own subsistence. The military have had their pay augmented, to insult as well as to enslave you. Be not appalled. We will adopt the words of a celebrated motto [the royal one: Dieu et mon droit] and defy all attempts to deceive us. We do not wish to adopt the plan of a neighbouring nation [i.e., France], however it may have been suggested; but we sell our lives dearly to maintain what we have demanded. Nay, countrymen, more: We have already discovered the tricks of Government in supplying our enemies with different commodities, and a few days will probably lead to something more. In the meantime,
We remain, Dear Countrymen,
[Your loving Brothers, Red for Ever][1]

(R. W. Postgate, *Revolution From 1789 to 1906: Documents Selected and Edited with Notes and Introductions.* New York: Harper Torch, 1962. 73–74)

5. Proclamation by Robert Emmet, 23 July 1803

[Robert Emmet (1778–1803) went to an early death as a martyr for Irish independence from British rule. He is interesting as an example of a disaffected member of the protestant elite, as a reminder of the close but problematic links between revolutionary France and long-suffering Ireland, and of the ironies and contradictions of

---

[1] This is how the copy for Lord Southesk ends. The version prepared for the printer concludes more diplomatically, "Yours affectionately."

Britain formalizing its political union with Ireland in the new United Kingdom in 1801 while at the same time and throughout the nineteenth century requiring and resenting a substantial Irish presence in its military and labour force. After the abortive Franco-Irish rising of 1798, Emmet followed events in France carefully while reflecting on the political unreliability of the Irish middle classes. The rise to prominence of Napoleon Bonaparte intensified his concern about the consequences of depending on France to aid revolution in Ireland. He chose to work conspiratorially rather than diplomatically, building secret networks among the Irish working class and waiting for the right moment when Anglo-French hostilities would recommence and Ireland could rise up while Britain was distracted. However, his conspiracy was not as leak-free as he hoped. The British government knew more than he realised and may indeed have actually encouraged political action it knew would fail, except in facilitating another round of hanging and imprisoning Irish radicals. Emmet's preparations in the summer of 1803 included the making of green and white uniforms and flags, disastrous attempts to make rockets, and the printing of two "Proclamations," the shorter of which is reproduced here. It is much the same as a manifesto in tone and design, with a kind of patriotic hype that attributes to Hibernia a comprehensive unity of purpose it has never as yet enjoyed. The particular target audience are the "Citizens of Dublin" whose support will better enable the storming of Dublin Castle and transforming of the city into a symbolic and logistical equivalent of radical Paris. Despite the careful planning, a series of miscues led to early detection and dispersal of Emmet's patriots. He was soon apprehended by the authorities and became another eloquent martyr to the cause of Irish independence.]

CITIZENS OF DUBLIN,
A BAND of patriots, mindful of their oath, and faithful to their engagement as United Irishmen, have determined to give freedom to their country, and a period to the long career of English oppression.

In this endeavour, they are now successfully engaged, and their efforts are seconded by complete and universal co-operation from the country; every part of which, from the extremity of the north to that of the south, pours forth its warriors in support of our hallowed cause. Citizens of Dublin, we require your aid, necessary secrecy has prevented to many of you notice of our plan; but the erection of our national standard, the secret, though long degraded, Green, will be found sufficient to call to arms, and rally round it every man in whose breast exists a spark of patriotism, or sense of duty; avail yourselves of your local advantages; in a city each street becomes a defile and each house a battery; impede the march of your oppressors, charge them with the arms of the brave, the pike, and from your windows and roofs hurl stones, bricks, bottles and all other convenient implements on the heads of the satellites of your tyrant, the mercenary, the sanguinary soldiery of England.

Orangemen: add not to the catalogue of your follies and crimes; already have you been duped to the ruin of your country, in the legislative union with its tyrant;—attempt not an opposition, which will carry with it your inevitable destruction, return from the paths of delusion; return to the arms of your countrymen, who will receive and hail your repentance.

Countrymen of all descriptions, let us act with union and concert. All sects, Catholic, Protestant, Presbyterian are equally and indiscriminately embraced in the benevolence of your object; repress, prevent and discourage excesses, pillage and intoxication, let each man do his duty, and remember that during public agitation inaction becomes a crime; be no other competition known than that of doing good; remember against whom you fight, your oppressors for six hundred years, remember their massacres, their tortures, remember your murdered friends—your burned houses—your violated females;—keep in mind your country, to whom we are now giving her high rank among nations, and in the honest terror of feeling, let us all exclaim, that as in the hour of trial we serve this country, so may God serve us in that which will be the last of all.

(Postgate, *Revolution From 1789 to 1906*. 68–69)

6. Manifesto of the Productive Classes of Great Britain and Ireland, to the Governments and People of the Continents of Europe, and of North and South America, 13 May 1833

[With the conclusion of the Napoleonic wars in 1815 political reaction set in, but so did resistance. In France revolution burst forth again in 1830. Meanwhile in Britain increasing industrialization and agrarian reform was accompanied by enhanced working class consciousness and solidarity. The Chartist and trade union movements, for example, had within a decade used setbacks like the Peterloo Massacre in 1919 to sharpen their capacity for articulating proletarian goals and making effective public arguments in their favour. By 1833, when the present manifesto was published, the first Reform Act (1832) had already made concessions in response to working-class as well as to bourgeois pressures for the redistribution of power and opportunity, and the Owenite Association of all Classes and Nations was only two years away. Proletarians were claiming public spaces for themselves and developing truly national and proto-international organizations. But the piece reproduced here is more about revelation and rearrangement than about revolution. Punctilious in its disavowal of physical force, ardent in its belief in the social powers of reason and the transformative powers of education, this manifesto remains challenging in its rehabilitation of labour as honourable productivity to which everyone should aspire and have access, its preference of co-operation to competition, its wish to dissolve and remake the current "professions," and its anticipation of the earth as a peaceable kingdom. The millenarian or utopian dimension of the text may remind us of Marx and Engels' reference to "duodecimo editions of the New Jerusalem," while its identifying of "ignorance" as the source of the current evils seems to underestimate the role of knowledge, and of education in particular, in reproducing and legitimating hierarchy and injustice. The conciliatory and co-operative tone bespeaks both the power and the limitations of unanimity, while the recycling of a Lockean sense of land gone to "waste," looks forward to the mixed benefits of Home Colonization such as Robert Owen advocated and the colonization of wastes and *terra nullius* overseas as unused productive capacity and sources of disease. The "Productive Classes" mentioned here had recently been distinguished by Owen from the "unproductive industrious classes" (i.e., retailers and distributors) in a message he aimed primarily at the righteously named, year-old "Association of the Intelligent and Well-disposed of the Industrious Classes for Removing Ignorance and Poverty." The fledgling National Equitable Labour Exchange which hosted the meeting leading to this manifesto, tried hard to use the labour theory of value to attack unemployment, profiteering, and the limitations of legal currency, but religious friction and lack of legal security for labour and goods led to its demise in 1834.]

Men of the Great Family of Mankind,—

We, your relatives and friends, have been enabled, through past experience, aided especially by modern improvements and discoveries, and late political events, to acquire the knowledge of a *new life*, and, in consequence, to perceive all things through a new light. We have thus arisen from a mental lethargy, which had overwhelmed our reasoning faculties, and benumbed all our finest and best feelings. But we are now wide awake, and have become fully conscious of all the evils which we and you have so long suffered. Our eyes have been opened to our real position in society; and we have at length discovered the true source of our power, and the most effectual mode of applying it for the benefit of all future generations.

To accomplish the great work which we are about to undertake, many and most important changes in conducting the affairs of life must of necessity be made; and we now put forth this statement to obtain your approval and ardent co-operation, because we desire that these changes should be effected by reason, and not by force.

We, therefore, intend now to make manifest the necessity that has arisen at this period for the adoption of these changes, and also to convince the population of the world of their truth and justice, and thus to carry the minds of all with us; and, in the spirit of charity and kindness, to prevent all future revolutions of violence, by removing the causes which germinate and bring them to maturity.

We perceive that the evils which have afflicted the human race have arisen from ignorance; our remedy is to remove this ignorance.

The materials for the production of happiness superabound— they are now unused or misused. We mean to bring them into action, and to give them a right direction.

The materials for the production of happiness are the *earth* and *human beings*. The former requires but to be well cultivated, and properly arranged to produce abundance, and to form a terrestrial paradise. The latter, but to be trained from birth according to the laws of their nature, and all their faculties and qualities to be made available, and properly directed, to insure the perpetual happiness of each individual.

To effect these important results, another and a very different arrangement of society from that which has hitherto existed must now be made.

The whole powers of the *soil* and of *man* must be brought into action; no portion of either can lie dormant when population can be advanced to require the wastes and wildernesses of the earth, which are for now, for want of cultivation, fruitful sources of disease and discomfort to man.

But all our powers are now misapplied. The arrangements of society are random or chance proceedings, arising chiefly from the supposed private interests of one family, in opposition to all others.

We, the *producers of real wealth*, have been, and now are, held in disesteem; while the *unproductive*, useless, and injurious members of society, riot to their own hurt in riches, and are trained to consider us their servants and slaves. By these ignorant and unnatural proceedings, the Earth and his own nature have been made the perpetual source of evil instead of good to man.

We *will*, that this irrational state of society shall now cease, and that, henceforward, *all*, except those of the present generation too far advanced in life for the change, shall be trained to become producers of physical wealth or of intellectual gratification, and that none shall be maintained who are not occupied in producing or acquiring that which will benefit society, or be deemed equivalent to their consumption of its productions.

We now know that all will become far better and happier, by being made to be producers, physically or intellectually, or both, of the means of gratification to society, than they can be by living a life of idleness or uselessness, and that the individual who is not trained, and afterwards employed to effect something beneficial to society must be, of necessity, not merely a useless but a positively injurious member of the great family of mankind.

That it is, therefore, the first duty of all governments to adopt national measures to train and place all the population of their respective dominions within such arrangements as shall make them physically, intellectually, and morally useful members of society.

But, to effect this change, an entire new organization of society is necessary. None of the professions, as they are now exercised, will be required; nor can any of the modes of transacting the business of life be retained. Instead of these errors of the old world, arrangements will be adopted to re-organize the whole of society, and to re-model the proceedings of mankind. We know that, whatever shall be discovered and proved to be for the permanent interest of the human race, will of necessity be carried into execution; and we know it to be for the permanent interest of the human race that the natural powers and faculties of each individual should be fully developed and brought into action for the direct benefit of all, that he himself may thereby be the most permanently benefited.

That each individual should be trained to become, as his natural faculties may direct, a producer of wealth, or of something of real value to society; that is, of something that shall contribute to the well-being or happiness of some portion of the population; or, in other words, as all may be trained to be useful or useless, no one shall be formed to become a worthless or useless member of our new social state. We also know that, by arrangements founded on these simple principles, the human race may be emancipated from ignorance and poverty, and, consequently, from sin and all its frightful train of miseries and evils innumerable.

The union of these few principles, properly combined in practice, will constitute the foundation for a very superior local and general government of the human race; and the general business of society, which has been hitherto so complicated and perplexed, will become, as it ought to be, so plain that any individual may be trained easily to comprehend the principles, and apply them advantageously to practice.

We, therefore, now proclaim to you that a new *era* has commenced—one in which wealth of the most intrinsic value can be created to an unlimited extent, and in which the individuals of the human race may be trained and educated to become beings possessing all the good and superior qualities only which belong to their nature.

And this era we do not hesitate to pronounce the commencement of that period, which, under the term Millennium, the human race has been so long taught to expect.[1]

It is a period when all deception and artifice must cease—when man will know and acknowledge the laws of his nature, and act in perfect accordance with them, and when, in consequence, he will become a natural and superior being.

We invite you now to co-operate cordially with us to effect this great and glorious change—we invite you as relatives and friends, without desire to create hostile feeling of any description—we invite you purely from the affection which our newly acquired knowledge

---

[1] This appeal is much more limited than is admitted. Christian belief in one reading of Revelations XX. 1–5 consorts uneasily with various strands of utopian socialism while avoiding the serious historical analysis demanded by M and E.

of our common nature has created within us. We dismiss all fear and suspicion, and all the inferior feelings which a system of error had generated and matured within us; for we have now full confidence that we ourselves can attain these grand and noble results without the aid of any, and, notwithstanding the opposition of any, or all parties, whoever or whatever they may be. The old power of the old system of error is vanishing away as a mist disappears before the refulgent influence of the sun. It had no strength but that which it derived from *public opinion*, and from public opinion it can no longer obtain support.

And why should any of you lament that public opinion is withdrawn from giving power to an old system of error which has produced evil continually? Is there any one, from the occupier of the most powerful throne to the meanest individual of the lowest tribe, who is not most grievously injured by the necessary effects of this system? It makes now, of all mankind, slaves[1] to passions or to persons—a state of human existence which can never produce either virtue or happiness. Not one of you has a real interest in the longer support of this system; but, on the contrary, your future happiness must arise from its now dying a natural death.

Come, then, and for your own happiness co-operate with us as friends. We are the producers of all the wealth and means of comfort you have hitherto possessed—we can make arrangements by which, in future, you may enjoy these good things in safety, and without fear; but, were we so inclined, we could effectually withhold them from you and your children; and force applied to us, would demonstrate only the weakness and folly of our mistaken opponents. The reign of terror, of carnal arms, or of physical force of any kind or description in opposition, has for ever ceased. It is now useless to speak of these old worn-out means to effect any great or permanent object. We discard them as being worse than useless; as a means of power gone by, never more to be called into action by *beings* claiming a rational nature.

We call upon you to discard them also, and to turn your thoughts from the destruction of your fellow men, and of their wealth, to the acquisition of that knowledge which will enable you to assist materially to improve the former, and greatly to increase the amount of

---

[1] Britain abolished its slave trade in 1808 but slavery continued in its dominions in various forms. An insurrection of slaves in Jamaica in 1831 had been brutally repressed, fuelling a new wave of abolitionist activities and much public debate.

the latter. To act thus is your duty and your interest, for it is the only course that can insure you permanent satisfaction, or what can now give you a chance of happiness.

In conclusion, we again earnestly call upon you to unite cordially with us in our measures—

First, To produce a surplus of all kinds of wealth.

Second, To distribute wealth the most beneficially for all parties in all countries.

Third, To form a superior character for the rising generation, and to improve the adults of the present generation.

Fourth, To govern well and wisely for all parties.

Fifth, And to form arrangements to carry these measures into immediate execution, to stop the evident progress daily making toward a revolution of violence.

(Bronterre O'Brien, *Babeuf's Conspiracy for Equality*. 445–48)

7. Manifesto Addressed to the People of Canada by the Constitutional Committee on Reform and Progress, 1847

[As experience in the United States, Ireland, and elsewhere had attested, the loyalty and tolerance of its "own" colonists could not simply be presumed by the mother country. British greed and rigidity had fuelled a successful revolution in North America and continued to stimulate Irish "troubles"—and the domestic and colonial exportation of those "troubles"—after the death of Robert Emmet. In Canada, the desire for "responsible government" intensified as colonists and new immigrants measured events in Europe and the United States against their own situation. French Canadian nationalism in Lower Canada, and resentment of the Anglican "family compact" in Upper Canada, were important causes of the rebellions of 1837 which had made more pressing the question of reform or revolution as the better instrument for settling Canadian grievances. In the decade since the rebellions, the moderate reform movement associated with Robert Baldwin (1804–54), Francis Hincks (1807–85), and Louis-Hippolyte Lafontaine (1807–64) had made some headway, but it was faced with opposition from Governor Metcalfe as well as from radical republicans still supportive of William Lyon Mackenzie (1795–1861, still in exile in the United States at this time) and Louis-Joseph Papineau (1786–1871, who returned in 1845 from exile in

France). Neither the mix of trials and reparations that followed the rebellions, nor the recommendations of Lord Durham in his *Report* of 1839, had settled matters. The "Manifesto" produced here shows the channelling of resistance through existing institutions and the documenting of the need for institutional and governmental reform. It is a clever appeal for unity-in-diversity that foreshadows the next two main phases in Canada's progress toward political independence from Britain, in 1848 (with the first responsible government led by Lafontaine) and 1867 (the year of Confederation). The document represents an association whose very name aligns it with the broadly based reform movement in Britain rather than more radical or revolutionary examples and options (identified here explicitly and exclusively with France). Significantly, the rebellions of 1837 are termed *"insurrections partielles."* This "Manifesto" employs a discourse of interest, improvement, and effective consultation, and is itself the product of exchange and formal ratification before dissemination. Its employment of French is a pointed reminder of British discrimination against this language and its speakers, a point it emphasizes explicitly later. But its style is only too successful in imitating the complex details and convoluted procedures which are its main theme. That said, it skillfully and predictively positions itself between the libertarian traditions of Britain at its best and the economic dynamism of the republic to the south of Canada. In striving to be more patriotic than partisan, the "Manifesto" nevertheless remains ominously and prophetically silent on the matter of Canada's first peoples, their economies, political and language rights, and territorial entitlements. The defusing of political tensions in colonial and then sovereign Canada, as well as those in Britain and Europe, would of course depend to a significant degree on the dispossession and betrayal of the peoples whose roots in North America were much the deepest. The impulse to conciliation, inclusiveness, justice, and respect for difference, was not extended beyond the "two founding peoples," French and English, to Aboriginal Canadians, a pattern repeated far too often as Canada proceeded to extend westward and northward into its present territorial form.]

Fellow citizens,
Electors of the city and county of Quebec, rightly alarmed at the social and political condition of the country, assembled on 28th June and 29th July last, and put in place the basis for an association designed

to look after the political interests of the country and to promote the material interests of the district of Quebec in particular. This association has since its establishment been regularly constituted in Quebec with the name, "Constitutional Committee on Reform and Progress," and it is in its name that we invite you to associate yourselves with all the points about the country in order to monitor politics in general, and the measures of a purely local interest neglected in many respects by a government which makes of every public enterprise an occasion for corruption and a pretext for the ruin of the common treasury.

In a resolution adopted unanimously by the Assembly on 29 July, it is declared "that the number of members of the Legislative Assembly of Canada is insufficient to represent completely and accurately the wishes and needs of the people of this province, and that it is not at all proportional to the already considerable population of the province that continues to grow quickly," and it is urgently recommended to the Committee, "to take all the measures it believes appropriate to obtaining representation fuller and more reflective of the diverse parties in the province."

A quick glance at our political history and our current situation must suffice to convince us of the truth of this assertion and the urgency of this reform which we do not at all hesitate to declare indispensable to good government, to peace, and to the prosperity of this province.

Under the former Constitution of Lower Canada, the majority of the Legislative Assembly represented in effect the majority of the residents; but a very small minority, represented accordingly in the chamber, were the only source of the Governor's Executive Council, exempted by this from any responsibility to the people, themselves comprising almost the entire Legislative Council, and glorying in governing in defiance of the wishes of the majority of the residents of this region expressed by the majority of their representatives.

This system of governance was pushed so far that in its resolutions and address to the King of 1 April 1833, the Legislative Council publicly avowed the mission of representing the interests of a minority of residents of the country, and, in the parliamentary session which immediately followed, those members of the Assembly who supported the administration adopted the name of "members of the opposition."

An almost identical state of affairs prevailed in Upper Canada, and the result of this regime was a partial insurrection in both provinces, in the wake of which Lower Canada witnessed itself stripped of constitutional and elected government and accepted the grounds for legislative union of the two provinces.

Lord Durham, who, at this juncture was himself invested with this virtually unlimited power, declared that this state of affairs was but "but a temporary and necessary subjugation," and he calculated in addition that it would *cost Great Britain, in the most conservative estimate, an annual increase of one million pounds sterling in colonial expenses to make a temporary system permanent.*

At the same time he declared "that the former constitution (all of whose defects he noted) had functioned so badly that none of its various political parts would warrant restoration, and no friend of order and liberty would know how to envision the province anew while subject to [the Constitution's] pernicious influence."

"As for all the plans," which propose to make from a *"real minority an electoral majority, by new and foreign ways of voting, or unjust distributions of land* (added His Majesty's High Commissioner), I will restrict myself to saying that if it is necessary to deprive Canadians of a representative government, it would be much better to do so in a plain and direct way than to attempt to establish a permanent system of government on a basis which the entire world would regard as *unmistakable electoral fraud.* It is not in North America that one can fool people with an illusion of representative government, or that one can induce them to believe that one prevails over them numerically when in fact they are being disenfranchised."

This latter system thus styled a kind of hypothesis is precisely the one that has followed in practice for seven years and under which we are currently living. The terms used by Lord Durham in 1839 to discredit a simple proposition apply identically to the state of affairs which exists in 1847.

A minority governs, just as governed under the former regime, with the difference that by means of *electoral fraud* it has become an *electoral majority,* however weak and dubious; and it has seized control of every branch of the legislature. *Unfair assignments of land have been made,* Vast tracts have been brought together into single entities, while at the same time some counties with less than half that population have been broken into several pieces. Small towns, boroughs of between 2,000 and 4,000 souls, have been given the privilege of electing a representative, and have acquired a political importance of which their residents never dreamed. Some counties of between

45,000 and 64,000 souls who send a representative to Parliament witness each day the voice of their representative paralysed by the vote of someone from these small boroughs. The six counties of Montreal, Quebec, Dorchester, Huntingdon, Saint Hyacinthe and Two-Mountains, with a total population of 144,810, have only the same number of representatives as the five small towns of Cornwall, Niagara, Hamilton, Sherbrooke and Three-Rivers, and Russell County, which have a combined population of a mere 12,254 souls. Ultimately the current administration counts on a majority of one or two in the Legislative Assembly, while its supporters represent only 472,201 individuals and its opponents 795,177!

From another vantage, the elections for the first Parliament since the legislative union of the two Canadas, effected for the most part by violence, disenfranchisement, the choice of inaccessible localities, the intervention of bands hired and armed; and the election for the city of Montreal for the second Parliament of 1844, where other bands armed and organized under the eyes of the government and aided by regular troops ensured the election of two men who would never have been able to secure the majority of votes in a free and peaceful election; all these facts undoubtedly constitute *new and foreign forms of theft*.

These evils have been inflicted on the mass of the population of the country as a consequence of erroneous ideas which allow to occur among statesmen in the metropolis an unfair parallel between the races of men who reside in this part of the province, of an equally unjust exaggeration of their reciprocal national antipathies, and of a conclusion (contradicted however by the details of the picture they had produced) in favour of one race against another, by the eminent personage to whom we have already alluded [i.e. Lord Durham], and which in the same document which we have already cited, strives in vain to blend constitutional principles of the very wisest kind with regrettable biases. Some have even avowed an intention to punish the French population of Lower Canada for a partial insurrection provoked by forty-eight years of a situation declared pernicious and imposed on this colony by the Imperial Government and its agents. *Mercantile intrigues*, denounced in the House of Lords in these very terms by Lord Gosford, who had been the last Governor of Lower Canada, also contributed to the passage by the United Parliament of Great Britain and Ireland of the Act 3 and 4, section 35.

By this Act two provinces entirely different in religion, language, customs, social and political habits, for which a separate existence had been designed, were fused into one without the consent of one of them, and despite the formal opposition expressed by the 40,000 signatures appended to the solemn requests of the residents of Lower Canada.

That metropolitan states consider themselves entitled to play with the destinies of their colonies, that they think they can establish one day one regime, another day another regime, in line with the changes their own policies seem to demand—only force can guarantee the continuance of such arrangements. A society colonised or similarly constituted in law and recognized for political longevity would not against its will be united with another society, except by one of those abuses of power that could never be legitimated. It is very true that the serviceable expression *fait accompli* was invented as a temporary palliative of injustice, but one has seen even after the passage of centuries the sense of such injustice re-awaken; all the evils, all the miseries, all the corruption of society attributed to the foundational violence; and the *fait accompli* cited once again in the court of opinion of the civilized world.

In the present case, everything converged to render less legitimate an act arbitrary by its very nature. The details of the act have been as bad as its principles. The population of Upper Canada, a third less numerous, has been given representation equal to that of Lower Canada; a permanent civil list has been imposed in the Legislature for the illusory appearance of controlling the government; a debt of a million and a half contracted by and for Upper Canada before the union of the provinces has been imported into the consolidated fund of the United Province, and the French language, the language of the majority of residents of the country, admired the whole world over, imposed previously in England itself [via the Norman Conquest], has been excluded from the parliamentary archives and from the texts of the law.

One has not only violently changed the political condition of half a million men, all British subjects, descendants of the two greatest nations in the world, occupying one of the territories of North America colonized first, and larger than the mother country, and enjoying in fact a level of civilization more advanced than that of most countries in continental Europe; but one has again subjected this population to domination by a smaller population which is in no way superior in enlightenment or industry.

Therefore, even if one were to proclaim a legislative union, one would be sowing the seeds of a protracted political division. One would create between the subjects of a single empire, inhabiting henceforth a single province, a double distinction of nationality and locality. A British subject residing in Upper Canada is declared to be of greater political value, and has in fact a larger share of public power, and by the same token more liberty, than his co-subjects who reside in Lower Canada. The whole mass of the population of British origin in Upper Canada is pronounced superior to the mass of the population of Lower Canada of French extraction, and is endowed with a much more substantial share of public power, a much larger portion of independence and liberty. The new Constitution thus decreed in law, and established in fact, the oppression of Lower Canada as a region, the oppression of French-Canadians as a race.

The partisan spirit has frequently attributed the complaints of the oppressed to the desire for domination on their part, and it is by inspiring in them the fear of being tyrannised in their turn by the very people whom they tyrannise that the leaders of the oligarchy alarm and dominate their supporters. "Injustice is not at all natural to man (a great writer said) and it is only by inducing oneself to believe that one's liberty is in danger that one can bring oneself to make an attempt on the liberty of others." Because, moreover, French-Canadians, ill treated as they are, have found it necessary to complain and make reference to their origins, insofar as they are made a sign of inferiority, their complaints have been ascribed to a national jealousy; they have been burdened with exclusive views that contradict their whole political history; national prejudices have been stirred up against them.

However, they were not at all alone in complaining. A number of men of British origin in Lower Canada, distinguished for their knowledge and experience, were reclaiming the liberty of all, convinced that oppression was good for nothing and not at all consoled by the prospect of being bereft of some of their rights, while thinking that their fellow citizens of different origin were more badly treated than themselves.

Their apprehensions were as wise as their sentiments were generous. The political degradation of the majority of the inhabitants of Lower Canada would not have been achievable, but for the harming of local interests in this part of the province, and all classes of society have suffered equally. Those in the provincial administration who have professed to represent a Lower Canada minority have in fact represented only the interests or the impulses of their colleagues; they have been tools in their hands, always ready to be sacrificed to the increasing influence of the aforesaid colleagues. The day has arrived when the minority of inhabitants of Lower Canada must understand that their interests, well understood, are the interests of the majority; or rather, that there exists but one common interest, that of the moral and material prosperity of the country, a goal which cannot be attained except by the sacrifice of all prejudices and all nation-based antipathy, by a common effort for the development of the vast resources this country offers to all who live here. It must also be convinced that political equality is a condition essential to this harmony and to this common effort on which depends the happiness of all, and that sectional advantages based on electoral fraud will not operate (as in effect they have not operated) except to the detriment of those whom they have destined to serve them as lure and bait.

Seven years have not yet elapsed, yet the order of things based in injustice is already giving grounds for complaint to men of all origins, of all creeds, of all opinions, of all localities. The evil is everywhere so incontestable there is no longer any pretext for calumniating those who claim to be unhappy. There are no longer any principles which unite those who are bereft of power; there is no political denomination at all which can apply itself to their supporters; there is no injurious epithet which can be directed towards the mass in the country who repudiate them. There is for all distinction in one quarter an unprecedented corruption, and on the other an honest and universal indignation.

Only one thing could have forestalled such a deplorable outcome, a strict and sincere adhesion to the principles of government respected in the mother country, and without which any colonial constitution, whatever its representative base, could be nothing other than a dangerous parody, an unavailing instrument for good, equally fatal to the colonies into whose hands they have been rendered and to the metropolis which has brought them to this pass.

With the application of these principles, even under a vicious electoral redistribution, the real opinion of the country can make itself known, and the wishes of the real majority elicit respect from the artificial majority. We have had a brief experience of this.

The resolutions adopted by the Legislative Assembly on 3 September, 1841 contain an exposure of these principles; they mark an epoch in our parliamentary annals and are conceived in the following terms.

1st   Resolution "that the most important and the most incontestable of the political rights of the people of this province is to have a provincial parliament for the protection of its liberties in order to exercise a constitutional influence over the executive departments of its government, and in order to legislate on all matters of internal governance."

2nd   Resolution "that the leader of the executive government of the province being within the limits of his government the representative of his Sovereign, is responsible only to the Imperial authorities, but that nonetheless our local affairs cannot be directed by him except with the assistance or means, according to the judgement and information of lesser officials in the province."

3rd   Resolution "that in order to maintain among the different branches of the provincial parliament the harmony which is essential to the peace, well-being and good government of the province, the principal advisers to the Sovereign's representative, constituting under him a provincial administration, must be men who enjoy the confidence of the representatives of the people, and hence offer a guarantee that the well understood interests of the people, that Our Gracious Sovereign [Queen Victoria] has declared must on all occasions guide the provincial government, will be faithfully represented and defended."

4th   Resolution "that the people of this province have more right to expect of the provincial administration thus constituted that it will apply all its efforts to that which the Imperial authority within its constitutional limits may demand in the manner the most consistent with those well understood wishes and interests."

There is in this important document no provision for *cases which would in no way be adjudged of adequate importance*; and one has effectively *omitted to provide for antagonism* which might disclose itself between the representative of the Sovereign on the one hand and on the other her representatives who enjoy the confidence of the people's representatives. The Legislative Assembly which adopted these resolutions by a majority of 56 over 7, and the provincial government besides, which, via one of its members had proposed these resolutions, seemed equally convinced of the importance of all our local concerns, and, far indeed from imagining that the Sovereign's representative could harbour any ill will against the counsellors, as long as they may enjoy public confidence; far indeed above all from believing that the responsibility of the Governor to the metropolitan authorities must reduce to nothing the responsibility of his counsellors to the people of this colony; the last of these resolutions charged the provincial administration to use all its efforts in order that *the Imperial authority, within its constitutional limits, was exercised in the manner most consistent with the wishes and interests of the people.*

The one and the other of these results were achieved under the government of Sir Charles Bagot [1841–43], while on the one hand the greatest tranquillity, the greatest confidence prevailed across the entire country, the administration formed by this Governor who is greatly missed [since his death in May 1843], all the while maintaining with the metropolitan government the harmony and good relations so desirable in all circumstances, knew by his firmness and patriotism how to assure important concessions on the part of his government; and, although some of these have been ratified only since he left office, they are an important part of his major contribution.

A powerful majority in the Legislative Assembly ensured strong and moderate government, progressively conceding to the party that had brought it to power the just reforms for which it argued, and rallying around it by its wisdom the very people who might have opposed its political actions. A reciprocal confidence prevailed between the Sovereign's representative and his constitutional counsellors, with strong support from the people's representatives; in sum a perfect harmony existed among the members of this administration. These members, far from being preoccupied solely with making their individual and collective situation the most secure possible (which might have led them on the one hand to sacrifice some principles, and on the other into personal intrigues with the goal of replacing some by others) ever since they saw that the successor to Sir Charles Bagot [from 1843–45, Sir Charles Metcalfe] refused them the right of consultation in certain matters which he took upon himself to consider as of insufficient importance, and declared an antagonism which on his part could signify only a determination to bypass their opinions; these counsellors, we declare, from this moment sacrificed their collective status as an administration while simultaneously offering their resignation; and all of them, with only one exception, sacrificed their individual position by persisting in this course.

The difficulties which arose between the Governor and his coun-sellors, in the simple disclosure of the facts which had been the cause of their retreat, demonstrated how much they depend on having the confidence of their constituents in order to fulfil their mandate faith-fully. The Governor pretended that his counsellors had required of him unconstitutional stipulations by which they had expressed the desire to impose advice as if it were law, so that they ultimately aimed at noth-ing less than the absolute usurpation of the Royal Prerogative. It was, moreover, according to him, a conflict of opinion about a theory, a diffi-culty which had been brought up inappropriately and which he had in no way sought out. The counsellors, on the contrary, claimed to have insisted only on the right to be consulted first, to be informed subse-quently of the Governor's decision after he had weighed their opin-ions, which he was free not to follow, and that they were free not to accept responsibility for his decision because power did not reside with them. They affirmed, moreover, "that the difference of opinion between the Governor and themselves in no way existed only in theory; that it derived not only from nominations to positions contrary to their advice, nominations and offers of employment which had in no respect been brought to their attention until after the opportunity to provide their views on this matter had passed; but still the determi-nation on the part of His Excellency to reserve for the expression of the pleasure of His Majesty a *bill* introduced into the provincial Parliament with the knowledge and consent of His Excellency, as a government measure without informing the members of the Executive Council that it would probably be reserved. They found themselves (they added in the memorandum forwarded to the Governor in their name by Monsieur Lafontaine) in the abnormal situation, after their own declarations and their public and solemn undertakings to be responsible for all the Acts of the executive government in Parliament, at the same time deprived not only of the opportunity to offer their advice relative to these Acts but also of knowledge of their existence until they were informed of them by private, unofficial sources."

To begin with, men who would not have enjoyed the complete confidence of the country, would have struggled under disadvantages against the word and protestations of the Governor; and for having done their duty they would perhaps have been punished by an unfavourable vote in the Legislative Assembly. Thus on the contrary, as the majority who had supported the ex-ministers during their administration, and done so out of conviction rather than servility, they received from this majority, after what was termed their disgrace, a mark of esteem and confidence which would undoubtedly not have been forthcoming in similar circumstances from an administration whose strength was signified only by a majority of one or two votes acquired and retained by intrigue. Such flattering testimony is conveyed in the following resolution, passed in the Legislative Assembly on 2 December 1843, by a vote of 46 to 23:

"Be it resolved—That a humble address be presented to His Excellency the Governor-General, in order to explain humbly to him the intense regret this chamber feels as a result of the withdrawal of certain members of the provincial legislature on the question of the right they reaffirm to be consulted relative to the nominations for employment which we unhesitatingly declare to belong to the Prerogative of the Crown, and in order to assure His Excellency that the defence of this principle gives them the right to the confidence of this chamber, in that it is strictly consistent with principles expressed in the resolutions which were adopted by this chamber on 3 September 1841."

Calumnious assertions against his former counsellors, a direct intervention in the elections on the part of the government, which did not hesitate to make its name a partisan slogan, procured for him an approval from the body politic visible although numerically very weak. He obtained thus from the new Parliament what he had been unable able to attain from the preceding one. It was on this occasion that the majority, the immense majority of the country's population, had to complain more than ever before of the unfairness and inadequacy of representation. After having set aside the true principles of government, one took advantage of means already employed by the minority to prevail over the majority, and it is affirmed today that if, with a sincere and impartial Governor, a strict adherence to British principles might in some fashion cause to be forgotten the fundamental defect of our Constitution, it would have been no less permissible to any ill disposed Governor to avail himself of corrupt elements who offered an electoral redrawing in order to give victory to one party against the will of the mass of the population.

Such an act seemed so odious, that one might think it incapable of repetition; and despite the efforts of the current administration to keep itself in power, despite its having been allowed to open the third session of Parliament with a majority of one in the Assembly and the vote of the Speaker of the Legislative Council, himself an entirely supportive member of this administration in the latter body; however, we did not at all expect from the next general election scenes of violence and intimidation such as had dishonoured the government in 1841 and in 1844, nor the direct or indirect intervention of the leader of the Executive in the struggle between his counsellors and public opinion. But the immediate dangers are not the only ones to be avoided; and it seems to us prudent, on the contrary, to take advantage of the happy circumstance which makes remote any appearance of offensive allusion to the representative of Her Majesty, in order to demand a reform which will make impossible in future abuses which we have just exposed.

Like us, England itself had at the same time responsible government and a vicious redrawing of electoral boundaries. Its men of state, its true patriots, never considered its Constitution to be perfectly developed except insofar as it rested on the solid base of *electoral reform*. The former Constitution of Lower Canada, vicious because of the lack of accountability on the part of the executive power, had to succumb, and the new Constitution, where this vice was replaced by unjust and inadequate representation, lacks the wherewithal to do better.

The history of three sessions of Parliament which are about to finish, during which the small number of representatives, and the shameful trading in small electoral colleges, which here as in England bear the name of *rotten boroughs*, has produced an administration which has itself admitted its impotence and unpopularity, the means to prolong its life and renew itself in almost all its departments without at all improving any of them; this history unfortunately presents to the people of this colony a spectacle so deplorable as to discourage any serious seeking out of the causes of such political disorder, so that they do not loudly clamour for the only effective remedy.

The evils that result from this disorder are not imaginary. All the departments of the public service are affected by it. All the interests of a large part of the population are neglected. The instability of the laws, the continual uncertainty which directs the fate of men in power, the even greater uncertainty concerning the fate of the measures they propose one after another, with no other object most often than to acquire or conserve partisans' own hesitations, their constant avowals of personal weakness, their continual efforts to secure the recruitment of men drawn from the ranks of their adversaries, the continual changes in the various departments of the public service, the frequent vacancies caused in the Legislative

Assembly—all that can but discredit in the eyes of the people the laws of the land and those who are charged with upholding them.

The material interests of a large portion of the country are neglected. The needs of partisans, who put to the test a weak and unscrupulous ministry, is cause that the public funds, instead of being spent where they would produce real improvements and a source of revenue for the province and of prosperity for its residents, are on the contrary spent where it is thought they will create *political capital*, to purchase a temporary support for men in power. Lower Canada and the region of Quebec in particular demanded in vain numerous improvements indispensable to the development of their commerce and industry; they also demanded in vain the concessions on Crown lands at lower prices and easier conditions of payment; this favour, or rather this promise of justice, is constantly deferred, and during this time immense sums are voted each year to be spent in another part of the province. The surplus of the sums spent in Upper Canada for public works combined with the surplus of its part of the public debt contracted before the Union gives counter to Lower Canada a balance of $2,622,128; and the credit and resources of this province have for a long time been engaged in the payment of an enormous public debt, which already reaches $4,248,689, and for which it will soon be difficult to supply the interest without recourse to direct taxation.

Within this debt there figures a sum of no less than $139,570, spent in large measure on the Welland Canal [joining Port Weller on Lake Ontario with Port Colborne on Lake Erie] without prior appropriation. Further sums have also been spent in this manner, in contempt of the laws of Parliament and the Constitution, in order to compensate public officials whom the government saw fit to let go.

The important measures complained of in our new position on commercial relations are little understood; and while in all civilised countries one is busy establishing or preparing for free trade, a new customs tariff higher than the former one has been the fruit of the economic reflections of the men of state in this colony. Lord Grey [1799–1802, erstwhile Judge-Advocate-General, and now Home Secretary], in a recent dispatch, invited the English provinces of North America to plan together on the important subjects of customs, mails and means of communication among themselves; and the government of this colony is the only one which seems to have set no store by this appeal. The Irish troubles [especially in the "hungry forties"] marked an emigration extraordinary both for the number of emigrants and for the calamities they encountered; however, the government let the moment of danger arrive without having made preparations which simple prudence suggests. The legislation created in the past three years is insufficient, equivocal and contradictory. In this short space of time, Lower Canada has had on its account two new systems of education and two new systems for municipalities. Each year the government proposes to repeal the law it passed the previous year in order to substitute a new one. The municipal organization in the country, and public education, which constitute the two most powerful instruments for intellectual and material progress, are thus continually put into question; and having itself proposed to substitute compulsory tax assessment for voluntary assessment, the government is publicly accused, and with the strongest appearances of culpability, of favouring and inciting resistance to its own laws, in order to make its political opponents unpopular.

Questions so important for Upper Canada—of the sale of lands held in reserve for the clergy, and of a more liberal use of the endowment of *King's College*[1]—have not been resolved in the sense of the protestations of ministers outside the chamber; and the last of these questions, discussed every year, remains in the same condition. The history of the inconsistency of government regarding this last measure is not the least convincing proof of its weakness.

The revenue from goods belonging to the former Jesuit order has been appropriated in a manner displeasing to the entire population of Lower Canada and especially the Catholic population, and was hitherto used to defray expenses from the consolidated fund itself, what was equivalent to a sharing of the revenues between the two sections of the province. The costs of the administration of justice in Upper Canada have been borne by the consolidated fund contrary to the provisions of the Act of Union [of 1841] already so unjust towards Lower Canada. Government properties, which in the towns of Lower Canada had been taxed until then as municipal entities, were for the future exempted from taxation. Forty thousand louis and more were voted to compensate the residents of Upper Canada for the

---

[1] One seventh of the public land in Upper Canada was reserved for the "Protestant Clergy," in effect the Church of England. George IV approved a charter for King's College in 1827 but various forms of resistance and intrigue meant that building began only in 1842, and the early years of what would become the University of Toronto continued to politicize higher education.

losses incurred during the Rebellion [of 1837–38], while a law passed to compensate losses of the same sort in Lower Canada has not yet been acted upon. Another law passed to come to the rescue of those residents of Quebec City whose houses were destroyed by the fires of 1845 was not implemented for a full year, and was subsequently modified to their disadvantage. At last all the spoliations imaginable, and some even that were difficult to imagine, have been committed to the detriment of the residents of Lower Canada.

The nominations to employment presented the spectacle of the most deplorable bias; and the Prerogative of the Crown which has been so much discussed has been constantly prostituted by the selection of notoriously incompetent men. The tribunals of Lower Canada have been assigned the useless and even dangerous burden of appointees whose professional reputation is most absurd; and it seems the better title to high judicial office may now be an absolute unfitness for any other task. Judges have been drawn from inferior judiciaries to be schooled in political struggles like members of the government, and two members of the government, tired with the struggle, found in the judiciary a lucrative retreat. The tribunals have thus been exposed to party influence, and the sanctuary of justice profaned and degraded in public opinion.

Not only respect for the law, for the government, for the tribunals, for all the institutions has been seriously shaken from one end of the province to the other, but the morality of its residents has also been exposed to the pernicious influence of the sorriest examples. The refusal of an inquiry into the violations committed in the last election in the city of Montreal; the decision of a committee of the Legislative Assembly sworn to arbitrate in a contested election to find in favour of a man whom the committee declared not to have received a majority of the votes, and who, to his great surprise, has become a member of the legislature; the nomination of a sitting member in another committee, charged with deciding another contested election, to *three positions* of cumulatively lucrative benefit to him, before this committee had made its final report; the vote of the honourable William Draper [1801–77, English-born member of the family compact, leader of the Conservative Party and soon to be Metcalfe's Attorney General] bestowed on a vital question decided by two votes, at the same time as he declared publicly that *in a few hours* he was going to accept a judicial appointment which, according to the law, rendered his place as deputy vacant; the confirmation of the election of another representative made by virtue of an authority which the chamber itself had already declared null; the frivolous difficulties raised concerning the competence of the representative of the county of Champlain, difficulties which deprived this county of its voice in Parliament for almost an entire session; the delay imposed on issuing an order for the election of a representative for the county of Dorchester, to replace one of the members of the administration named to a judicial appointment on the eve of a session (these four latter facts giving two illegal votes to the ministry, and depriving the opposition of two legitimate votes, forming thus an artificial and illegal majority of four votes), all these acts are apt to persuade the people of this colony that everything is permissible to public officials in order to acquire or preserve lucrative appointments under this government. Hence each individual is invited to conclude that everything is also permitted to him in the sphere of action to acquire, conserve or increase his well-being and that of his family; and the complete obliteration of all sense of morality and justice would be the consequence of such examples, if by a happy accident one did not often see the honour and virtue banned from the high ranks of society take refuge in, and illuminate with greater intensity, the bosom of public conscience.

At last, the principle of the responsibility of the legally recognized executive government is rendered ridiculous and discredited in practice by the most flagrant contradictions.

In law, it was declared that the leader of the Executive must be surrounded by counsellors responsible to public opinion.

In fact, you have seen for a period of nine months a government isolate itself from all counsellors to gradually form by agglomeration a Council which, in announcing at the end of this time its own existence, had to have recourse to an electoral struggle marked on its part by fraud and violence, in order merely to try to survive.

In law, you are told that the Governor, representative of the Sovereign, politically incorruptible like she whom he represents, must remain remote from party squabbles.

In fact, you have seen an election fought with the name of the Governor as a battle cry, and men who call themselves British in their principles and values vote to sustain *Lord Metcalfe and his policies!* Can you imagine a voter in London or Manchester voting for Queen *Victoria and her policies!*

In law, you are told that the provincial administration is responsible, alone responsible, for all legislation created under all auspices.

In fact, each day you see this administration flinging back to the opposition the responsibility for its own actions.

In law, you are told that the constitutional counsellors of the leader of the Executive must enjoy the confidence of the public.

In fact, you see these counsellors maintain themselves in power long after having themselves recognized their impotence, in offering a part of their responsibility to their opponents, in negotiating with them the formation of a more effective administration, and a long time after the Governor himself officially recognized their unpopularity, in inviting one of the leaders of the opposition and some of his friends to join the administration on terms which it was declared had to be equally honourable for the former and the new ministers.

In law, you are told that you have the same constitutional government as they have in Great Britain, and while the men of state of this great Empire retreat before public opinion, while they utterly lack a majority sufficiently imposing to command the respect of their political adversaries, you have heard in this colony an Attorney General, a powerful cabinet minister, say that a majority of one or two votes is as good as twenty or thirty; and in fact the government is conducted in the manner of an ostensible majority of one or two votes, a veritable minority if one subtracts the votes of ministers, and if one takes account of the tactics employed to form this artificial advantage.

A state of affairs such as we have just depicted seems grounds for discouraging those who might be tempted to remedy it; but one must remember, wherever the elective principle is to some degree admitted, one may achieve the necessary reforms without the shock of violence and without going beyond the ambit of the Constitution.

When the Union was imposed on Lower Canada without its consent, the greatest energy was expended by the population to resist this measure within the bounds of order and legality. The solemn protest by those of the representatives of Lower Canada who had been freely elected was entered in the record of the Legislative Assembly, in an amendment proposed in the address in response to the speech by the Governor General. The point of order of the Liberal Party of Lower Canada concerned the modification of the unjust details of the Act of Union without which there would have to be immediate agitation for repeal of the Act. The subsequent recognition by the mother country of the principles of constitutional government in all the colonies of North America, and the putting into practice of these principles under the government of Sir Charles Bagot, nourished hope that there would be no delay in obtaining the changes which alone could make tolerable the regime of the Union, and save the country from the renewed pain of a violent shock, a new disturbance. The retrograde tendency that Lord Metcalfe wished to imprint on public opinion necessitated a countermove by the Liberal Party, and the general election of 1844 produced a moral result (although the Governor had obtained a majority of two or three and consequently an apparent endorsement of his conduct), the most energetic affirmation of the principles put into question; and at the present moment there is universal acceptance of it in theory; at the same time as the implementation is nothing less than effective, since a parliamentary majority of one or two is what one finds best for safeguarding the uncorruptibility of the Sovereign's representative.

Among the modifications of the Act of Union demanded from the outset, there is electoral reform, and we believe we have demonstrated how necessary this measure is to the functioning of responsible government. Already two of the radical evils of the Constitutional Act identified in the Liberal platform of 1841 can be considered eliminated. The Act of the provincial Legislature that provided for a permanent civil list has received royal assent, and at the same time as the Imperial Parliament will set this law to work by the repeal of the provisions of the Act of Union which contain in this regard a usurpation of the laws of the people of this colony; we have assurance that the clause unfit for modern civilization which forbids the use of the French language from being used in legislation and parliamentary records will also be repealed. Although in connection with the first of these measures it remains a matter of profound regret that the Executive may not be what it ought to be—dependent on subventions freely voted on each year—the recognition of the law of the colonial Legislature to approve these subventions is nonetheless an important improvement.

What the resoluteness and wisdom of the Liberal Party has accomplished in these two connections, combined with the recognition of the responsibility of the counsellors of the leader of the Executive, must be for all Liberals an indication of what they will be able to achieve with a more active organization, and with a stronger expression of public opinion in favour of the reforms required in the present state of our affairs.

From our standpoint, these measures are, in political and constitutional order:—

1st THE ELECTORAL REFORM required for the whole province, the greatest political inequality being the result of the insufficiency and inequality of representation and the undue influence accorded to small localities subject to corruption and intimidation.

2nd THE IMPLEMENTATION OF CONSTITUTIONAL PRINCIPLES RECOGNIZED IN THE RESOLUTIONS OF 1841.

In the economic and material scheme:

1st FREE TRADE WITH FOREIGN COUNTRIES; AND FREE NAVIGATION IN THE ST. LAURENCE which will open to the civilized world a country scarcely known to other nations and will facilitate the development of its vast resources; a double freedom rendered necessary and strictly equitable by the financial measures adopted by Great Britain itself, and by the great example it offers the whole world.

2nd THE PROGRESSIVE AMORTIZATION OF THE PUBLIC DEBT which, contrary to legislative arrangements and the actions based on this principle, goes on increasing year by year. It must furthermore be represented to the Imperial Government that the abandonment of all or a part of the claims pre-existing the Union would be merely an act of justice; for a start, justice for the whole colony whose commerce no longer finds in the markets of Great Britain the protection it had secured to undertake and continue gigantic public works; justice above all for the residents of Lower Canada who have been made liable for this debt by the sole fiat of the Imperial Parliament and without a shade of law or equity.

3rd THE CEDING OF CROWN LANDS AT LOWER RATES AND WITH EASIER REPAYMENT ARRANGE-MENTS; *in small lots, and directly to the colonies who must establish themselves there.*

4th THE REFORM OF THE POSTAL DEPARTMENT, reform which has not been so happy in England and the need for which makes itself so vividly felt in this country where exorbitant postal rates, especially for newspapers and publications originating abroad, imposes a detestable tax on knowledge, a tax which a bad administration of this department over which there is no effective control renders barren of revenue.

In order to attract public attention to these measures, so as to agree on and concentrate on their details, in order to discuss and explain them to people in public assemblies and to urge their adoption by means of petitions, an organization of the Liberal Party throughout the province has become indispensable. Besides, by means of this organization this Party will have to triumph in the next elections, and the choice of men entirely devoted to the programme we have just sketched is the best evidence which could be adduced in favour of this programme and the most reliable gage of its accomplishment. In spite of the unfairness of the current electoral divisions, the last election and all that has occurred since prompts us to believe that that will in fact be the outcome of a free and peaceful election.

We cannot say it too often: success cannot be attained except by united action, by an organization strong, resolved, enlightened. It is to this end that the Constitutional Committee for Reform and Progress, instituted by public demand in the former capital of Lower Canada [Quebec City], not to dominate but to clear the path, resolved to declare plainly its opinion about the past and its views about the future in order to attract compellingly the attention of all those who desire that their country thrive to a course of action which seems to be dictated by justice, by prudence and legality, and for the adoption of which it calls solicitously on their sincere uniting, their unremitting zeal, their constant vigilance.

In order to effect a prompt and comprehensive organization of the country into a vast constitutional association for reform and progress, consider the path that the central and venerable branch of Quebec believes has to be suggested and whose details are contained in the instructions which it will next address to all people of influence in the various localities.

On receiving these documents eminent or enthusiastic persons in each parish will have to bring together the electors of their locality to constitute themselves immediately in a provisional assembly in order to consider the important object of the desired organization, then to name a president, a vice-president, a secretary, a treasurer and a parish committee, etc. These officers and these parish committees will form a county council which at its first meeting will elect a president, two vice-presidents, a secretary-archivist, a corresponding secretary, and a treasurer-general. These county councils whose assemblies will have to be held as much as possible in a central location will consider the projects of rules which will be provided for them by the central association in Quebec, and will transmit them thereafter to all parish associations which will adopt them with or without changes. After this county organization has been completed, it will be necessary to give it advice and to convey all its details to the association of Quebec which will consistently apply itself to keeping the county councils up to date with matters in which it considers they have an appropriate interest and which will even include all lessons useful for the general cause. These exchanges between the mother association and the regional branches will also have to be as frequent as possible in order to nourish a good accord among the country's Liberals while enabling them to consult each other in all challenging situations. It is easy to imagine that each district firmly united in this way by an ever-ready organization will constantly have available to itself the means effectively to combat corruption, to avoid division, mutual defiance, the inevitable and lethal result of isolation. Beyond the advantages it will offer in electoral struggles, this organization will present at ordinary times and even after victory inestimable advantages by giving to the electors the means to consult among themselves on the needs of their localities, and will furnish them with a natural intermediary concerning their representatives who often have no means of learning the opinions of their constituents or of conveying to them the instruction of which they may have need.

The committees established thus will be moreover an excellent means of working for moral and material progress throughout the whole province. For several years, respectable citizens, among whom the worthy clergy of the country are prominent, have made enormous efforts to achieve a social regeneration which will have for itself all its vows, and in the objects which will lie more particularly within its remit, the complete support of the association. Already we owe to this spirit of improvement the progress in primary education, the palpable decrease of the ravages caused by the hideous vice of drunkenness, the perfecting of agriculture, the establishment of savings banks in the towns; and, if there remains much to do unfortunately in all these areas, it is nonetheless comforting to think that in a very brief space of time public attention has been attracted with some success towards so many and so important objects. More than any other means, the rapid establishment of public lands seems apt to improve the moral and material condition of the population of Lower Canada. We have already spoken about these land concessions; but it seems to us important also to engage the superabundant population on both banks of the St. Laurence themselves to turn their attention towards the localities where their futures lie. In recommending this point to the most immediate and serious consideration of the committees which will have to organize themselves in each county, we believe we will have accomplished an important part of our mission. This grand object, like all the local improvements of a public utility which will be projected in every county, will have to form an essential part of the correspondence between the central committee and its various branches.

In the fulfilment of duties that this association requires of itself, in the efforts it will have to make to realize its projects, no consideration must intimidate the citizens which comprise it: neither the difficulties of organization, nor the obstacles that may be placed in its way, nor the very magnitude of the undertaking, nor the considerations of personal interest or friendship, nor finally this false sense of shame, that low opinion of themselves which prevents a great number of men from combining their labours with those of others, esteeming as they do their own participation useless and inconsequential. The day has come for every man to devote himself completely to his country: the more and more brilliant destiny of this continent draws to it all the talented, all the ambitious, all the brave, and no-one would be able to refuse his share of the efforts and sacrifices without incurring great culpability.

History, and contemporary history especially, teaches us that, however long and difficult the struggle of peoples against the obstacles impeding their development, a wise and persevering energy assures them of success in the end. The growing prosperity of the vast republic which is our neighbour, which already extends civilization and liberty from one ocean to the other, shows us what patriotism and a spirit of association can do. Political struggles for which Great Britain has been the theatre afford no less useful instruction. Catholic Emancipation, electoral reform, the repeal of the Corn Laws,[1] all these measures which in the course of this century have marked the intellectual progress of this great nation, have been the

---

[1]   Catholic Emancipation became law in 1829, largely as a result of the efforts of Irish nationalists like Daniel O'Connell. Thereafter, Catholics were once again eligible to hold a range of public offices. The Reform Act of 1832 was passed three times in the House of Commons before the House of Lords accepted this first of three major extensions of the franchise. The Corn Law passed in 1815 was modified in 1828 and repealed in 1846, after graphic illustrations of the political potency of the price of bread. As well as addressing widespread starvation in Ireland, repeal of these protectionist laws also cunningly cast the landed aristocracy as the friends and protectors of the working poor.

fruit of persevering, collective efforts of a citizenry united in a common commitment to the same principles. Less fortunate, France has paid more dearly and with its noblest blood for the liberties it enjoys and whose foundation it also wishes to extend by an electoral reform. Finally, closer to us, the Liberals of Nova Scotia[1] have just given us an example which applies just as well to our situation in that, down there like here, one wished to stifle in their cradles the nascent liberties to which one seemed to have given birth only reluctantly.

For us, for the Liberals of the two sections of the province, a common and energetic effort will have to assure us for ever of the rights which we claim for all of us as British subjects. The talents deployed in this noble struggle by the leaders of the Liberal Party of Upper Canada, and the numerous public demonstrations ["*manifestations*"] which have taken place in that part of the province, are a sure sign of the success which awaits us.

Our fate, the future of our native land [*patrie*], lies therefore in our own hands, and our memory will be responsible to our posterity for the sum of the good fortune more or less substantial which we will have bequeathed them.

CONSTITUTIONAL COMMITTEE FOR REFORM AND PROGRESS

At a general assembly of this association held November 5, at M. Dion's school, presided over by JOSEPH LÉGARÉ Junior, Esquire, joint president of the Committee, it was reported on behalf of the special committee struck to prepare a manifesto conforming with the instructions and resolutions of the public assembly of last July 30; the following resolution was then adopted unanimously.

On a motion by J. P. Rhéaume, Esquire, seconded by Ls. Bilodeau, Esquire,

That the manifesto which has just been read be adopted and addressed to the principal citizens of the various localities in the province, and that the French and English newspapers of the country be asked to publish it.

After which the assembly adjourned.

---

[1]   Under the leadership of Joseph Howe reformers won the election of 1847 and would secure responsible government for Nova Scotia the following year.

N. AUBIN,
Secretary-Archivist.

Quebec, 8 November, 1847.

Here, according to the last census, are the official details of the populations of the counties discussed above.

Montreal,	64,895	Cornwall,	1,439
Quebec,	45,676	Niagara,	2,090
Dorchester,	34,826	Hamilton,	2,152
Huntingdon,	36,204	Thr-Riv.,	3,297
Two-Mountains,	26,936	Russell,	2,481
St.-Hyacinthe,	21,273	Sherbrooke,	795
	229,810		12,254

Difference of the population
of the towns of Quebec and
Montreal   85,000

144,810

8. "Manifesto to Europe," 2 March 1848

[Alphonse de Lamartine (1790–1869), one of France's leading romantic poets, was also a great orator, experienced diplomat, and prominent political figure. His Royalist sympathies dissipated after the July Revolution of 1830, and he travelled in great style in Greece and the Middle East before becoming an independent, idealistic member of the Chamber of Deputies in 1833. An effective advocate for freedom of the press, abolition of slavery and the death penalty, and other progressive causes, Lamartine exemplified a kind of populist utopianism which Marx and Engels both criticized and envied. His passionate apology for the Reign of Terror in his *History of the Girondins* (1847) struck a chord in the swelling numbers hostile to the reign of Louis-Philippe, and he found himself suddenly and charismatically occupying a radical republican place in French consciousness. He played a dramatic part in the revolution of 1848, led the provisional government, and was rewarded with high office in the Second Republic (1848–52) while being burdened with unreasonable expectations from its socialist and anti-socialist elements alike. The bravado of the piece reproduced here, addressed to all European powers ("Manifeste aux puissances") as well as to the professional diplomats who will represent the new French republic to its wary neighbours, is fuelled by a sense of his own celebrity but also by a well-founded fear of reactionaries inside and outside France. Lamartine is no Robespierre, and appeals to contrast, maturation, and pluralism rather than an incorruptibly revolutionary ideology. He offers more reassurance than defiance— that, and a poetic pacifism ("The people and peace, are the same words") within a broader, often hyperbolic, political poetics and semantics. Marx and Engels would agree with Lamartine's sense of the French Revolution of 1789 as restrictively bourgeois, but would see as neo-bourgeois his analogy between individuals and nations and his oxymoronic pitch for "conservative freedom," and as typically wishful thinking his claim that classes and class struggle have been dissolved and pre-empted in a newly inclusive republican patriotism and harmonious internationalism.]

CIRCULAR
of the Minister of Foreign Affairs
to the diplomatic Agents of the French Republic.

Sir,—
You are aware of the events in Paris, of the victory of the people, of its heroism, its moderation, its pacification, and of order re-established by the aid of all citizens, as if in this interregnum of visible power, reason alone was the governor of France.

Thus has the French Revolution entered into its definitive period. France is a Republic; and the French Republic does not need to be recognised to exist. It lives by natural right and by national right. It is the will of a great people whose credentials can only be demanded by itself. Nevertheless, since the French Republic desires to enter into the family of established governments as a regular power and not as a disturbing element in the European order, it is desirable that you should promptly make known to the government to which you are accredited the principles and tendencies which henceforward will guide the foreign policy of the French Government.

The proclamation of the French Republic is not an act of aggression against any form of government in the world. Forms of government are legitimately as diverse as the characters, geographical situation, and mental, moral and material developments of the peoples. Nations, like individuals, vary in age, and the principles which guide them follow in successive phases. Monarchic, aristocratic, constitutional and Republican Governments are the expressions of the different degrees of maturity in the popular mind. Peoples demand more freedom as they feel themselves capable of supporting more: they demand more equality and democracy as they are the more inspired by justice and love for the people. A question of time. A people is as much lost by anticipating the hour of maturity as it is dishonoured by letting it pass uncaught. In the eyes of true statesmen, Monarchy and Republicanism are not two absolute principles which must fight to the death; but contrasting facts which may exist side by side, respecting and understanding each other.

Hence war is not a principle of the French Republic, as, in 1792, it was its mortal and glorious necessity. Between 1792 and 1848 lies half a century. To return, after half a century, to the principle of 1792, the principle of the conquest of an empire, would be retrograde and not progressive: and yesterday's revolution is a step forward, not a step back. We and the world both desire to advance towards fraternity and peace.

If the position of the French Republic in 1792 explains its warlike character, the difference between that epoch of our history and the present epoch explains its pacific character now. Let it be your endeavour to understand this difference and make it clear to those around you.

In 1792 the nation was not one. There were two peoples on the one soil. A terrible struggle was carried on between the classes that had lost their privileges and those that had but recently gained liberty and equality. The dispossessed classes joined with captive royalty and jealous foreigner to deprive France of the Revolution and to re-impose on her by invasion monarchy, aristocracy and theocracy. To-day there are no more distinct and unequal classes: liberty has freed all, equality before the law has levelled all: fraternity, which we proclaim and whose benefits the Assembly will organise, will unite all. No citizen of France, whatever his opinions, fails to rally to the principle of "Our country before all," nor, by this very unity, to make her free from anxiety or attempt at invasion.

In 1792 it was not the whole people that possessed itself of the Government, but the middle class alone which desired to exercise and enjoy liberty. The triumph of the middle class, as of any oligarchy, was selfish: it wished to keep to itself the rights conquered for all. To do this, it had to make a serious diversion in the people's advance, to hurry it to the battlefield to prevent it seizing its own government. This diversion was war. War was the desire of the *Monarchists* and the *Girondins*, not of the more advanced Democrats, who, like us, desired the true, complete and orderly reign of the people, understanding by that word all the classes without exception which make up the Nation.

In 1792 the people was the instrument and not the object of the Revolution. To-day the Revolution is made by it and for it. In itself it is the Revolution, and entering into it brings with it its new needs of labour, industry, education, agriculture, commerce, morality, prosperity, property, livelihood, navigation—in fine, of civilisation. And all these are the needs of peace. The people and peace are the same words.

In 1792, the ideas of France and Europe were not prepared to understand and accept the mutual harmony of nations, to the general good. The thought of the dying century was hidden in the heads of a few philosophers. To-day, philosophy is popular. Fifty years of freedom of thought, of speech and of writing have produced their effect. Books, newspapers and speeches have been the apostles of European enlightenment. Reason shining around and across the frontiers of peoples has created that great intellectual nation which will give the final achievement of the French Revolution and the institution of international fraternity to all the world.

Finally, in 1792, liberty was novelty, equality a scandal and the Republic a problem. The right of the people, scarcely unveiled by Fénelon, Montesquieu and Rousseau,[1] was so forgotten, buried and profaned by the old traditions of feudalism, monarchy and priesthood, that the most legitimate intervention of the people in its own affairs seemed a monstrosity to the Statesman of the old school. Democracy shook at once the thrones and the foundations of society. To-day thrones and peoples are used to the word, to the forms and orderly operations of liberty exercised in various proportions

---

[1]   François Fénelon (1651–1715) was an eminent theologian, educator, and author whose didactic romance, *Télémaque* (1699), offered reflections on politics which were applied by many readers to the absolutist régime of Louis XIV. Charles de Secondat, Baron de Montesquieu (1689–1755) made a major, enduring contribution to political philosophy in his *Spirit of the Laws* (1750). Jean-Jacques Rousseau (1712–78) is perhaps the most celebrated of all French political thinkers. An accomplished dramatist, novelist, and aesthetician, his contributions to the *Encyclopedia* and *Social Contract* (1762) provided important intellectual underpinnings for the French Revolution of 1789.

in nearly all States, even those monarchic in form. They will grow used to the Republic, in its most complete form in the ripest nations. They will realise that there is such a thing as conservative liberty: that in a Republic may exist not merely better order, but that better order must exist in a government by all for all than in a government by a few for a few.

However apart from all these disinterested motives, the mere need of the consolidation and permanency of the Republic will inspire French statesmen with thoughts of peace. In war it is not our country that runs the worst risks. It is liberty. War is almost always a dictator. Soldiers forget institutions and remember persons. Thrones excite ambitious men. Glory dazzles the eyes of patriotism. The prestige of a victorious name covers an attack upon the national sovereignty. The Republic, indeed, desires glory, but for herself, not for a Caesar or a Napoleon.

Yet make no mistake. These ideas, which the Provisional Government instructs you to present to the Powers as guarantees of European safety, are no requests to pardon the Republic for her audacity in coming to birth: still less humble prayers for the place of a great and legal European state. Their aim is nobler: to provoke sovereigns and peoples to thought and prevent involuntary mistakes concerning the character of our Revolution: to give light and its true character to this event: finally, to give pledges to humanity before giving them to our rights and honour if ever these are theatened.

The French Republic, then, will attack no one. Needless to say, war will be accepted, if conditions of war are forced upon the French people. The thought of the present rulers of France is of the happiness of France, if war is declared on her, and she is forced to grow in strength and glory despite her moderation: of her terrible responsibility if the Republic declares war without provocation. In the first case her martial genius, her impatient spirit, the strength she has accumulated during so many years of peace, would make her invincible at home and perhaps dangerous beyond her frontiers. In the second case, she would rouse against her the memories of the conquests which turned the nations against her, and comprise her first, her widest alliance: the soul of the peoples and the spirit of civilisation.

In accordance with these principles, Sir, the considered principles of France, principles presented without fear and without defiance to friends and enemies alike, you will be good enough to take note of the following declarations.

In the eyes of the French Republic the treaties of 1815 [concluding the Napoleonic Wars] exist no longer in law: nevertheless the territorial limits of these treaties are facts which it acknowledges as a basis in its relations with other nations.

But although the treaties of 1815 exist now only as facts to be mourned by common consent, and although the Republic openly declares that its right and mission is to obtain these modifications pacifically and in a regular manner, the Republic's good sense, moderation, conscience and wisdom remain and are for Europe a better and more honourable guarantee than the letter of these treaties which it has so often broken or altered.

Exert yourself, Sir, to make this liberation of the Republic from the treaties of 1815 understood and genuinely admitted and to show that this frankness need in no way disturb the peace of Europe.

Thus we openly say that if we think that the decree of Providence has sounded the hour for the reconstruction of certain oppressed nationalities in Europe or elsewhere; if Switzerland, our faithful ally since Francis I, be repressed or threatened in her growing movement at home to add fresh force to the *fasces* of democratic governments; if the independent states of Italy be invaded; if limits or obstacles be placed to their internal changes; if armed force be used to prevent their joining in alliance to form an Italian motherland; then the French Republic would consider it its right to take up arms to protect these legitimate governments of growth and nationality.

You observe that the Republic has passed in one step the age of proscription and dictatorship. Decided never to veil liberty at home, equally decided never to veil her democratic principles abroad, it will not permit anyone to place his hand between its peaceful radiance of freedom and the eyes of the peoples of the world. It proclaims itself the enlightened and cordial ally of all rights, progress and legitimate development of all nations who wish to live by the same principles as its own. It will not undertake dark and incendiary propaganda ["propagande"] among its neighbours. It knows that durable liberties can grow only from the native soil; but by the light of its ideals, by the example of order and peace that it hopes to give to the world, it will start the only true proselytising, that of admiration and sympathy. That is not war, but nature; not the disturbance of Europe, but life: it is not to set fire to the world, but to shine on the people's horizon to precede and guide them at once.

For humanity we desire, we even hope, that peace may remain. A year ago a question of war arose between France and England. Not the Republic caused it to arise, but the dynasty. The dynasty carries away with it the danger of a European war which it had caused by the purely personal ambition of its family alliances in Spain. Thus this domestic policy of the fallen dynasty [of Louis Philippe] which for seventeen years degraded our national dignity, threatened also peace and our liberal alliances by its claim to a second crown in Madrid. The Republic has no ambitions and no nepotism to serve; it does not inherit a family claim. Let Spain rule itself, let it be independent and free. France, to cement this natural alliance, trusts rather to common principles than the succession of the House of Bourbon.

Such, Sir, is the mind of the Republic. Such will invariably be the character of the frank, strong and moderate policy you will represent.

At its birth, in the heat of a struggle unsought by the people, the Republic pronounced three words which revealed its soul and will call to its cradle the blessings of god and man: *Liberty, Equality, Fraternity.* The next day, by abolishing the political death-penalty, it gave the true commentary on these words at home; do you give them the true commentary abroad.

The meaning of these three words applied to our foreign relations is this: To free France from the chains which weighed down her principle and her dignity; to recover her proper rank among the European great powers; to make a declaration, finally, to all nations of alliance and friendship. If France is aware of her part in the liberal and civilising mission of the century, not one of these words means *war*. If Europe is wise and just, there is not one that does not mean *peace*.

I am, Sir, etc.,

LAMARTINE,
Minister of Foreign Affairs.

(Postgate, *Revolution from 1789 to 1906.* 193–96)

Further Reading

Andréas, Bert. *Le Manifeste Communiste de Marx et Engels: Histoire et Bibliographie 1848–1918*. Milan: Feltrinelli, 1963.

Beamish, Rob. "The Making of the Manifesto." In Panitch and Leys. 218–39.

Benjamin, Walter. "The Task of the Translator." *Illuminations*. Ed. and intro. Hannah Arendt. Trans. Harry Zohn. London: Fontana, 1973. 69–82.

Berman, Marshall. *All That Is Solid Melts Into Air: The Experience of Modernity*. New York: Simon and Schuster, 1982.

Bourdieu, Pierre. *Rules of Art: Genesis and Structure of the Literary Field*. Trans. Susan Emanuel. Stanford: Stanford UP, 1996.

Bowditch, John and Clement Ramsland. *Voices of the Industrial Revolution: Selected Reading from the Liberal Economists and Their Critics*. Ann Arbor: U of Michigan P, 1961.

Callinicos, Alex. *An Anti-Capitalist Manifesto*. Cambridge: Polity, 2003.

Carver, Terrell, ed. and trans. *Marx: Later Political Writings*. Cambridge: Cambridge UP, 1996.

——. *Marx and Engels: The Intellectual Relationship*. Bloomington: Indiana UP, 1983.

——. *Friedrich Engels: His Life and Thought*. Basingstoke: Macmillan, 1981.

Chua, Amy. *World on Fire: How Exporting Free Market Democracy Breeds Ethnic Hatred and Global Instability*. New York: Doubleday, 2003.

Cohen, G. A. 1978. *History, Labour, and Freedom*. Oxford: Clarendon P, 1988.

Cormack, Patricia, ed. *Manifestos and Declarations of the Twentieth Century*. Toronto: Garamond P, 1998.

Coutts, Ian. "Say, isn't that Karl Marx?" *Globe & Mail*, July 18, 1998: D9.

Cowling, Mark, ed. *The Communist Manifesto: New Interpretations*. New York: New York UP, 1998.

Davidson, Rondel V. "Reform versus Revolution: Victor Considérant and the *Communist Manifesto*." *Social Science Quarterly* 58 (1977): 74–85.

Derrida, Jacques. *Specters of Marx: The State of the Debt, the Work of Mourning, and the New International*. Trans. Peggy Kamuf and intro. Bernd Magnus and Stephen Cullenberg. New York: Routledge, 1994.

de Soto, Hernando. *The Mystery of Capital: Why Capitalism Triumphs in the West and Fails Everywhere Else.* New York: Basic Books, 2000.

Draper, Hal. *The Marx-Engels Chronicle: A Day-by-Day Chronology of Marx and Engels' Life and Activity.* New York: Schocken Books, 1985.

———. *The Adventures of the Communist Manifesto.* Berkeley: Center for Socialist History, 1994, 1998.

Findlay, L. M. "Runes of Marx and *The University in Ruins.*" *University of Toronto Quarterly* 66 (1997): 677–90.

———. "The Cunning of Education or the Democracy Staple? Which Should Canada be Promoting in its Communities and the World?" *Community Values in the Age of Globalization.* Ed. Marsha Hanen, Alex Barber, and David Cassels. Calgary: Shumir Foundation for Ethics in Leadership, 2000. 171–91.

———. "Content Providers of the World Unite! A Critical Analysis and Canadian Agenda." *Topia* 9 (2003): 15–33.

Fukuyama, Francis. *The End of History and the Last Man.* New York: The Free P, 1992.

Furet, François. *Marx and the French Revolution.* Trans. Deborah Kan Furet. Ed. and intro. Lucien Calvié. Chicago: U of Chicago P, 1988.

Gane, Mike. "The *Communist Manifesto*'s Transgendered Proletarians." In Cowling. 132–41.

Gooch, G. P. *History and Historians in the Nineteenth Century.* Boston: Beacon P, 1959.

Gross, John. *The Rise and Fall of the Man of Letters: Aspects of English Literary Life since 1800.* Harmondsworth: Penguin, 1991.

Hobsbawm, Eric, intro. *The Communist Manifesto: A Modern Edition.* London: Verso, 1998.

Hunley, J.D. *The Life and Thought of Friedrich Engels.* New Haven: Yale UP, 1991.

Kuczynski, Thomas. *Das Kommunistische Manifest: Marx und Engels.* Trier: Karl-Marx-Haus, 1995.

Janowitz, Anne. *Lyric and Labour in the Romantic Tradition.* Cambridge: Cambridge UP, 1998.

Lawton, Anna, ed. and trans. with Herbert Eagle. *Russian Futurism Through its Manifestos, 1912–1928.* Ithaca: Cornell UP, 1988.

Lyon, Janet. *Manifestoes: Provocations of the Modern.* Ithaca: Cornell UP, 1999.

Macfarlane, Helen, trans. *Manifesto of the German Communist Party. The Red Republican,* nos. 21–24 November 1850.

Marx, Karl and Frederick Engels. *Collected Works.* London: Lawrence and Wishart; New York: International Publishers; Moscow: Progress Publishers, 1975–. 50 vols. planned. [MECW]

Niethammer, Lutz, with Dirk van Laak. *Posthistoire: Has History Come to an End?* Trans. Patrick Camiller. London:Verso, 1992.

Osborne, Peter. "Remember the Future? The Communist Manifesto as Historical and Cultural Form." In Panitch and Leys. 190–204.

Panitch, Leo and Colin Leys, eds. *The Socialist Register 1998.* Rendlesham: Merlin P, 1998.

Postgate, R. W. *Revolution from 1789 to 1906: Documents Selected and Edited with Notes and Introductions.* New York: Harper Torchbook, 1962.

Rose, Jonathan. *The Intellectual Life of the British Working Classes.* New Haven:Yale UP, 2001.

Rowbotham, Sheila. "Dear Dr. Marx: A Letter from a Socialist Feminist." in Panitch and Leys. 1–17.

Sewell, William H. Jr. *Work and Revolution in France: The Language of Labour from the Old Régime to 1848.* Cambridge: Cambridge UP, 1980.

Siemann, Wolfram. *The German Revolution of 1848–49.* Trans. Christiane Banerji. New York: St. Martin's P, 1998.

Smith, Adam. *An Inquiry into the Nature and Causes of the Wealth of Nations.* Ed. R.H. Campbell, A.S. Skinner, and W.B. Todd. 2 vols. Indianapolis: Liberty Classics, 1981.

Sprinker, Michael, ed. *Ghostly Demarcations: A Symposium on Jacques Derrida's 'Spectres of Marx'.* London:Verso, 1999.

Stiglitz, Joseph. *Globalization and its Discontents.* London: Penguin, 2002.

Tucker, Robert C. *The Marxian Revolutionary Idea.* New York: Norton, 1969.

Wheen, Francis. *Karl Marx.* London: Fourth Estate, 2000.

Credits

"Letter from Engels to Marx, Nov–Dec 1846," from *Marx and Engels, Collected Works*, vol 38, pp. 89–94, London: Lawrence and Wishart; New York: Publishers, 1982.

"Engels, of a Communist Confession of Faith, 9 June 1847," from *Marx and Engels, Collected Works*, vol 6, pp. 96–103, London: Lawrence and Wishart; New York: Publishers, 1976.

"Marx, Communism of the *Rheinischer Beobachter*, 1847," from *Marx and Engels, Collected Works*, vol 6, pp. 220–234, London: Lawrence and Wishart; New York: Publishers, 1976.

"Letter from Engels to Marx, 23–24 November 1847," from *Marx and Engels, Collected Works*, vol 38, pp. 146–150, London: Lawrence and Wishart; New York: Publishers, 1982.

"Engels, 'On the History of the Communist League,' 1885,' from *Marx and Engels, Collected Works*, vol 26, pp. 312–330, London: Lawrence and Wishart; New York: Publishers, 1990.

"Engels, 'The Labour Movement in America,' 'Preface to the American Edition of *The Condition of the Working Class in England*,' 26 January 1887," from *Marx and Engels, Collected Works*, vol 26, pp. 434–442, London: Lawrence and Wishart; New York: Publishers, 1990.

"Engels, 'Notes on My Journey Through America and Canada,' September 1888," from *Marx and Engels, Collected Works*, vol 26, pp. 581–583, London: Lawrence and Wishart; New York: Publishers, 1990.

"Engels, 'Impressions of a Journey Round America,' late September," from *Marx and Engels, Collected Works*, vol 26, pp. 584–586, London: Lawrence and Wishart; New York: Publishers, 1990.

Stewart, John Hall, *Documentary Survey of the French Revolution*, 1st Edition, © 1951. Reprinted by permission of Pearson Education, Inc., Upper Saddle River, NJ.

Postgate, R. W., "Manifesto of the Delegates to their Countrymen, 6 June 1797," from *Revolution from 1789 to 1906: Documents Selected and Edited with Notes and Introductions*. New York: Harper Torch, 1962.

Postgate, R. W., "Proclamation by Robert Emmet, 23 July 1803," from *Revolution from 1789 to 1906: Documents Selected and Edited with Notes and Introductions*. New York: Harper Torch, 1962.

Postgate, R. W., A. de Lamartin, "Manifesto to Europe, 2 March 1848," firom *Revolution from 1789 to 1906: Documents Selected and Edited with Notes and Introductions*. New York: Harper Torch, 1962.